Workin

A major new series from Falmer Press

Gender and Society:
Feminist Perspectives on the Past and Present

Series Editor: June Purvis,
School of Social and Historical Studies,
Portsmouth Polytechnic, Milldam Site,
Portsmouth PO1 3AS, UK

This major new series will consist of scholarly texts written in an accessible style which promote and advance feminist research, thinking and debate. The series will range across disciplines such as sociology, history, social policy and cultural studies. The series editor is interested in hearing from prospective authors. Before submitting proposals, a copy of the guidelines for contributors to *Gender and Society* should be obtained from June Purvis at the address above.

Working Out:
New Directions
for Women's Studies

Edited by

Hilary Hinds, Ann Phoenix and Jackie Stacey

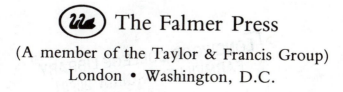 The Falmer Press

(A member of the Taylor & Francis Group)
London • Washington, D.C.

UK   The Falmer Press, 4 John St., London WC1N 2ET
USA   The Falmer Press, Taylor & Francis Inc., 1900 Frost Road, Suite 101,
      Bristol, PA 19007

First published 1992

**A Catalogue Record for this book is available from the British
Library**

ISBN 0 75070 043 2
ISBN 0 75070 044 0 pbk

**Library of Congress Cataloging-in-Publication Data are
available on request**

Typeset in 9.5/11pt Bembo
by Graphicraft Typesetters Ltd., Hong Kong

*Printed in Great Britain by Burgess Science Press, Basingstoke on paper
which has a specified pH value on final paper manufacture of not less than
7.5 and is therefore 'acid free'.*

Contents

Contents

For everyone whose love and support has helped Jackie on the road to recovery, and, most especially, for Audre Lorde, whose *Cancer Journals* have given so much strength to so many women.

Acknowledgments

We would like to thank our institutions, Fircroft College of Adult Education, Birmingham; The Thomas Coram Research Unit, Institute of Education, London; and the Sociology Department, University of Lancaster, for their support for the organization of the Women's Studies Network (UK) Conference in July 1991, and also for the preparation of this book.

Thanks, too, to all the contributors for keeping, against all the odds, to a set of very tight deadlines; and to Jacinta Evans, our editor, for her part in the speedy publication of this volume.

Jackie Stacey, Ann Phoenix and Hilary Hinds

Introduction

Working Out: New Directions for Women's Studies

Jackie Stacey, Ann Phoenix and Hilary Hinds

Looking Back, Moving Forward

Women's Studies is a burgeoning field of academic study in many Western societies. In Britain, for example, the Women's Studies Network (UK) list includes details of Women's Studies courses[1] taught at over fifty institutions, requiring constant additions to keep it up to date. Such rapid growth is indicative of the popularity of Women's Studies and its appeal to new groups of students.

Yet it is precisely because Women's Studies is flourishing that it is important not simply to accept it as a 1990s success story, but to take stock of where it has been and where it is going. This is particularly the case since Women's Studies is generally considered to be too 'soft' to be of high status in many colleges, polytechnics and universities. As part of the increasing emphasis on 'efficiency' and 'value added', it is not only student numbers, but also publications and attracting large research grants, that score highly in educational institutions. As a result, Women's Studies is vulnerable to cut-backs and marginalization when compared, for example, with some science subjects.

A number of issues need to be addressed if we are to reflect on the past and current state of Women's Studies in order to inform our thinking about its future directions. What, for example, is the interrelationship between feminism, in all its expressions, and Women's Studies, given the 'difficulty Women's Studies is seen as experiencing in maintaining an unequivocally feminist stance' (Aaron and Walby, 1991, p. 5)? What, if anything, unifies Women's Studies courses and the teaching done on them? Is Women's Studies typified by particular disciplinary approaches? Which new directions within Women's Studies are particularly innovative, insightful or useful ones? Indeed, is Women's Studies still necessary, or have the achievements of feminism in what some have called a 'postfeminist era' made it redundant? In the words of some younger students of Women's Studies, 'What about the men?'

The Women's Studies Network (UK) annual conference provides an opportunity to address these kinds of issues: to look forward to new directions in Women's Studies, while not forgetting that the future arises out of what has gone before. This book is a selection of the 1991 Women's Studies Network conference papers re-worked for publication. The title, *Working Out: New Directions for Women's Studies* deliberately plays with a number of ambiguities relevant to the consideration of Women's Studies and its future directions. It celebrates the success of Women's Studies over the last decade: it has been, and is, 'working out' for many students, teachers and academic programmes, which, as Beatrix Campbell points out in her chapter, is no mean achievement after years of Thatcherism. The title also recognizes the challenges that Women's Studies faces; these emanate both from its context, educational institutions where it is seen as a marginal subject, and from the internal dynamics of a perspective that is predicated on debate, process and political change. Consequently, Women's Studies is still 'working out' its responses to such challenges. Moreover, the fact that the title is in the present tense indicates that such 'working out' for Women's Studies has to be a continuous process, rather than a once-and-for-all event; thus women new to writing or teaching within academia are as important to the project of Women's Studies as are more experienced ones. So the ambiguities multiply: the title hints at the mental activity of striving to forge 'new directions', specific ways of theorizing the world; it presents an image of women in employment, working outside their homes; and, as Women's Studies is a relatively new discipline, it suggests the working out of apprenticeships. The very ambiguity of the title reflects the ambiguities that have characterized and strengthened feminist politics over the last decade or so (see Beatrix Campbell's chapter).

The particular kind of new directions that have to be worked out are twofold: to do both with theoretical developments in Women's Studies, and with the ways in which Women's Studies is practised. The intention here is not to suggest that theory and practice are either dichotomous or clearly separable, but to give recognition to the fact that Women's Studies both reflects and constructs developments in feminist practice as well as theory. Thus the work presented in the chapters which follow both reassesses the past and points us in new directions for Women's Studies.

Many of the 1991 conference papers have been substantially rewritten for this volume. They continue to deploy, however, a variety of styles and a variety of material and disciplinary approaches. Thus personal as well as more formal modes of written presentation are included here; some styles bear little relation to the spoken papers from which chapters were produced, whilst others retain a more colloquial style. These stylistic differences partly reflect the variety of material which is relevant in Women's Studies, and partly reflect the ways in which particular women choose to write. Rather than giving a résumé of each of the chapters to follow, we will instead outline the structure of the book, mentioning some chapters, and then introduce some of those and the other chapters more fully through a discussion of two specific themes which emerged from this collection: the increasingly interdisciplinary nature of Women's Studies, and the changing classificatory labels of different feminist perspectives used therein.

Each of the book's four sections deals with issues which are central to the development of Women's Studies, taking both Women's Studies and feminist thinking into new directions. It is worth noting that contributions from Black and/or lesbian women and contributions on 'race' and/or sexuality have not been brought together into separate sections in this volume, but instead appear throughout. This is a deliberate decision to reflect the fact that Black and other minority women (whatever their sexuality) and lesbian women (whatever their colour or ethnicity) address a variety of themes and issues that have relevance for all areas of Women's Studies.

Section I: The Politics and Practice of Women's Studies

The book starts by engaging with the issue of the interrelationship between feminist politics and the ways in which Women's Studies is practised. This issue is clearly a crucial one for clarifying what constitutes, and hence unifies, Women's Studies. It is thus a section which lays the foundations for the sections which follow.

Some of the work here concerns looking back and taking stock of the past; Maureen McNeil, for example, examines some pressing issues facing feminist teachers in a 'postfeminist era', when questions of differences between women have made it more challenging to teach about gender relations than it was in the 1970s; similarly, Deborah Philips and Ella Westland review the thorny issue of men in Women's Studies. Both chapters raise crucial questions related to future practice in Women's Studies pedagogy. Other chapters in this section push forward into new areas so far barely discussed in Women's Studies: Helen (charles), for example, reflects on the fact that feminist work dealing with race and ethnicity has almost exclusively focused on Blackness, and raises questions about what a feminist analysis of whiteness would look like.

Section II: Commonalities and Differences

The issue of commonalities and differences between women has been one of the most pressing and painful areas within feminist thinking in the last two decades. It is, however, also an area that has encouraged promising new ways of theorizing women's situations and gender relations as well as political practice within feminism. The chapters in this section bring feminist issues of commonalities and differences onto the Women's Studies agenda in varied ways. Again, some work addresses issues which have long been debated, yet which still need further attention, such as lesbianism and ethnicity. Others address issues seldom covered in feminist debate. In this latter category comes Nasa Begum's chapter, which addresses the question of the importance of theorizing disability within feminism, and challenges Women's Studies to address this issue at a political and theoretical level.

Section III: International Feminisms

Changes in global politics such as the dissolution of Eastern bloc 'communisms', the popularity of fundamentalisms both in East and West, the rise of nationalisms, and yet the emergence of a united European 'free' market, pose important questions for the feminist agenda. International links between individual feminists and between feminist organizations have come sharply into focus within Women's Studies as 1992 approaches with the promise of dissolving rigidity of thinking about national boundaries. This section presents feminist perspectives on issues within particular countries and from more international perspectives.

The longstanding feminist concern with universals and particulars is taken into new contexts by Shaheen Sardar-Ali and Siobhan Mullally in their case study of women's rights in Muslim countries. Naila Kabeer offers an appraisal of the impact of liberal feminism on the theory and practice of 'Women in Development', and, opening up a hitherto neglected area of interest within Women's Studies,

Chris Corrin looks at the question of Women's Studies in central and Eastern Europe.

Section IV: Theories and Methods

The final section of the book is interlinked with the first section, in that the politics and practices of Women's Studies are necessarily related to the theories, methods and approaches that we use. This section comes at the end of the book, however, to allow an examination of innovative thinking about theories, methods and approaches after substantive issues have been discussed. In this section there is, once again, some rethinking of questions about which substantial debate already exists. Liz Stanley, for example, uses letters written by women to Edward Carpenter to challenge some contemporary ideas about 'romantic friendship'; Liz Kelly, Linda Regan and Sheila Burton enter the debate about feminist methodology to suggest that the belief that feminist research must necessarily be qualitative, rather than quantitative, reproduces dualisms that feminism has sought to challenge. Other chapters in this section push feminist theory into new areas; Lynne Pearce, for example, suggests the employment of a new theoretical approach to the understanding of women's writing, that of Bakhtin's dialogic theory.

Working out(side) Disciplinary Boundaries?

Women's Studies has had a contradictory relationship with academic disciplines. As we move into the 1990s, educational institutions are supporting an increasing number of interdisciplinary initiatives, amongst them a steady proliferation of Women's Studies courses. This enthusiasm for interdisciplinary courses has generally been welcomed by the educational establishment in terms of 'student demand' and 'market forces'. In her chapter, Beatrix Campbell raises the question of the contradictions in the introduction of 'market' principles to education: on the one hand, feminists have rightly been opposed to the extension of capitalist values and practices to their institutions; on the other, if student demand means that Women's Studies is enabled to flourish, according to such principles, then there are positive spin-offs. Thus, the move towards more courses, more students and new markets has, in some institutions, led to the welcoming of interdisciplinary courses such as Women's Studies, previously perceived as too threatening to the disciplinary boundaries which structured education at all levels.

When Women's Studies first emerged, much of its output aimed to challenge the patriarchal content and assumptions of the existing academic disciplines. In some disciplines this has been more thoroughly and successfully implemented than in others: literary studies in the 1990s, for example, is hard to imagine without the feminist critiques of patriarchal culture which have been so vital to the development of this field. The impact of feminism on the study of science and technology, on the other hand, has been much less visible. In the case of relatively new disciplines, such as film and television studies, feminist work has not only made an impact, but has often formed a central part of the disciplinary agenda: studies of stars, genres and audiences, for example, have all taken gender as a central concern.

To what extent, then, does Women's Studies aim to offer a critique from within conventional disciplines, with the hope of transforming them, and to what extent does it aspire to an interdisciplinary, autonomous place of its own? The contributions to the 1991 Women's Studies Network Conference provide an interesting gauge by which to measure this. Of course, the obvious response to the above question is that Women's Studies does both: it both works within disciplines to challenge and transform them, and it seeks some autonomy through which to develop new models and understandings. Some feminist work can be seen to be interdisciplinary in that it explicitly borrows material from one discipline and reworks it in the context of another. This can both highlight the limits of particular disciplines, and expand the boundaries of others. Other work could be called interdisciplinary in that it addresses questions of relevance to all disciplines, but contained by none. Still other work poses a direct challenge to academic disciplinary boundaries, seeing them as part of the problem of patriarchal thought itself.

From our knowledge of the changes within our educational institutions, and on the basis of the papers at the 1991 conference, we would suggest that Women's Studies is developing an increasingly interdisciplinary focus, with women using insights from more than one discipline to present their arguments. This is not true of all the chapters in this collection, and we are not suggesting that feminists should *not* continue to work within disciplines, but rather that one of the striking features of many of the chapters which follow is that they cross disciplinary boundaries in a variety of important ways.

Tamsin Wilton's chapter, for example, defies disciplinary boundaries by extending and challenging the already interdisciplinary work on sexuality and representation in which feminist theory has always been a key component. Drawing on theories of visual and sexual pleasure to analyze representations in 'safer sex' materials, she skilfully moves in and out of the usual academic compartments, offering the reader an innovative place from which to reassess controversial feminist debates.

Some chapters in this collection concern questions of clear relevance to feminists in all disciplines. Helen (charles), for example, in challenging the restriction of feminist discussions about ethnicity to questions of Blackness, and outlining what a notion of Whiteness might mean for feminism and for Women's Studies, raises an issue that could be described as 'interdisciplinary' in the fullest sense. Felly Nkweto Simmonds, likewise, in her analysis of the continuing marginalization of Black feminist perspectives within Women's Studies, raises issues of importance for all Women's Studies teachers and students about questions of power, knowledge and the academy. Both these chapters challenge those working in Women's Studies to examine critically questions of feminist practice as well as theory. Similarly, Maureen McNeil's reflections upon her own experience of teaching about gender puts feminist practice firmly on the agenda in terms of pedagogy. Examining developments within feminist theory (such as the impact of poststructuralism) and changing political contexts (such as the importance of differences among women), McNeil calls for a more open approach to the difficult questions of pedagogy which are relevant to feminist teaching in all disciplines.

Many of the chapters in this book demonstrate in a variety of ways the increasing importance of feminist interdisciplinary work in the 1990s. Such loosening of long-established academic disciplinary boundaries, however, may produce new uncertainties: where, for example, are the boundaries to our fields

of investigation, and which theoretical frameworks are appropriate to their interpretation? In addition, what institutional changes do we desire to support this
interdisciplinary work: what are the advantages of Women's Studies departments,
for example, as opposed to our existing rather scattered bases in different departments? Despite these uncertainties, the innovation of feminist interdisciplinary
work provides a necessary dynamism in the working out of new directions for
Women's Studies.

Beyond the 'Big Three'!

Beatrix Campbell's theme of ambiguity is also pertinent to the reassessment of the
conventional feminist perspectives, so often used in Women's Studies teaching.
The 'Big Three', radical, socialist and liberal feminism, have dominated the political and theoretical agenda in Women's Studies for many years now. Traditionally, these perspectives have been seen as incompatible, if not in conflict with each
other. Indeed, of the 'Big Three', the third, liberal feminism, has, to some extent,
taken a back seat in British feminism,[2] and thus debates have historically been
divided between radical feminism and socialist feminism.

These two perspectives have been characterized by a difference in focus, and
a difference of explanation, in their approach to women's subordination. Radical
feminism has typically been characterized by its concern with issues such as violence against women, sexuality, and reproduction, drawing on an analysis which
sees men as a group benefiting from women's oppression. Socialist feminism, on
the other hand, has been characterized by its emphasis on the role of capitalism in
reproducing gender inequality and women's place in a class-structured society,
and has therefore tended to focus on areas such as women's paid and unpaid work
and the state.

It is ironic that, despite the fact that feminists have been so critical of the
binary oppositions produced in Western patriarchal thought (mind/body, black/
white, male/female and so on), they have also contributed to binary thinking by
reducing complex questions to the two oppositional standpoints of radical and
socialist feminism. Nowhere could this be more true than in the history of feminist perspectives in Women's Studies in Britain. There are certainly important
differences between feminist analyses of gender inequality, but the antagonistic
binarism of socialist versus radical feminism has not proved productive; the fact
that much recent feminist work (including many of the contributions to this
collection) goes beyond the creation and reification of such dualisms is to be
welcomed.

Indeed, the issues have always been more complex than the usual division
of feminism into three perspectives would suggest. The 'opponents' begin to
fragment and multiply when considered more closely. The category 'socialist
feminism' immediately begs for further elaboration in relation to the history of
Marxism and of Left politics more generally. A distinction between Marxist
feminism and socialist feminism is often drawn: the former suggests a closer tie
to economic determinism and to class politics more generally, whilst the latter
may indicate a belief that fighting capitalism is necessary for women's liberation,
without prioritizing economic questions over sexual or reproductive ones. Similarly,
the category 'radical feminism' is often inclusive of 'revolutionary feminism'

and/or lesbian separatism. Whereas the former may include women who believe in the importance of transforming heterosexuality from within, as it were, the latter is more committed to directing all energy, including sexual energy, towards women.

In addition to the diversity within the categories of radical and socialist feminism, the third of the 'Big Three', 'liberal feminism', also requires further definition. Liberal feminism is traditionally associated with a belief in women gaining access to the choices and freedoms they are denied in this society, through the reform of institutions such as the law and education, to enable women to be equal with men. However, feminist struggle within institutions has not only been the practice of liberal feminism. Indeed, as feminism has enabled women to have an effect within institutions, as well as outside them, feminists of all 'persuasions' have found themselves working towards institutional transformation in ways that have complicated the previously easy distinctions drawn between reform and more radical transformation. Be it changing police practices about violence against women, introducing Women's Studies courses within education, or transforming local government through, for example, the feminist work done within the former Greater London Council, many feminists who would not call themselves 'liberals' have fought to challenge and transform practices within existing institutions. As Christine Wieneke asks in her chapter in this collection, 'Does equal opportunities legislation and practice serve the Women's Movement?' Here the traditionally liberal strategy, equal opportunities, is shown to be more complex than such a classification would suggest. Indeed, through this case study, Christine Wieneke highlights the diversity of equal opportunities strategies and their varied rates of success.

One of the problems with the way the 'Big Three' have been used to classify feminist perspectives within Women's Studies is that many other kinds of feminism are excluded. There has always been more diversity among feminists than such a rigid characterization would suggest. Eco-feminism, for example, has linked a concern for the environment with a critique of patriarchy; and the women's peace movement has, through Greenham Common and other direct actions, highlighted the connections between male domination and militarism. Similarly, 'materialist feminism' aims to combine the Marxist focus on the expropriation of labour with the radical feminist claim that women's oppression is separable from capitalism. These forms of feminisms do not fit easily into the usual classifications of feminist thought within Women's Studies courses.

Another problem with these standard categorizations of feminism is that of stereotyping. Feminists have been keen to challenge offensive stereotypes with which we disagree, but we have also been guilty of our own kinds of stereotyping, which has led to reductionist analysis and knee-jerk responses to other feminists' work. For example, feminists interested in questions of sexuality are assumed to take a radical feminist perspective, and those interested in paid work to take a Marxist or socialist feminist perspective; those feminists who are against censorship are assumed to be liberal feminists, whilst those opposing pornography are assumed to be radical feminists. Any mention of lesbianism is assumed to be allied with radical feminism. In her chapter 'Difference, Power and Knowledge', Felly Nkweto Simmonds challenges the ways in which such stereotyping has resulted in an unhelpful construction of differences between feminisms. Such stereotypes have often meant that the full complexities of certain topics have not been analyzed, debates dissolving instead into a rigid positioning of opponents. According to Felly Nkweto Simmonds, this has had particular implications for the ways in which Black feminists have been marginalized within Women's Studies: she counters, for example, the assumption that all radical feminists in the 1970s and 1980s were white.

A further problem with the rigid classification of feminist work into three categories is that it ignores the shifting and multiple feminist identities which one woman may have either at different times in her life, or indeed about different issues at one time. In other words, a woman may take a radical feminist perspective on sexuality and violence, and yet hold a commitment to some socialist principles, or another may have moved through a variety of feminisms and no longer be classifiable within a single category.

In her chapter, Felly Nkweto Simmonds also addresses this ambiguity, the fluidity of differences among women. Drawing on her plenary conference address, she explores the complexities involved in thinking through our commonalities and differences, given the shifting nature of the categories of insiders and outsiders, depending on the particular context. Class, ethnicity, sexuality, physical ability and employment may all combine to produce contradictory aspects of our identities, some of which may connect women to power and some of which may not. Emphasizing the multiplicity of our identities, she challenges feminists to rethink difference within a more positive and productive framework of 'dialogue and autonomy'.

Some contributions to this collection challenge such stereotypes and bring together issues and perspectives frequently held apart within Women's Studies. Both Gill Dunne's 'Difference at Work', which uses ethnographic interviews with women about their expectations, aspirations and experiences of paid work and sexual relationships, and Lisa Adkins and Celia Lury's 'Gender and the Labour Market', which analyzes the place of female sexuality in the relations of production, challenge the assumptions that it is only Marxist feminism which is concerned with women's paid work, and that Marxist approaches can best explain women's position in the labour market. Furthermore, both chapters combine two areas usually kept separate within feminist analysis: sexuality and paid employment.

The conventional classification of feminist perspectives as the 'Big Three' has also often meant that all Black feminist work appears under the unified category 'Black feminism'. This is not only problematic because it suggests that White feminism is diverse and complex, needing three categories, whilst Black feminism can be constructed as a single category, but also because it necessarily marginalizes 'Black feminism' (which becomes the fourth category) as other to the central three categories of feminist thought which are thus, by implication, all white. In her chapter, Helen (charles) challenges the taken-for-grantedness of such assumptions about race and ethnicity within Women's Studies by exploring a category previously largely left untheorized within feminist work — Whiteness. Why have feminist discussions about race and ethnicity always focused on Blackness, and what would an analysis of Whiteness include, she asks? In offering an account of the workshop on this topic in which participants were asked to 'politically colour the "non"' assumed in categories such as 'non-white', Helen (charles) suggests that Whiteness is invisible for white women and wonders whether Women's Studies in Britain is ready for Whiteness yet.

Given the proliferation of feminist work within the last ten years, classifying feminisms within a small number of neatly compartmentalized perspectives has become increasingly unworkable. Psychoanalysis, poststructuralism and postmodernism, for example, have all been important theoretical frameworks for some feminist work of the late 1980s and early 1990s, all of them defying the conventional classifications of feminism and the boundaries between them. In her chapter 'Desire and the Politics of Representation', for example, Tamsin Wilton employs theoretical tools and political arguments from a variety of traditionally incompatible sources, such as radical feminism and Foucauldian discourse theory. Refreshing in its innovative combination of such diverse positions, this chapter deconstructs 'safer sex' materials targeted at lesbians, gay men and heterosexual men and women, arguing for the need for a different approach which would enable an autonomous female desire to be represented.

Some chapters in this collection introduce new issues onto the agenda which cut across existing classifications of feminist thought and do not fit into one of the 'Big Three', or, indeed, any of the other perspectives mentioned above. For example, Nasa Begum's 'Disabled Women and the Feminist Agenda' offers a thought-provoking account of the connections between assumptions about gender roles, body image, sexuality and disability. Chris Corrin's chapter, 'Women's Studies in Central and Eastern Europe', reminds us that the changes in Eastern Europe in the late 1980s and early 1990s pose crucial questions not just for those feminists with a continuing commitment to some form of socialist politics, but for all those interested in the notion of international feminist politics. As Beatrix Campbell's plenary address stated, such political changes necessitate a fundamental rethinking of the meaning of radical politics in the 1990s.

The above critique aims to highlight the limitations of previous models of classification of feminist thought within Women's Studies. This does not mean that such classifications are not an important part of the history of feminism and the Women's Movement, and, as such, form a significant agenda for Women's Studies courses. Neither does it deny the usefulness of classifications and categories in general, despite their inevitable reductiveness, in understanding crucial differences between feminist approaches. However, what emerges very distinctively from the chapters in this volume is the way in which much feminist work in the 1990s requires us to rethink the old models of classification, and not to try to squeeze new work into existing categories it does not fit.

Notes

1 The Women's Studies Network (UK) Course Listings, 1991–2, was compiled by Lisa Adkins and Jackie Stacey. It was based upon a questionnaire conducted at the Women's Studies Network (UK) Annual Conference (1990) held at Coventry Polytechnic. Only the institutions represented at that conference, or in the Network more generally, are included and thus the actual number of Women's Studies courses available far exceeds those listed. Copies of the booklet are available from Lisa Adkins or Jackie Stacey, Department of Sociology, Lancaster University, LA1 4YL.

2 The impact of liberal feminist thinking has varied, however; see Naila Kabeer's chapter in this volume.

Reference

AARON, JANE and WALBY, SYLVIA (1991) 'Towards a Feminist Intellectual Space', in AARON, JANE and WALBY, SYLVIA (Eds) *Out of the Margins: Women's Studies in the Nineties*, London, Falmer Press.

Section I

The Politics and Practice of Women's Studies

Chapter 1

Feminist Politics after Thatcher

Beatrix Campbell

A key to thinking about feminism in the post-Thatcher period, and feminism as we move towards the end of the century, is the notion of ambiguity, of things which are both positive and negative — of moving backwards and forwards. I want that notion to infuse what I am saying here, partly because it helps counteract the hopelessness of political pessimism.

This notion of ambiguity helps us to deal with the things that have been difficult — absolutely awful, actually — about the last ten years and which will become very difficult for the rest of the century. But it is important to hold on to some of those difficult things because they may have an important message for us: that the last ten years have not just been terrible; that we did not go away, we did not die; that our politics did not disintegrate and disappear; that we were not defeated; that we are here today.

First, there is the oddness of the disappearance of Thatcherism itself, which tells us something about changes in our political culture. Then there is the politics we have created for ourselves and the 'us' that we have created through those politics. Thatcherism: the disappearance of the woman, the end of the regular afternoon circus on the television at parliamentary question time, was devastating for some of us; a kind of sport went out of parliamentary politics.

One of the interesting things about her reign is that Thatcher was only able to speak truthfully about her experience as a woman during her time in power at the end. She was only able to establish a kinship with women in her moment of defeat. It was as if feminism only became useful to her once she had lost and once she had to own up to the pain of being defeated by what had seemed to her — and was described by all our national newspapers — as a coup by men.

Even though there was 'shock horror' when she was elected as the leader of the Conservative Party, there was also belief among Conservatives that they had pulled off a consummate political coup. They knew themselves very well; they knew that they had done something consummate when they put her into the position of supreme power in the Conservative Party because they also knew that her presence was contingent and conditional.

This was at a crucial moment in history: the second wave of modern feminism; a time when women's insurgence, women's presence, women's nerve and audacity was palpable. The Conservatives couldn't ignore it; they had to do something about it and what they did was very brilliant. They put in power someone who would give women's politics no endorsement at all, but who would, in her own way, express something of the audacity of the moment — and Thatcher was nothing if not audacious. She was someone who would lend to the regressive, patriarchal politics of traditional Conservatism the endorsement of the feminine, not the *feminist*. She only endorsed the feminist import of her election as leader of the Conservatives when she was ousted, and then she called up a feminist language, a kind of feminist grief, to explain the pain of her dispatch.

The way Thatcher wielded power is a good example of the conditions under which women are or are not allowed to exercise power. She clearly enjoyed power, and wielded it with a panache unrivalled by any of her contemporaries. But she also exercised it in a way which demanded that she banish, dismiss, disown her sense of connection to the real world of women. That world had, for Conservative politics, become impossibly contradictory; but the Thatcher project could not be seen to endorse the experience of women. Their ploy was to produce a spectacular example of a woman in power.

So she got kicked out in the end, and The Times — even The Times — scripted her demise in a language of gender consciousness. It described it as 'the march of the men'. When she was first elected, that just would not have been thinkable. In those days, the world was ruled by men: men of a certain colour, a certain age, a certain girth. It was not seen as a problem then. Now it is, and it is significant that they did not celebrate the march of the men when they booted her out.

Uncertain Future

It is now not really clear what the ambience of British politics will be in the future. Nor is it clear what our part in that is going to be. But we will be there. The problem for us is to define what the terms of feminism's dialogue with other political institutions could be. The second half of the 1980s was very different from the first. Even if it was awful in the first half, there were sanctuaries — Greenham, for instance, where you could find a reinvigorating politics of spectacle and theatre, a robust energy, a politics of opposition which reminded you that you belonged to something called the Women's Liberation Movement — and which, a few years earlier, you had thought was not there any more. That kind of politics of spectacle in the public domain has not been around for a long time now, and we have a problem when it is not there because movements think they do not exist if it is not there.

But we need to think about the ambiguities of the global situation as well as our own domestic situation. The events of 1989 changed the world and it is very important — and especially important for Women's Studies — to address what was so extraordinarily dramatic, for women as well as for men and humankind, about the demise of the existing socialist regimes, so-called, in 1989. It is particularly salient when we are thinking about the people involved in Women's Studies and the spaces women have created in institutions that survived the 1980s.

One of the contradictions in Thatcherism is that it enabled the survival of something like Women's Studies. The introduction of a market principle, which is, of course, appalling in many ways, none the less meant that there was room for manoeuvre for some women's initiatives, because those initiatives were popular, were consumer-led, consumer-defined, were in dialogue with consumers — and the consumers of education are very demanding.

So one of the contradictions in the 1980s was that we discovered that terms like 'the market' are much more ambiguous than we had thought. We had banished them to the swamps of capitalism, forgetting that of course feminists and socialists have a long tradition of creating initiatives within the market-place. The cooperative movement, for instance, operated in the market; it was all about the market. A moralism surrounds the notion of the market, but we only need to look towards eastern Europe to discover the consequences of the abolition of those kinds of spaces. It is going to be very difficult for women to secure their place in the new, apparently pluralistic, post-socialist economies, precisely because the old orders abolished or undermined open markets and civil society, and with them disappeared a certain degree of flexibility and capacity.

The market has enabled British feminists to hold on to fastnesses of scholarship, initiative, energy and service to each other, which ten or twelve years ago we probably would have been utterly pessimistic about our capacity to sustain.

But in the allegedly egalitarian 'socialist' East, the absence of democracy, of markets, of civil society, conspired to produce patriarchal, conservative and atavistic gender politics amidst the movements for renewal.

Letting Go

This is not to say that the survival of feminist politics in Britain is thanks solely to Margaret Thatcher and the open market. But the fact is that women's movement politics, feminist politics, indeed many feminisms, have survived and continue to thrive in all sorts of ways and in all sorts of spaces — institutional and other — to which we had no access fifteen or twenty years ago.

Clearly, we no longer have a women's liberation movement in the old form of the 1960s and 1970s. So what does our feminism look like now? What kind of room has it created for itself? Why is it different from other political forms? What makes it flexible, rather than dead?

It is very important for us not to get paralysed by comparing our politics to other traditions. For instance, I remember a long time ago reading and feeling moderately inspired by the Communist Manifesto. The end is horrible, very butch language about dictatorship, but there are some nice things in it about the creation of popular people's politics. And I can remember thinking very fondly of a particular phrase which was about this: the need to protect the movements of the future in the movements of the present. I remember thinking at the time, 'That's lovely'. You know the way you search these texts for little homilies to help you define the kind of politics you think you are trying to make and preferably get it down to three words?

There is an implication in this particular little homily that you can control the future — but you can't; the last fifteen years have shown us that. But there is some generosity in it still, once you deal with the notion of control, because it helps us to review the way feminism aligned itself to political traditions which were not helpful. Our way of going about our business is quite different from some of those traditions, particularly of the left, which represented a controlling and a bullying megalomania; a sense of impregnable isolation that dared not be contaminated by negotiation, by networking, by allowing a conversation with the rest of society because it felt dangerous. What comes to mind is the title which the Irish republicanist movement has chosen for itself: 'Sinn Fein', meaning 'We ourselves alone'. It is a deadly notion, absolutely deadly, because what it does is produce a notion that we cannot actually exist in the society which we inhabit.

Everything that the Women's Studies Network is about testifies to the opposite. It is about trying to create forms and spaces that enable people to do exactly that thing that feminism was always about. It is not about creating political forms that celebrate women, ourselves, in completed form, in heroic isolation. It is about creating a political form that allows women to become something else.

In our society, access to education has become absolutely critical as part of people's — particularly oppressed people's — access to the society in which they live but from which they feel exiled. And that is what also happens inside institutions, even those that apparently have a quite different project. So what you do is utterly subversive.

We do not have a women's liberation movement with a mailing address and an annual conference and march and all that. We stopped having a national conference when they got so horrible that no one would organize it any more. But that did not mean we committed suicide. Unlike the trade union movement — people like Arthur Scargill and Eric Hammond who go to the TUC every year for their annual joust and ritual slaughter — we do not need a formal national structure to survive. When we found ourselves ritually slaughtering each other, sensibly we stopped. We abandoned a political form that produced a compulsion, a controllingness; we let go, and relaxed, and turned our energies instead to things that were useful.

Ambiguities

What we have learned about feminism's ability to survive into the rest of the century is that it is ephemeral and enduring; that it is critical — because it is critical of everything around us, ourselves included — and self-critical. It is a politics which is about being anti-authoritarian while at the same time attaching authority to women's experiences. It is a politics which rests upon autonomy and alliances: the necessary autonomy of all those who feel the need to gather, find recognition, find each other, discover difference, discover that difference is survivable, discover the mechanisms of negotiation that, for example, enable Black women and white women to be in the same room and share a project, that enable women to negotiate with men.

It is a politics that moves from autonomy to alliances: things break up and reform all the time. It is a politics which is about mobility, crossing boundaries; it is transgressive; it adopts multiple forms.

So if we can all hang on to all the contradictions and ambiguities that are embedded in that, then what we discover is a kind of strength that is supple, not brittle. We should not be frightened of the destruction of our own traditions, because we are inherently about recreating ourselves constantly; ours is a politics that is always critical, a politics of becoming.

So we should be confident about holding on to the ambiguities in our own history. So long as we hang on to the fundamental and generous principles of modern feminism — principles of commitment, contemplation, discovery and usefulness — we will not disappear.

Note

This is an edited version of an opening address given at the Women's Studies Network (UK) Conference in London, July 1991, and was published in *Trouble and Strife* 22, Winter 1991.

Chapter 2

Pedagogical Praxis and Problems: Reflections on Teaching about Gender Relations

Maureen McNeil

Introduction

If someone had told me in the late 1970s as I struggled with my first full-time teaching job, on a temporary contract in a department where I was the only female member of the teaching staff (with nine male lecturers) that some thirteen years later I would be nostalgic about that period I would have laughed. Nevertheless, now I *am* quite nostalgic about those 'good old days'. There I was: relatively young, terribly enthusiastic, ready to take on the world and fighting for any crumbs I could get. My main allies were my first two postgraduate students. (There were only three female postgraduates in the whole department.) They were mature students, not much younger than myself, and committed feminists. They were peers and hierarchy seemed irrelevant in our relationship. The battles were clear and the targets obvious: creating space (*any*) for women, by increasing women's access to higher education and by drawing attention to women's oppression in research and teaching. We were discovering the delights of collaborative work — its tabooed nature increased our pleasure. Our pure hunger for mutual support and for new knowledge about the neglected half of the species kept us buzzing. Of course it is easy to romanticize, but looking back on those years now, I am nostalgic for a period when the 'we' and 'them' seemed so clear, when the strategies in the classroom seemed so obvious. Just to mention 'women' or 'gender relations' or to get a course on the curriculum with some Women's Studies content seemed achievements, particularly in teaching like mine which was mainly about science and technology. Indeed, remaining employed in higher education was itself an achievement.

Now, some thirteen years later, my situation has changed, some would say, dramatically for the better. There is no doubt that I am in an extremely privileged situation. I now have a permanent, full-time job and a number of female (indeed, feminist) postgraduate students. Although I would not want to lose one of them, my problem now is that I have too many of them. I teach mainly about gender relations in an unusual department which has made an open political commitment to feminism (however unevenly and imperfectly realized this is in practice). I have an undergraduate and a postgraduate course each devoted to gender issues. As of this past year, I even have two full-time women colleagues who are on permanent contracts. By the standards of a working-class scholarship girl or that naive, enthusiastic young teacher of the late 1970s, I might well consider myself as having reached feminist utopia!

Despite these positive changes, I'm worried, uneasy: this last year or so has been a period of crisis for me. This is the proverbial 'mid-life crisis' in a 'new-wave' feminist form no doubt. Indeed, in the last few months when I have woken up depressed about the state of my life, I feel that the global politics represented on the radio news — the death of socialist aspirations, endless proliferation of civil wars, and so on — provide a global mirror to my own inner turmoil. Nevertheless, there is a version of *'my* crisis' which would locate it historically as the crisis of 1970s and 1980s feminism confronting the multifarious problems of diversity and its own roots.

In this chapter I focus on one aspect of this crisis — my uncertainty about being a 'feminist' teacher, teaching about gender relations. My strategy for survival as a feminist (and I am struggling both to survive and to remain a feminist or, more exactly, to know what it means to be a feminist now) draws me to a 1990s version of the 'personal as political'. That is, I see my own crisis about teaching as part of a broader loss of confidence amongst feminists and about feminism in early 1990s Britain and North America which may also extend to other parts of Western Europe, Australia, and New Zealand.

I am offering a preliminary set of reflections about difficult experiences, so this is sketchy. My aim is to explore some neglected problems within feminist (and feminist-influenced) pedagogy. To make this more concrete, I refer to some of my own teaching practices. I am mindful that these practices (and those of others) have developed in a context of scarce resources and extensive cut-backs in the social sciences and humanities within higher education in Britain. Nevertheless, I treat these developments as the crucial but unexplored backdrop for the issues I shall consider. The core of my argument is an appeal for more open forms of feminist pedagogy that will address some of the problems which have inhibited me and, I suspect, many other higher education teachers.

Feminism and Education

In considering teaching I have encountered the perennial problem that university teachers do not speak often about what they actually do. I was reminded by Charlotte Brunsdon of Judith Williamson's remarks: 'teaching . . . is like sex — you know other people do it, but you never know exactly what they do or how they do it' (Williamson, 1981/2, p. 41; Brunsdon, 1991). What goes on behind the closed doors of the classroom or lecture theatre is private property — information about which is carefully guarded. For the most part, higher education teachers in Britain are never trained as teachers (short induction courses notwithstanding). The Oxbridge tradition of courses as private projects has acted as a further barrier in the British university sector in contrast to the polytechnic sector where CNAA (Committee for National Academic Awards) panels, however problematically, do provide some openings for discussion about teaching content and practices. Some of this is changing, unevenly and not necessarily for the better, with the introduction of new forms of higher education management.

There was little published material to help me in my current dilemmas. In Britain there was a wave of publications about feminism and education in the late 1970s and early 1980s. However, much of that was about access and women's exclusion. Also there seems to have been much more written about the nature of schooling than about the nature of higher education teaching. There is some material from the USA on pedagogy within Women's Studies, some of which is relevant here (see Penley, 1986; Treichler, 1986; hooks, 1989, chapters 6–11). With a few notable exceptions (Culley and Portuges, 1985; Thompson and Wilcox, 1989; Humm, 1991; Lubelska, 1991) my feeling is that in Britain, we have mostly got on with transforming the content of our disciplines.[1] Women's caucuses or groups have had an impact on most of the arts and social science disciplines, in some cases with remarkable success. We have fought for space in classrooms, in the lecture theatres and for new texts and curricula. As we have done this new teaching methods have evolved. However, I am not sure how critically these have been explored. Of course, students often provide course evaluations (formal or informal) and criticisms, but many of us have not had the resources to undertake this for ourselves or to compare notes. Indeed, I would suggest that there has been more explicit reflection about feminist research practices than there has been about feminist teaching in British higher education (see Roberts, 1981; McRobbie, 1982; Stanley and Wise, 1983; Stanley, 1990).

The fact is that feminism is very different now than it was at the end of the 1970s as is reflected in the titles of some recent publications: *Feminism and the Contradictions of Oppression, Conflicts in Feminism, Patterns of Dissonance* (Ramazanoglu, 1989; Hirsch and Keller, 1990; Braidotti, 1991). Amongst the changes which have been crucial are: the growing awareness of diversity amongst women; the emergence of notions of 'postfeminism' and the backlash against feminism; the end of a feminist movement which was orientated primarily around concerted public action. Yet, as Andrea Stuart has observed: 'most of the social problems that prompted the rise of Feminism in the early 1970s still remain with us' (Stuart, 1990, p. 29). So, as Bea Campbell has argued, feminism has dispersed (see her chapter in this volume). She gives this a positive gloss by claiming that this has been a protective development as 'there is now no address where they can get us'. In contrast, I would contend that a few addresses have come to be identified with feminism and one of these is higher education where Women's Studies and teaching about gender relations are amongst the identifiable locations of 'Professional Feminism' (see Stuart, 1990).[2]

My interest is in what is happening to feminism 'at this address'. There are many observations that could be made about the forms of feminism within academia in the 1990s. These could be developed through reference to published materials and/or to the content and form of teaching which is relatively less visible. Bearing in mind both these profiles, my list of key developments would include (in no particular order): the emergence and burgeoning of feminist theory; complex explorations of subjectivity and engagement with a range of therapeutic modes; increasing awareness of, and concern for, divisions and diversity amongst women; and the explosion of Men's Studies.[3]

In this setting, the project of feminist teaching about gender relations is a far more complex one than that undertaken by this naive, enthusiastic young feminist lecturer thirteen years ago. I have chosen to address some of those complexities under three somewhat idiosyncratic and provocative headings: 'The personal is political, but how personal and whose politics?', 'The feminine and the feminist: critique and romance' and 'My mother made me a feminist'.

The Personal Is Political, But How Personal and Whose Politics?

Some of us 'new-wave' feminists carried the motto 'the personal is political' into the classroom. The appeal of this strategy was clear since, under this banner, space has been created for a range of women's experiences (and, indeed, often more critically, of men's experiences) which have been neglected by traditional scholars. Moreover, the slogan lies at the centre of a now highly developed set of epistemological challenges about detached objectivity which feminists have put forward (see especially Harding, 1987). There have by now been many forms of teaching that have this as one of their main touchstones, however implicit and unarticulated this might be. Moreover, this strain within feminist pedagogy intersected with other contemporaneous developments, particularly 'progressive education'.

In my own teaching, there are a number of practices that are linked to the notion that 'the personal is political'. For example, in my second-year course on Gender in Contemporary British Society (which focused on a case study around 'work' broadly defined) I asked my students to write an essay based on their own experience of gender relations at one particular work site. In a first-year, team-taught course on Media, Culture and Society, my colleagues and I ask our students 'to put themselves in the picture', in a project about a social group or site with which they have been involved, and to relate this to issues raised in the course.

Assignments such as these side-step complex theoretical debates about essentialism versus social constructionism, identity versus dispersed and fragmented subjectivity, and so on. This does not worry me much. Like Denise Riley (1988) and Diana Fuss (1989), I have found much of this debate a rather time-consuming cul-de-sac. Like them, I feel that we have to be *carefully strategic*: deploying essentialist arguments and terms (like 'women', etc.) strategically and recognizing the dangers of so doing.[4] Furthermore, in my experience, there are more immediate problems which arise from such projects.

Amongst these are a cluster of difficulties which I link to often unacknowledged power relations *within* the classroom. Given the fact that education (even feminist education) is under the jurisdiction of the state, that an aura exists around the professions (even Women's Studies lecturers), the link between power and knowledge, not to mention the constant context of assessment, teachers' calls to expose personal experiences are not necessarily experienced as liberating. Hence, for some students, invoking 'the personal as political' can seem a threatening imperative, associated with surveillance and scrutiny which provokes unease and possibly resistance.

Moreover, I suspect that I am probably one of many teachers who has not honestly confronted the diversity that emerges from such invocations. Increasingly I feel that exploring the political dimensions of 'the personal' requires different sorts of work with different sorts of students. Minimally, I feel that such an exercise works differently for those who are relatively more advantaged than it does for those who are relatively disadvantaged. Hence such an assignment, potentially, could reinforce power differentials that already exist. What I have in mind here is the fact that so much 'established knowledge' is already based on the experience of white, middle-class, heterosexual men; while 'speaking' of the experience of the underprivileged in an academic setting can itself be an achievement. Depending on the students, we could be (and here I am being rather metaphorical) helping some students to 'find a voice' or helping others to recognize how their voice 'has silenced others'. Less positively, we run the risk of amplifying some powerful voices and continuing the silencing of others.

This is further exacerbated by class, race and other inequalities which cross-cut gender inequalities. Will I be able to recognize the difficulties which a black, working-class women experiences in articulating her experience? Moreover, given deteriorating conditions of higher education in Britain, including greater numbers, I often do not know very much about where students are coming from, about who we are working with. Assumptions can be dangerous and misleading, under-estimating the complexities of styles, images and identities.[5]

This brings me to further problems relating to the skills of teachers. Dealing with 'the personal as political' can unleash considerable emotion and/or distress. For those who have had experience of women's consciousness-raising groups this should be neither new nor surprising. Yet, a classroom can be a difficult environment in which to cope with such emotions. Moreover, teachers do not necessarily have the personal resources or counselling skills to cope with some of these situations.

It is also possible that, anticipating such difficulties, students might call us up short and resist any would-be imperative. Here, I recall a striking incident in which two of my students declared that they were not willing to talk about sexuality in our seminar. I can remember thinking that unpacking precisely that deeply engrained view of sexuality as 'our most private, inner self' was part of the agenda. I did try to work with this in the session. Nevertheless, their refusal was both deeply ironic and yet absolutely understandable.[6]

I have also been increasingly aware of feminism's own constructions and conventions. The autobiographical form has been honed and polished in new-wave feminism. I and many other feminist teachers are very cagey about our own presentation of versions of 'the personal as political'. Speaking for myself, I know that I am very selective and that I am rather good at packaging my personal experiences for more public presentation in a safe and manageable version. Perhaps this is one way in which I have become (and I cringe when I think of it) one of those 'Professional Feminists' to whom Andrea Stuart (1990) refers. I became particularly self-conscious about this during a course on gender which I taught recently. I did not encourage students to discuss their own experience of gender relations very much in part because I was feeling too raw and fragile due to my own recent embroilments in gender relations and because they might have been able to identify some of the actors in my would-be narrative. This exemplifies the teacher's power to regulate and control the conditions of working with experience.

Finally, there is a constant danger of narcissism and of turning inwards, which I find an occupational hazard in the non-ivory tower in which I work. I want to encourage many of my students to push *outside* the confines of their own current experiences. Given the relatively privileged nature of higher education institutions in Britain and the enormous social problems looming all around them, there is no guarantee that encouragements to pursue the personal will become an opening-up, rather than a closing-down.

My review of these difficulties should not be interpreted as a call for detached, objective modes of learning. Indeed, I am frightened by the retreats which have occurred when teachers have been confronted with some of these difficulties. I take some slavish emphases on theory and exclusive focus on texts as retreats in the face of difficulties such as these. Nevertheless, I am convinced that these problems must be directly addressed and the ways we invoke 'the personal as political' have to be much more carefully considered.

The Feminine and the Feminist: Critique and Romance

One way of illustrating the depth of my current crisis about teaching is to consider my use of the term 'woman' or 'women' in the classroom. In the late 1970s, it was a triumphant invocation, as if I had scored a point in the struggle for women's liberation each time I managed to use it in my teaching. Now, I avoid it like the plague, conscious that I am in dangerous territory unless I qualify and specify: 'white, middle-class, middle-aged, able-bodied, British women, from the south-east' as the caricature, which is not quite caricature, might go. This is no joke, because I know that the presumptions, assumptions and blindness that made that clear invocation possible were destructive and very misleading (see Riley, 1988; Spelman, 1990). Yet Diana Fuss (1989, p. 4) is right to insist that the process of specification is potentially endless — we can never get it 'right'. More pragmatically, developed sensitivities about diversity not only make every sentence unwieldy, but make teaching a course which is, after all, *about gender* extremely difficult.

This key semantic issue is linked to another dimension of the epistemological and political project of feminism. Charlotte Brunsdon has recently argued that at the core of feminist film and television studies has been the establishment of a feminine 'Other' as the focus for the feminist critic (Brunsdon, 1991). This pattern has not been restricted to feminist film and television studies. Returning to many of the early classics of 'new-wave' feminism we encounter a righteous anger in the identification of 'duped women' and of the foibles of the feminine woman. Germaine Greer's scathing indictment of Mills and Boon readers is a classic example of this mode (Greer, 1970). In part I attribute this to the uncritical use of certain theories of ideology and false consciousness in the early stages of the recent phase of feminism. However, that is another story. . . . What concerns me here, and Charlotte Brunsdon in another context, is the moralism, sense of superiority, hidden aesthetic judgments and failure to address diversity that lie behind some of this trajectory of critique. Undoubtedly, feminist analysis has become much more sophisticated, moving far beyond the 'false consciousness' and 'blinded by ideology' mode. Nevertheless, as Ang (1988), Winship (1985), Brunsdon (1991) and others have illustrated the critic often drifts back into the role of adjudicator between the 'feminist' and 'the feminine'.

Of course, this tendency has not gone unnoticed during the past twenty years. Some of the most valuable feminist work, in my opinion, has begun from the acknowledgment that we cannot afford to be disdainful about existing forms of feminine culture. As Janice Winship and others have acknowledged in their work, forms of femininity in our culture are the basic materials of feminism.

Confronted with this facet of feminism, some critics have rebelled and presented themselves as the celebrants of 'feminine culture'. At this opposite end of the pole, there have been various romances with specific 'feminine' cultural forms.

This, in turn, is not without its own difficulties. Lynne Segal has described some of these as based on the fruitless attempt to carve out a 'pure' version of feminine culture which is removed from patriarchy (Segal, 1987). In addition to this general difficulty, the celebration often flies in the face of the growing awareness of diversity and specificity. 'Women's cultural forms' are often specific to class, race, or age (to mention but a few key categories). Unless this is addressed, then exclusions and silences are the inevitable result.

Striking political transformations can be traced in attending to these two tendencies within feminist scholarship. For example, there seems to have been a dramatic change in attitudes towards motherhood during the course of 'new-wave' feminism. In the early years, mothering was seen as equivalent to being a Mills and Boon reader — to be avoided at all costs as a trap of femininity. Sometime in the mid 1980s feminist analyses began to shift and motherhood emerged as a feminine experience which was to be celebrated and recovered as 'feminist'. Ann Snitow has traced her version of this sea change (Snitow, 1992). For my purposes in this chapter, I see this shift as indicative of the way feminist scholarship has been drawn between the poles of feminist condemnation and feminist celebration of feminine cultural forms.

My elaboration of these two tendencies — the construction of the feminine as 'Other' and the celebration of forms of femininity — has enabled me to understand more of my own unease about teaching. As a teacher it is difficult to avoid some version of one of these. Charlotte Brunsdon discusses the ways in which female students react to certain teaching materials such as soap operas or feminist avant-garde films (Brunsdon, 1991). Their responses can be deeply embedded in the specificity of female diversity (class, race, sexual orientation, age, and disability are amongst the key factors here). In short, students may experience the use of such material as a moment of aesthetic and political statement and judgment on the part of the teacher. In these instances and, indeed, in virtually every decision or resource allocation we make as teachers, we speak or can be viewed as adjudicating through these paradigms. We can be seen as presenting either forms of feminine culture to be criticized (or even condemned) or to be celebrated. The versions of this can be more or less subtle, more or less hidden, more or less conscious. What matters is that they hover around the teaching situation and students can respond positively or negatively.

It is little wonder that my awareness of these poles of feminist analysis has haunted me as a teacher. Each time I choose a novel, a short story, a magazine, a film, or a theory, or introduce any ingredient into the teaching context, I am courting these dangers. In some sense these are inevitable. They are not just the result of who we are, what we do and how we do it, but of students' perceptions of us and of the power structure which shapes the teaching situation. Nevertheless, it does seem important to acknowledge this and to consider its implications for our daily teaching practices.

My Mother Made Me a Feminist

Thinking of who we are and what we bring to the teaching situation reminded me of the familiar graffiti slogan which I have taken as the subheading for this section. My memories are of finding this in women's toilets together with follow-ups such as 'What kind of wool did she use?' 'Will she make me one too?', and so on. I want to use it as a reminder of the specificity of *my*, and by extension, *all* relationships to feminism and to explore what this might mean for teaching. My interest here is understanding more about my investment in teaching and the impact of that investment on my interactions with students. If we go back to my original account of the enthusiastic young lecturer that I was I can recognize that much of my energy came from a sense of mission. Yet, as Angela McRobbie has suggested, there are dangers in such 'recruitist' forms of feminism (McRobbie, 1982, p. 52).

In employing the phrase 'my mother made me a feminist', I am reminding myself of the need to acknowledge the specificity of my own shaping as a feminist. In short, our feminism is a selection from a diverse and complicated range of priorities and issues. This is something about which I have recently become increasingly and sometimes painfully aware. Although I was politicized by the broad political movement which was feminism in the late 1960s and 1970s, I carved out my own particular version of it. As a white, heterosexual scholarship girl from a working-class family in affluent Canada I attached particular importance to economic independence and contraceptive access and rights.[7] Much of my feminism around these pivotal issues was in dialogue with my mother and my understandings and, possibly, misunderstandings of her life. These are areas which I have only begun to explore but they have encouraged me to be more open about the varieties of feminism and more wary of any missionary zeal.

As a teacher I am dealing with students with a variety of backgrounds and experiences — none of which are likely to be the same as mine (although there may be some shared elements). The point is not that I impose my version of feminism on my students in an evangelistic mode. Rather, I am concerned about a more subtle process. Inevitably those priorities and that particular version of feminism I inhabit shape my day-to-day operations in teaching. I can see some of the ways that my repertoire of pedagogic priorities has been influenced by that specific feminist route. For example, as I mentioned earlier, I just happened to choose 'work' as the site to be explored in my course on gender! This exploration seems to suggest the need to be more open about this process, negotiating with students and acknowledging very different starting points.[8]

The graffiti line of my subheading also has a further dimension. I have come to see those priorities which have shaped my feminism as both strengths and weaknesses. This reminds me of many feminist novels about generations of women who learn from their mothers' lives and thereby both make themselves freer, whilst encountering new forms of entrapment. One lesson I take from this fiction and from my own experience is that patterns of reproduction and change are extremely complex. Hence, even if we could as feminist teachers instil our priorities in our students, we might be creating new constraints as well as new freedoms.

In all of this I am advocating more open exploration of pedagogy and some stepping back from a definite sense of 'recruitism' within feminist teaching. This sense of mission apart, there needs to be more consideration of the power relations in the teaching situation and more awareness of our priorities in this context as precisely *our* priorities.

Conclusion

This chapter is more about explorations than it is about conclusions. The reflection on some of my own difficulties in invoking experience and 'the personal as political' within the classroom was one starting point for exploration. Here I found myself advocating caution and more consideration of power relations in the pedagogic setting. My second avenue of exploration was of feminist paradigms of critique and celebration of feminine cultural forms. Again, this pointed to the need for more awareness of how these function in the teaching context. Finally, I investigated some aspects of my own version of feminism as a shaping determinant of my teaching. Self-consciousness was the watchword here, as I appealed for the abandonment of missionary zeal and for greater openness within feminist teaching.

In considering some of my own unease about being a feminist teaching about gender relations in Britain today I am only beginning to see the wider connections. My concerns are not, I am sure, unique. The emergence of feminist theory and the *retreat* into that, which I would distinguish from the continuous and ongoing need for rigorous intellectual work and theoretical clarification, seems to be one response to such a crisis.[9] Another is to 'hide behind the text', in a world where textual analysis becomes all. Some forms of this work are relatively uncontroversial within the academy and can become quite hermetically sealed, so that the social problems which inspired feminism cease to be on the agenda. It may even be that the new vogue for 'Men's Studies' represents another response insofar as it involves turning away from the problems of diversity amongst women. This is not a sweeping judgment on specific work or teaching associated with these developments: theory is important, textual analyses are crucial and there must be good work on masculinity. Rather, I would contend that it is when these modes become ends in themselves or escapes from engagement in an open feminist teaching practice which is about political transformation that something has gone wrong. This paper has been about questions and beginnings, rather than answers and closures: I think I am one of a number of women who are struggling to understand what it means to be a feminist teacher in the 1990s. There is no room for nostalgia here, but there is a great need for openness and exploration.

Notes

1 For an early review of feminist efforts to transform various disciplines see Spender, 1981.
2 Of course, not all teaching about gender in higher education is necessarily feminist.
3 There is considerable debate about all of these developments. However, some would dispute whether Men's Studies should be identified with developments within feminism. I have included this in my list because the emergence of this field is clearly, for better or worse (and the crux of the debate is about whether it is for better or worse), in relation to feminist academic work.
4 Fuss's interesting chapter 'Essentialism in the Classroom' (Fuss, 1989, ch. 7) is to be recommended. However, I do think that it provides a rather decontextualized account of the higher education classroom in the USA.
5 This was illustrated at graduation this year when I and some of my colleagues were rather surprised to find a young woman we had assumed to be working-class arrived with her clearly middle-class, highly educated mother! Conversations with her mother seemed to suggest that a working-class accent and resistance to higher education were part of this young woman's rebellion against her family background.

6   This sense of our sexuality as our most intimate dimension — 'our real self' — is a key element of Western industrial culture, which we cannot ignore and in which we are all implicated. This was not just my students' problem! Moreover, in this particular incident it is likely that these students' reactions reflected their lack of confidence in my ability to tackle what might be unleashed in such discussion.

7   It is probably not insignificant that I have changed the wording of this section several times in what has been an illuminating process of clarification. Initially I thought of my feminism as focusing on contraception. I then considered changing this to *birth control*, but realized, in fact, that I had been precisely caught up with *contraception*, rather than *birth control*. This is a crucial distinction and acknowledgment in my early forties as I face childlessness.

8   For an interesting exploration of this in a rather different domain, see Janice Winship's article on magazines for young women in Britain in the early 1980s (Winship, 1985).

9   My fears about the direction of much feminist theory and its implications for pedagogy were fuelled by comments at a recent conference. In discussion at the Feminist Theory Conference held in Glasgow in July 1991 Nancy Miller acknowledged her own dismay that in preparing an undergraduate course she felt unable to use anything published since 1975! What does this say about feminist work in the academy and about the failure of feminist scholars to speak to their students?

References

ANG, IEN (1988) 'Feminist Desire and Female Pleasure', *Camera Obscura*, 16, pp. 178–91.

BRAIDOTTI, ROSI (1991) *Patterns of Dissonance*, Cambridge, Polity Press.

BRUNSDON, CHARLOTTE (1991) 'Pedagogies of the Feminine: Feminist Teaching and Women's Genres', *Screen*, 32:4, pp. 364–81.

CULLEY, MARGOT and PORTUGES, CATHERINE (1985) *Gendered Subjects*, London, Routledge and Kegan Paul.

FUSS, DIANA (1989) *Essentially Speaking: Feminism, Nature and Difference*, London, Routledge.

GREER, GERMAINE (1970) *The Female Eunuch*, London, Granada.

HARDING, SANDRA (1987) *The Science Question in Feminism*, Milton Keynes, Open University Press.

HIRSCH, MARIANNE and KELLER, EVELYN FOX (Eds) (1990) *Conflicts in Feminism*, London, Routledge.

HOOKS, BELL (1989) *Talking Back: Thinking Feminist, Thinking Black*, Boston, South End.

HUMM, MAGGIE (1991) ' "Thinking of things in themselves": Theory, Experience, Women's Studies', in AARON, JANE and WALBY, SYLVIA (Eds) *Out of the Margins: Women's Studies in the Nineties*, London, Falmer Press, pp. 49–62.

LUBELSKA, CATHY (1991) 'Teaching Methods in Women's Studies: Challenging the Mainstream', in AARON, JANE and WALBY, SYLVIA (Eds) *Out of the Margins: Women's Studies in the Nineties*, London, Falmer Press, pp. 41–8.

McROBBIE, ANGELA (1982) 'The Politics of Feminist Research: Between Talk, Text and Action', *Feminist Review*, 12, pp. 46–57.

PENLEY, CONSTANCE (1986) 'Teaching in Your Sleep: Feminism and Psychoanalysis', in NELSON, CARY (Ed.) *Theory in the Classroom*, Urbana and Chicago, University of Illinois Press, pp. 129–48.

RAMAZANOGLU, CAROLINE (1989) *Feminism and the Contradictions of Oppression*, London and New York, Routledge.

RILEY, DENISE (1988) *'Am I That Name?': Feminism and the Category of 'Women' in History*, Basingstoke, Macmillan.

ROBERTS, HELEN (1981) *Doing Feminist Research*, London, Routledge and Kegan Paul.
SEGAL, LYNNE (1987) *Is the Future Feminine?: Troubled Thoughts on Contemporary Feminism*, London, Virago.
SNITOW, ANN (1992) 'Feminism and Motherhood: An American Reading', *Feminist Review* 40, pp. 32–51.
SPELMAN, ELIZABETH (1990) *Inessential Woman: Problems of Exclusion in Feminist Thought*, London, Women's Press.
SPENDER, DALE (Ed.) (1981) *Men's Studies Modified: The Impact of Feminism on the Academic Disciplines*, Oxford, Pergamon.
STANLEY, LIZ (Ed.) (1990) *Feminist Praxis: Research, Theory and Epistemology in Feminist Sociology*, London, Routledge and Kegan Paul.
STANLEY, LIZ and WISE, SUE (1983) *Breaking Out: Feminist Consciousness and Feminist Research*, London, Routledge and Kegan Paul.
STUART, ANDREA (1990) 'Feminism: Dead or Alive?', in RUTHERFORD, JONATHAN (Ed.) *Identity: Community, Culture, Difference*, London, Lawrence and Wishart, pp. 28–42.
THOMPSON, ANN and WILCOX, HELEN (Eds) (1989) *Teaching Women: Feminism and English Studies*, Manchester, Manchester University Press.
TREICHLER, PAULA (1986) 'Teaching Feminist Theory', in NELSON, CARY (Ed.) *Theory in the Classroom*, Urbana and Chicago, University of Illinois Press, pp. 57–128.
WILLIAMSON, JUDITH (1981/2) 'How Does Girl Number Twenty Understand Ideology?', *Screen Education*, 40, pp. 80–7.
WINSHIP, JANICE (1985) ' "A girl needs to get street-wise": Magazines for the 1980s', *Feminist Review*, reprinted in BETTERTON, ROSEMARY (Ed.) (1987) *Looking On: Images of Femininity in the Visual Arts and the Media*, London, Pandora, pp. 127–41.

Chapter 3

Whiteness — The Relevance of Politically Colouring the 'Non'

Helen (charles)

A strange and interesting atmosphere was created at a workshop situated in the large and spacious room called the 'studio'. Strange, because in the years of studying 'race' issues, I had never discussed whiteness. Interesting, because I was finding out about the colour politics of women.

Let me explain that the following is not a formal paper, as such. This writing is a piece of my thinking around the exclusion politics that are rife in British Women's Studies, and has come about as a reflection upon the notion of 'whiteness' which was the subject of debate at the workshop. What follows forms the important possibility of greater accessibility and understanding of the changing faces of 'race' and 'racism'. By the very quotation marks that frame them, the concepts have entered the field of Women's Studies as terms that are ripe for deconstruction and examining. The political colouring of a skin-tone which is not independently colourized ('white' = 'non') or politicized, makes a statement in the multi-inter-cultural society of contemporary Britain.

The 'Non' as Whiteness

In highlighting the 'non', I believe that to speak of, for example, 'non-white', directs the listener, reader or writer to a place where 'white' people can silently inhabit a whiteness that is problematic at best and depoliticized at worst. If the 'non' refers to the homogeneity of Black people, then the 'white' assumes a place of control out of which all 'others' are categorized. It is the 'non' which indicates that 'white' is not being addressed. It never admits the presence of Blackness. There is only the relative safety of a displaced reference to 'other' or 'ethnic minority' — a highly charged assumption which is always trying to escape being pinned down. Non-politicization and non-recognition of whitenesses within Women's Studies means that so-called 'white women' are not part of the relevance of their own political colouring.

The purpose of my wanting to do a workshop on the notion of 'whiteness' was to find out how 'white women' saw themselves in relation to colour politics. The question of how so-termed 'women of colour' saw whiteness was not so difficult to ascertain, but in terms of a space where women could discuss the issue, the workshop proved to springboard an inter-colour debate.

Is the concept of 'whiteness' new? Not really. There are many of us who think about it, either directly or indirectly, all the time. In the public, historical, literary and theoretical sphere, though, there is a curious absence of analysis. An absence which is striking in the women's networks when we remember the relative ease with which the word 'white' is used in conjunction with 'middle-class men' or in the abbreviated WASP (White Anglo-Saxon Protestant). If the description of 'white women' occurs, it is laced with perceptions of 'otherness' that do not include all 'white women' (class, mobility, lesbianism). Yet all[1] Black, Asian and/or people of Colour have been and are perceived under the kinds of concepts that give an appearance of uni-formity: 'minority/ethnic', 'other', 'difference'. Sometimes the upper-casing of a concept can make the issue in question more important; thus, Black specifies an identity which has been thought and fought about constantly and consistently here in Britain.

'Race', 'Racism' and Women

In the Women's Movement, the uni-formity of perceived notions potentially has the ability to transfer across assumptions. The resolution does not seem to lie in 'white women' making friends or contact with one or more women of Colour (we have all been patronized by men who call themselves feminists). 'White women', in their interest in fighting against racism, appear to deny their own existence, culture, and/or identity. Could it be that it is far easier for some 'white women' to speak of racism from an assumed Black woman's point of view? What happens to the 'white woman' who feels more confident about anti-racist strategies than her own place in the dominant whiteness that we live in? The concept of 'racism' is changing. It now has the ability to take extremely subtle, but recognizable, paths. Perhaps there is a confusion about where 'racism' stops, but since it is an issue that is nowhere near being resolved in Britain, I believe it to be imperative to listen carefully to the perceptions and assumptions of writing, thinking, and speaking people. In so doing, the movement towards a truer understanding of what 'race' and 'racism' have evolved into (post-colonially) may be clarified. Because it is obvious that people of Colour write, think, or/and speak about 'white people' in the strain for recognition, equality, understanding and so on, it is becoming conspicuous that the vast majority of 'white women' operating in the field of Women's Studies are not able to discuss at any great length 'being white'. Instead, we have listened and read how: Black women are being Black; Asian women are being Asian; (bizarrely-termed) 'Third World' women are being 'Third World', and now the probable take-up in a new lesson on how these women and more are *being* 'of Colour'. All this may be fine if women can learn something about whiteness being actually and directly related to questions of ethnicity. Why shouldn't whiteness be discussed as openly as, say, the issues around Blackness?

But listening and reading does not necessarily produce white-awareness in 'white people'. The blockages that seem to make up 'white women's' inability to make connections with 'race'/'racism' as 'white women' are perfectly visible to Asian and/or Black women at some point in their daily experiences of exclusion politics: living, working, studying in Britain. It was those blockages that I found myself thinking about when I tried to prepare a workshop on 'race' which was not going to fall into the same 'culturally-interesting-and-therefore-entertaining' slots that I had seen other debates fall into.

The workshop on 'whiteness' was a conscious attempt to think openly about occlusion in 'white women'. As such, it was exploratory in the first instance which led to aspects of need, accessibility, diplomacy and political spotlighting. I hope that the twenty-nine women who attended went away thinking about colour politics in ways that they never had, or gave themselves the credit due to past and future efforts of surfacing the problem of whiteness. Some hopes have been rewarded by post-workshop communications from women who saw the workshop space as 'a challenge to white women in the group', 'interesting', 'insightful', and 'something that has to be discussed up-front'.

When I look for unambiguous thoughts about whiteness from other people's words (written or spoken) I find that bell hooks has written about certain aspects of it; she tells us about Coco Fusco who writes about the unprogressive nature of ignoring 'white ethnicity' (hooks, 1991, p. 171). Hooks has also spoken about whiteness in London (Black and Third World Radical Bookfair, 1991) — an issue which was not on the agenda but nevertheless became part of her discussion. You can also read whiteness *into* various feminist and womanist texts, but it is a challenge and a sign of change when you see that 'white' is discussed as a racial category in *Third World Women and the Politics of Feminism* (Mohanty, Russo and Torres, 1991, p. 24) and is accordingly indexed. In the index to *'Race', Writing and Difference* (Gates, 1986), 'white women, racism of' is listed. Look up the page reference and Hazel V. Carby is speaking about a woman called Anna Julia Cooper who, almost a century ago, stressed the importance of challenging 'white women' to: 'revolutionize their thinking and practices'. These are just a few references to whiteness in the existing literature.

'Real' White Women?

Do 'white women' exist? The structure of the question positions what I have also been attempting to clarify within the discourses of feminism and womanism. Owing to the vicissitudes of language and terminology, the British Women's Movement apparently has difficulty spotlighting something which is ever-present, and yet appears to be always out of focus. Discontent in Women's Studies networks arise when exclusionary practices take place. In order to exclude, there must be groups of women who take for granted certain privileges and use them to facilitate exclusion politics. The problem lies in the fact that many 'white women', in appearing to *include* women of Colour and the issues arising from race-oppression, create oppositional and dual registers that ignore or displace the position of 'white women' on the racism agenda. When we say 'I am . . .' do we exclude or include? If whiteness is saying 'I am non-Black', is the frame of reference solely dependent on the concept of 'of Colour'? If political colouring can stand on its own, as it does in the existence of numerous groups beginning and ending with 'Asian', 'Black', 'South-East Asian', 'of Colour', then what happens when whiteness is isolated? *Can* it be isolated?

The Workshop

Do 'white women' exist? — a possible re-naming for this workshop. The question was posited, doubtless, as a challenge. The participants, some of whom were of

Colour but most of whom were 'white', had had discussions in small groups following the individual answering of a set of questions I had prepared. The nine women of Colour were interspersed — symbolizing an important presence within the groups. The list of questions we used are re-presented below:

- Do you have a colour?
- What colour are you?
- What do you understand by the term 'woman of colour'?
- Have you ever heard or used the term 'non-white'?
- Is there a difference between 'non-Black' and 'white', and, if so, what?
- What associations do you have with 'white'?
- What image(s) do you have when you look at the phrase 'white woman'?
- Does white skin pertain to colour, and why/why not?
- Is white visible?
- On 'ethnic monitoring forms', what do you understand about the category 'White'?
- Do you think the colour of one's skin can be politicized, and, if so, how?
- What do you understand by the term 'coloured'?
- What do you understand by the term 'Other'?
- Which do you speak/write of most, 'race' or 'colour', and is there a difference between them?

For the allocated sixty minutes of the workshop, I was aware that just one of these questions could have taken up an hour-long discussion. My point was not to narrow the issues down, and so dilute their individual importance, but to place on one side of A4 paper some of the many questions that I considered necessary and relevant to begin discussing, if not answering. Why the subtle negativity ('non'), and why the poignant absence ('whiteness'), were questions begging to be analyzed. The set of prepared questions did not take long to compile as they localize issues that are raised every day, consciously or unconsciously, by and to people of a noticeable but minoritized colour and/or feature. Hazel Carby asked white women to listen in 1982, but it seems to me that there has been little change in the last decade in the way women perceive each other inter-culturally. Yes, 'white women' have listened and in some cases have become experts at listening to the voices of Black and/or Asian women, but how has this listening affected their own voices and understanding? Can 'white women' in politics and/or in academia only see the colour of their skins in relation to women of colour? Does whiteness exist only from an Asian/Black point of view? Are 'white women' to be perceived as those 'without skins' like the white slaveocracy in *Beloved* (Morrison, 1987)? Why have 'white women' not politicized themselves as 'non', or 'not'? Why have 'white women' in general not deemed it necessary to politicize 'white' with an upper-case 'W'? In view of this last question I have seen writers of Colour visibly showing the capitalized 'White'. I see this as more than prompting the realization that there is a tempting *laisser-faire* attitude towards fighting racism within the Women's Movement. On the same note, it is with a mixture of relief and suspicion that I see what might be an editorial policy to use upper-case 'W' for 'White' as well as 'B' for Black, in the journal *Women: A Cultural Review*. Strangely, there is no mention of why in the editorial or style notes, nor in the introduction.

Coming Out as White

I feel it is now time for some verbal and textual 'outness'. It is negatively exhausting teaching 'white women' what it is like to be Black, although it has been crucial in the development of my own analysis of the every-day effects of 'race' on Black people in England, Wales, Scotland and Ireland. What this teaching has highlighted is the incredible silences that pervade the seminar room and the conference hall, where the debate on racial colouring is seen as embarrassing and, therefore, non-debatable. It is well worth reading what Shantu Watt and Juliet Cook (1991) have to say about the ownership of racism in Women's Studies, as well as Avtar Brah's paper in the same volume, which discusses the conceptualization of 'difference'. In this day and age it is embarrassing and inappropriate to be talking/teaching race-, ability- and class-awareness, when there appears to be a fashionable rush towards 'post' concepts ('postfeminism', 'postmodernism' and so on) in some critical discourses. The power of white silence might draw some women into guilt-awareness but how long should we wait for it to move beyond the sinking-in stage? In the meantime there is an overt politics of exclusion going on in Women's Studies.

Becoming highly interested in exclusion politics, I realized (on a conscious level) that if you are looked at as a 'minority figure' there is a danger of inadvertently assuming the place of Object whilst re-placing the self as Subject. In other words, speaking out as Black, of Colour, someone who has a disability or is poor, working-class, zami, lesbian or gay, appears to be seen by dominant cultures as categorizations of mere convenience. The minority Self is placed in this ghettoized space where subjects of the dominant classes, castes, sexuality and colour can look at you and, if possible, 'help' you to fight against that which is silently deemed 'your problem'.

If women of Colour are part of Women's Studies, then there has to be a great deal more than just listening to 'them' as guest speakers, friends and colleagues. Putting into practice the valuable debate-material that is offered will make important moves, not towards a global feminism, but towards a space where 'white women' can get to grips with their own racial and cultural identities. (I was warmed to see that some of the workshop participants took away copies of the questions and told me that they intended using them in the educational field). With or without the spotlight, the shadowy images of 'whiteness' for white women in this culture will encourage the slippage of who or what is 'non' into an arena of self-denial and lessen the possibility of real coalition between the politics of women in Britain. The give and take of women within the Women's Studies framework is heavily weighted at one end and I, for one, am interested in seeing some action on how 'white women' really see themselves in relation to women of Colour as well as in relation to themselves.

Shifting the focus of 'race' and colour into the protected sphere of whiteness enables us to look carefully at how to speak, read, think and write of 'feminist whiteness' as a politic. It is never very clear how the apparent neutrality of (non-) colour is perceived in Women's Studies literature, let alone the assumptions that are left trailing. There was a great deal to talk about at the workshop and women did talk — well over the allotted time. We debated whether 'white' was a colour and from the twenty lists of questions that were returned to me, two women described themselves as other than Black, Brown or white: 'beige' and 'pink'. Obviously, there was little time to debate most of the questions but out of the several that were discussed, the one 'What image(s) do you have when you look at the phrase "white woman"?' spiralled outwards into some intriguing perceptions. What appeared to be paramount was that 'white women' had difficulty existing. They were people that only Black people saw or spoke about; they were ethereal beings; they were people who condoned racism in the nineteenth century; they were called Scarlett O'Hara; they were idealistic, powerless, blonde, middle-class; they were Scandinavian, gentile, moral; they were self-righteous, size 10 and aesthetically beautiful. The phrase itself ('white woman') brought up notions of male-determined language; apartheid and racial 'superiority'; religious fanaticism; positions of racial privilege; and sometimes it 'depended on the context'. Some women of Colour expressed views on exclusionary practices of the 'white woman' and asked 'white women' in the room whether any of their perceptions of the phrase included themselves. It was this challenge which led to the question of whether 'white women' existed, especially in the Women's Studies, highly selective, network.

Being Challenged

I once asked Pamela, a school friend, if she was 'coloured'. Her answer was angry and articulate. Did I see pink? Blue? Green? Did I see a rainbow on her face? No, she was brown, she said. At 14, we were verbalizing what I now see, in retro-spect, as a *mise-en-scène* depicting the puzzling and stalwart gazes of two brown teenagers. We had no words with politicizing capital 'B's in our vocabulary but we did have the beginnings of a debate, and our skin colours surrounded a scene of inquiry as I looked at my peer's face and tried to understand the irritation, for both of us, that my question had evoked. But we were not actors in this scene.

Those of us who have been called 'non-white', 'ethnic minorities', 'minority ethnics' and 'coloured' — to name a few of the more or less subtle subordinate terms — have been politically placed into the kind of homogenizing category that is intended to keep 'them' (that is, 'us') in their (our) place. But manipulation of the 'other cultures' or the 'between cultures' has not been easy. There is always room for challenge in Britain. Out of the vast number of questions that can be asked about whiteness, one focuses on the strategy of movement. What strategies of challenge make those moves? What makes a movement move? Whether we are talking about colour phenotypically or politically, whiteness needs to be addressed because at the moment, in some cases, it is relevant.

My challenge to 'white women' is to ask the same question I asked Pamela: Are you coloured — in any way?

Spiralling inwards, the issue of 'race' can be anchored to what some know as 'racism'. Its many forms are well-known. Its subtle forms are not. Debating whitecentricism (as opposed to Eurocentricism) attempts to bring 'white women' in the Women's Movement and/or in the Women's Studies field to a place where they are visible to themselves as well as in relation to other ('white') women.

The African-American adage, *the world is not yet ready for white people with dreadlocks*, has a nice ring to it. It also says something which cannot be submerged as guilt-awareness or any other deadlock repression. Is British Women's Studies ready for whiteness — yet?

Notes

I am indebted to Terry McBride and Riet Bettonviel for their invaluable support in the preparation of the workshop, and to the women who participated in a frank and encouraging way. Special thanks are also due to my brother Dennis, to Kimi Takesue, and to Tina Papoulias.

1   Whilst not wishing to amalgamate (Black and Asian) people of Colour into one category and thus into homogeneity, I find that the Black Lesbian and Gay Centre Project offers a very accessible definition of *Black* which is specific to Britain and can be referred to accordingly (see below). The term *Black* runs parallel to the African American *people of colour*, and I have upper-cased *Colour* in the text to illustrate its politicization as Black British, whilst also respecting its African American roots. This is the Project's definition:

> [All lesbians and gay men] descended (through one or both parents) from Africa, Asia (i.e. the Middle East to China, including the Pacific nations) and Latin America, and . . . descended from the original inhabitants of Australasia, North America and the islands of the Atlantic and Indian Ocean.

References

BRAH, AVTAR (1991) 'Questions of Difference and International Feminism', in AARON, JANE and WALBY, SYLVIA (Eds) *Out of the Margins: Women's Studies in the Nineties*, London, Falmer Press, pp. 168–76.

CARBY, HAZEL V. (1982) 'White Woman Listen! Black Feminism and the Boundaries of Sisterhood', in CENTRE FOR CONTEMPORARY CULTURAL STUDIES, *The Empire Strikes Back: Race and Racism in 70s Britain*, London, Hutchinson, pp. 212–35.

CARBY, HAZEL V. (1986) ' "On the Threshold of Woman's Era": Lynching, Empire, and Sexuality in Black Feminist Theory', in GATES, H.L., JR. (Ed.) *'Race', Writing, and Difference*, Chicago, University of Chicago Press, pp. 301–16.

GATES, H.L., JR. (Ed.) (1986) *'Race', Writing, and Difference*, Chicago, University of Chicago Press.

HOOKS, BELL (1991) *Yearning: Race, Gender, and Cultural Politics*, London, Turnaround.

MOHANTY, CHANDRA TALPADE, RUSSO, ANN and TORRES, LOURDES (1991) *Third World Women and the Politics of Feminism*, Bloomington and Indianapolis Indiana University Press.

MORRISON, TONI (1987) *Beloved*, London, Chatto and Windus.

WATT, SHANTU and COOK, JULIET (1991) 'Racism: Whose Liberation? Implications for Women's Studies', in AARON, JANE and WALBY, SYLVIA (Eds) *Out of the Margins: Women's Studies in the Nineties*, London, Falmer Press, pp. 131–42.

Chapter 4

Men in Women's Studies Classrooms

Deborah Philips and Ella Westland

'There is no room for men in women's studies, none whatsoever', Renate Duelli Klein argued fiercely in a polemical article of the 1980s (Klein, 1983, p. 413). Many feminist teachers in Britain still share this principled position,[1] but, in the 1990s, they find themselves working in a Women's Studies field which has expanded dramatically over the past decade and, in the process, admitted more men. In theory, Women's Studies coordinators may wish to preserve the Women's Studies space for women, but in the real world of academic institutions they often agree to pragmatic compromises. The attitude of Women's Studies students also seems to have shifted: the research project described in this article shows that many female students now believe that men have a place as teachers and learners in Women's Studies classrooms. These new pressures mean that there is an urgent need for feminists responsible for developing and teaching Women's Studies in all its varied forms to face the fact that men are a fixture on many programmes, and to adopt some appropriate new strategies for dealing with them.

The Men Problem

The use of male staff remains a subject for impassioned debate in many Women's Studies teams. The potential problems are well recognized, ranging from the threat of direct sexual harassment to subtler influences on course ethos and classroom dynamics. Male leadership inevitably affects the treatment of sensitive subject matter in class discussion, and male academics are less likely to be committed to the 'gynagogical' teaching methods and unorthodox modes of written work which Women's Studies courses frequently encourage (Humm, 1989; Lubelska, 1991).

In spite of these acknowledged risks, the significance of male involvement is sometimes underplayed in the search for solutions to local difficulties. In many institutions, the development of Women's Studies is a long and gruelling process, and male involvement at a minimal level is considered a small price to pay for bringing Women's Studies into the curriculum. A recent account of the 'five-year struggle' to establish a master's degree at Hull University is typical in this respect: it concedes the reality of the 'men problem', but reports that in their case the small input from male teachers was 'trouble-free' (Stoneman, 1989, pp. 96–100). Practical staffing considerations are the primary reason for opening the doors of Women's

Studies classrooms to male lecturers, but some Women's Studies coordinators may see an additional tactical advantage in expanding their course team to secure a broader power base in the institution.

Male staff, then, present a problem to female course teams, but our study shows that in the classrooms themselves the issue of male students is much more contentious. Men cannot be legally excluded from any non-vocational course, as validating bodies and college managers are well aware (for the only exceptions, see sections 47 and 48 of the 1975 Sex Discrimination Act). Postgraduate Women's Studies degrees attract applications from a small number of male students, and the recent proliferation of undergraduate Women's Studies courses is encouraging a steady stream of male enrolments. The new wave of gender studies, growing in spite of opposition from Women's Studies campaigners (Evans, 1991; Klein, 1991), implies male involvement at both staff and student level.

There is longstanding research, backed up by more recent studies, to show that men in mixed classrooms upset the learning process for women (Spender, 1980; Kramarae and Treichler, 1990; Thomas, 1990; Kelly, 1991). Teachers often find that even a minority of men in a mainly-women class tend to be more dominating in discussion and less supportive of the group. In the eyes of many feminists, any male presence invalidates the essential project of Women's Studies, which aims to give women opportunities to talk openly about personal experiences and patriarchal attitudes *among themselves*. Some Women's Studies organizers therefore conduct damage limitation exercises to protect their courses against men, carefully selecting male colleagues with the personal and political qualities likely to be acceptable to women staff and students, and actively discouraging male students from enrolling, but increasingly these tactics cannot be guaranteed success. They may indeed be deemed inappropriate in the current environment, for our research suggests that, though female postgraduates tend to support a women-only policy, many female undergraduates express a preference for working in mixed Women's Studies groups with male staff input. It is not only the influx of men, but also the expectations of a younger generation of women students, that require us to re-examine our current philosophy and practice.

The Study

Our research is based on questionnaires completed by ninety-six students in eleven Women's Studies classes, including three classes of our own. (Table 4.1 shows our sample categories.) With five of the groups, the administration of questionnaires in class was followed by a discussion session; the remaining six groups were surveyed through questionnaires only.

Our findings showed a crucial divergence between undergraduate and postgraduate students, and in the account below we deal with these groups under separate headings.

The Undergraduate View

We received fifty-eight questionnaires from the seven undergraduate classes (see Table 4.2); all the classes included male students, ranging from one to one-third

Deborah Philips and Ella Westland

Table 4.1 Women's Studies courses: total sample

The table gives the number of courses in each category and (in brackets) the number of completed questionnaires.

Staff	Students			
	BA courses		MA courses	
	Mixed groups	All-women groups	Mixed groups	All-women groups
Mixed teaching teams (i.e. one or more men)	3 (20)	—	1 (9)	2 (22)
All-women teaching teams	4 (38)	—	—	1 (7)

Total number of courses in sample = 11
Total number of questionnaires completed = 96
Number of questionnaires completed by men = 11

Table 4.2 BA courses

Mixed teaching teams = 'Group M'	20 questionnaires from 3 classes
All-women teaching teams = 'Group W'	38 questionnaires from 4 classes

Total number of classes = 7
Total number of questionnaires completed = 58
Number of questionnaires completed by men = 10

(eight out of a class of twenty-four). In every case, younger students were in the majority: over half fell into the 19 to 21 age-group, and only eight students (all female) were over 30. Few had previously encountered women's groups or Women's Studies in any form.

These undergraduate courses, covering literature, history and sociology/film, all had 'women' or 'gender' in their titles. Although they were not specifically labelled as Women's Studies, they represent the kind of courses where much of the feminist teaching in our colleges now takes place: they were run by feminist lecturers, whose concept of the courses was in some degree consciousness-raising, and many of their students testified to the changes which the classes brought about in their own attitudes to gender issues.[2]

Undergraduate Attitudes to Male Staff

An unexpectedly large majority of BA students welcomed the involvement of male staff on Women's Studies courses. Nineteen out of the twenty students in Group M, who had been taught by women and men, saw it as an advantage to have had a male lecturer, and thought that future courses should 'definitely' (13) or 'if possible' (6) be co-taught. By contrast, a third of the students in Group W, who had not been taught Women's Studies by men, were happy with an all-women teaching team, though only one woman 'definitely' wanted female staff. This response suggests that a good proportion of students who have experienced

Women's Studies courses taught exclusively by women will express a preference for that mode, and indicates that the virtually unanimous support from Group M for a mixed teaching team primarily reflects students' actual experience. But it is important to note that half the students in Group W shared the view of Group M that male lecturers would make a welcome contribution to Women's Studies courses.

Three of the classes in Group W, who had not experienced a male Women's Studies teacher, were asked whether they noticed any differences between the approach of their Women's Studies staff and the lecturers they had encountered on other undergraduate courses at the same institution. They nearly all recorded examples, and though a few criticized their female Women's Studies teachers for being too 'one-sided' or 'pushy', a far larger number commented with enthusiasm on such features as the 'more relaxed approach and . . . more honest attitude' of the Women's Studies class, and the apparently unusual experience of meeting a teacher who 'values what students have to say'. But only half noted any differences that they felt could be attributed to the gender of the lecturers, and these usually related to the adoption of an explicitly feminist theoretical approach. Teaching methods that might be seen as successful examples of Women's Studies 'gynagogy' were not interpreted by undergraduates in such terms.

Three-quarters of the students in Group M noted differences in the approaches and attitudes of their Women's Studies lecturers that they attributed to gender. In some cases, the less 'objective' approach of the women was expressed in positive language: female lecturers were more 'enthusiastic', 'sympathetic', 'sensitive', and 'at home with the subject'. The most articulate comment read:

> Male lecturer appeared to speak from a purely academic point of view . . .
> I felt [the female lecturer] knew what she was talking about, not just academically, but with the spirit that is female. She understood the 'difference of view', the woman's voice. (Female student, age 39)

However, for a larger number of students, to be 'academic' was evidently a cardinal virtue, and female lecturers were criticized for their lack of detachment. Women were said to 'press', 'push', 'insist' and 'force', and to show 'indignation over sexism . . . rather than any real examination'; on the other hand, male lecturers gave 'a more objective view to compare to the strong feminist critique'. Two male students lapsed into the plural to refer to their one male lecturer, claiming as a universal truth that: 'Males [are] far more prepared to look at things from both viewpoints'.

Students repeatedly justified the usefulness of male teachers in terms of providing 'balance' and redressing 'bias', believing that male lecturers ensured that they were 'being taught about feminism on neutral grounds'. They had unexpectedly different perceptions from the staff of the women and men who had taught them, setting up male authority against female subjectivity: even where male lecturers were seen by their female colleagues as feminist allies, the men were viewed by their students as 'objective' and the women as 'biased'. These findings warn us of the danger of seeing sympathetic male colleagues exclusively from our own point of view. We can fail to realize how the students are responding to the gender of their teachers, or to consider thoroughly in what ways male involvement changes their learning experience and the nature of the course.

Undergraduate Attitudes to Male Students

The biggest surprise in this batch of undergraduate questionnaires was the virtually unanimous vote in favour of mixed classrooms. Only three students out of fifty-eight viewed men as a definite disadvantage, and forty-eight saw a positive advantage in having male students on the course. In response to the question 'Ideally, should the course be available only to female students?', fifty-seven out of fifty-eight students answered with a resounding 'No'.

There were three main arguments for including male students, which can be labelled as: discrimination, education and balance. Female students frequently supported the opening of Women's Studies courses to men on the grounds of 'equality'. One black student who saw the involvement of male *teachers* as a disadvantage, and recorded her experience on another course of 'a typically white, male, heterosexual bigot who often made fun of "English students" and "black women" of which I am both', was adamant that the Women's Studies course should be available to male *students*:

> It is just as bigoted and prejudiced to exclude men from something as to exclude women. We complain at men suppressing women so how can we stop them from doing something that they must obviously feel some interest in and some sensitivity towards?

The concept of equality often went hand in hand with the concept of education. Many of the young women vehemently expressed their belief that 'men have to be educated!', and nearly all the male students justified their involvement in Women's Studies on consciousness-raising grounds.

However, the overriding reason given for including male students, as for male lecturers, was that they benefited the group as a whole by giving 'balance'. Although the men seemed to believe that they were there primarily to learn to see things from the female point of view, it was assumed by the women that the men would bring 'different viewpoints/different experiences' to enrich the group, and many undergraduate women wanted the men to perform the function of representing the 'other' side.

Interestingly, this enthusiasm for inviting male students into Women's Studies classrooms was rarely a reflection of what had actually happened. In practice, the men were often criticized for being 'not at all forthcoming', and not playing the part in debate that the women had assigned to them. There was only one class in which the lone male student was seen by other group members as having satisfactorily performed the function of being 'particularly sensitive to women and women's issues whilst often arguing for men'. But if this is indeed what men should be there for, it seems a lot to expect of the average 19-year-old undergraduate!

It was not evident from these responses that the undergraduates had given much thought to the effect of a male presence on classroom dynamics. Unusually, there were no complaints of dominating men in our sample groups, and few comments suggested that their presence had inhibited discussion. Instead, some women perceived the male students as having been overwhelmed by the experience, and were critical of the hostile situation in which the men had found themselves.

Table 4.3   MA courses

Staff	Students	
	Mixed groups	All-women groups
Mixed teaching teams	1 group* 9 questionnaires	2 groups 22 questionnaires
All-women teaching teams	—	1 group 7 questionnaires

Total number of classes = 4
Total number of questionnaires completed = 38
* There was only one male student enrolled on these four courses who completed a questionnaire.

With such a small sample it is hard to draw serious conclusions about what the men thought, and it looks as if the classroom climates differed considerably. In one group, which was one-third men, the six male respondents all commented favourably on the course, claimed that their attitudes had changed a good deal, and showed none of the uneasiness that female students were attributing to them. In another class, where the male students were conspicuous by their absence, the only man who came to the last meeting of the course and completed a questionnaire definitely showed signs of wear!

For teachers of undergraduate Women's Studies, two important questions arise from these findings. Should our courses be taking the needs and contributions of this male minority more seriously? And how should we be responding to the express desire of young women to welcome men into their Women's Studies classrooms?

The Postgraduate View

This part of the study was based on thirty-eight completed questionnaires from four postgraduate classes, and discussions involving three of the groups. All the students were enrolled in diploma/MA programmes in Women's Studies, and our sample included students at the end of their first and second years. Although the level of male involvement varied (see table 4.3), this factor had little effect on the spread of student opinions on most issues.

Students opting for a Women's Studies postgraduate course are inevitably older than the majority of undergraduates. The youngest student in the sample was 25 years old, and two-thirds were over 35. A much higher proportion of MA students (over half) had some previous experience of Women's Studies or a women-only group, often through the Open University's 'Changing Experience of Women' course, WEA classes or feminist political groups. Many of the postgraduates were constructively critical of their courses and showed a greater interest than undergraduates in suggesting improvements. They displayed a tendency to deconstruct our questionnaires, demonstrating a sophisticated understanding of the complexities of the issues we were probing, and sometimes exhibiting a healthy frustration with our questionnaire's simplistic approach.

Postgraduate Attitudes to Male Staff

Postgraduates had stronger reactions than undergraduates to the issue of male staff participation, and one-third believed that only women should teach on Women's Studies courses. Nevertheless, the responses were divided, and student opinion was not as strongly biased against male involvement as we had expected, perhaps because women lecturers were correctly perceived to be in charge of the overall direction of study. On the MA programme without male staff input, only one of the seven student respondents was adamant that men would be a definite disadvantage, though the teaching team had felt strongly enough to take a policy decision excluding male staff.

A preponderance of women lecturers was valued highly by all the groups. Women lecturers were experienced as more 'woman-centred' and 'credible', and postgraduates evidently felt much more comfortable discussing certain issues, particularly sexuality, with female tutors. There was clear recognition, too, of the relationship between Women's Studies and teaching modes ('I liked their style . . . no guru-like posture'), and grateful appreciation of a learning environment which 'upholds mutual support and collective thinking'. Although some students perceived some men as effective and approachable teachers, many women felt that they were 'not on the same wavelength' as the male staff. They described them as distant or 'super-confident', and criticized their contributions for being too 'structured'.

A large majority of postgraduates (over three-quarters) finally favoured an all-women teaching team, while those who advocated the inclusion of men usually did so with some equivocation. Nearly half saw some advantage in involving men, partly because they threw the special qualities of the female staff into relief! Students also felt that their academic contributions could be useful, and maintained that men provided 'balance' and represented the 'other point of view' (phrases familiar from undergraduate questionnaires). Some students thought that it would be useful to test out their ideas on a male lecturer who could represent patriarchal attitudes; however, other students commented that any man accepted onto the teaching team should be obviously sympathetic to feminism. The general view was that male staff were 'acceptable only when in the minority and only for certain subjects'.

Postgraduate Attitudes to Male Students

Negative feelings about the participation of male students ran higher than feelings about male staff, and postgraduates expressed a striking preference for a women-only student group. Unlike the undergraduates we studied, three of the four postgraduate groups had experienced all-female classes. The whole issue of group dynamics became a major theme in discussions with MA students; the project clearly raised a subtext of the groups' experience which both staff and students seemed glad of an opportunity to air. Postgraduates often maintained that they found the absence of men 'freeing', and were capable of making strong statements in support of an all-women space that were almost completely lacking from undergraduate responses:

> I think Women's Studies should be about empowering women, not about pandering to 'interested' men.

The opinion expressed by one woman, of being 'naturally suspicious of men who want to study Women's Studies', was echoed across the groups, and a number of responses advocated 'Masculinity Studies' as a means of diverting men from Women's Studies programmes.

In one class, eleven out of thirteen postgraduates agreed with the proposition that Women's Studies courses should be offered only to women; several of these students had been asked at interview whether they would object to men as teachers or students and had expressed no concern at that stage, but their views had changed with the development of their ideas on Women's Studies and their personal experience of a very supportive all-women group. Another class which had meshed strongly over the first year of their course said that they would have no objections to a woman becoming a new member of their group, but they were vociferously opposed to the introduction of a male student.

Many women admitted to their own tendency to feel protective towards men in a group situation; in the class which included one male student the women thought that it was the personality of the individual man that inspired such maternal feelings, but similar comments elsewhere suggest that this has more to do with the way in which women generally respond to men in groups. One class had observed the influence of men on the behaviour of a female lecturer, who adopted a jokey style to soften the impact of her arguments when she was teaching an option including male undergraduates that she never used in an all-female situation. Students were aware of the time that could be wasted on accommodating the minority male viewpoint, and conscious of the ways in which a male presence 'defocuses the attention from the female point of view to a crass reference to the male point of view'. Although the potential for differences and conflicts in an all-women class was recognized, it was generally assumed that groups without men were more likely to 'share basic common ground' and could therefore go further in their thinking.

As feelings about all-women groups were so positive, it was surprising to find that only half the postgraduates were prepared to exclude men completely from Women's Studies courses. Like the undergraduates, some maintained that men should be there because they 'need enlightening', but more widespread was the concern that Women's Studies should not become deliberately 'cliquey' or 'ghettoized'. The comments provoked by this question were fascinating; students were clearly wrestling with this matter of principle versus preference, and felt that feminist theory gave them no absolute answers. As one woman put it: 'Women's Studies is ambiguous about "preventing"'.

Negotiating the Generation Gap

The sharp contrast between undergraduate and postgraduate views revealed by the study must be partly due to the nature of the courses: a 19-year-old taking a Women Writers option is making a different choice from a 49-year-old embarking on a full-scale MA programme in Women's Studies. To select a Women's Studies course for postgraduate study is likely to be a politically motivated decision; as one MA student expressed it, her enrolment was in itself 'a political act'. However, a commitment to a feminist perspective cannot be assumed for undergraduates, whose ideas about women and Women's Studies may well be much less clearly defined.

There was also a significant split between BA and MA students that can be attributed to age. Older undergraduates tended to respond like postgraduates, and one reason why our BA/MA results diverge so clearly is because our sample of undergraduate courses did not include a class with a high proportion of mature students. Clearly, younger and older women have very different expectations of and responses to a Women's Studies course. The question about all-women courses was particularly telling in the polarized reactions it provoked, with some post-graduates taking it as an insult to be asked to contemplate the inclusion of men in any capacity, while at the other extreme some undergraduates responded to the idea of an all-women course with 'Of course not', 'Definitely not!!!' or even 'A ridiculous suggestion!' Women under 25 saw no reason why male students should inhibit their discussion, and had apparently not considered the presence of men as an issue at all, whereas mature students, after more experience of men inside and outside the classroom, were more likely to appreciate the changes in group dynamics that occur when men are present and to acknowledge the political argument for a women-only space.

As Gloria Steinem long ago pointed out, women are radicalized by their life experiences, and younger women are often more conservative (Steinem, 1979). But in addition we are now dealing with a 'post-Thatcher' generation, primed with ideas about equality and open competition, and with a 'postfeminist' gen-eration, old enough to have been brought up by feminist mothers and taught at school by feminist teachers. For many undergraduates, feminism can be seen as old hat, and courses on women may not be perceived as radical. In a recent article on 'Teaching the Middle Ground of Feminism', Mary Eagleton has accurately identified 'a particular grouping' of young women on undergraduate courses, 'purposeful, politically unsophisticated, profiting from the work of older gen-erations but often unaware of the debt' (Eagleton, 1991, p. 4), and it is clear that many of our questionnaire responses came from a position of this kind. But this is a position that has frequently been underestimated by Women's Studies lecturers, who may assume a feminist commitment from their students that is not necessarily present.

What Next?

Our survey of postgraduate groups does not reveal any need for radical changes in course aims or methods on MA programmes, though there are two areas worth reviewing by course teams: the extent to which the students themselves are in-volved in decisions about male participation, and the opportunities afforded by the course to discuss the personal and political implications of a male presence.

However, the unexpected results from the undergraduate courses give real cause for concern. We know that men already occupy some of the space in Women's Studies classrooms, but our study forces us to recognize that many female students want them there. We have to learn that the arguments in support of a women-only space, which are at the heart of conventional Women's Studies wisdom, are not consciously entertained by the great majority of undergraduates, indeed that a majority of female undergraduates believe that male staff and male students have a rightful and useful place in a Women's Studies context.

This challenge from our undergraduate classrooms requires all Women's

Studies teachers to re-examine our principles and practice. If we want to hold on to the Women's Studies ideal of an all-women space, how do we respond to the reality of a male presence? If we are also committed to listening to our students, how do we deal with views on the 'men problem' that may differ markedly from our own?

Here are some of the questions which we have tried to address in our own teaching situations, and which other Women's Studies teachers working with male staff and male students on undergraduate courses might wish to consider:

- Do the course objectives need modification? Given that students may expect a subject-centred course, how far is it desirable and feasible to pursue a consciousness-raising agenda?

- How explicit should the consciousness-raising dimension of the course be? Should the 'men problem' be addressed as an up-front issue? Can it be part of a more sophisticated analysis in such areas as gender and 'fairness' or the social construction of fe/male 'viewpoints'?

- Do we implicitly have different goals for female and male students? Should they be different?

- In what ways do we anticipate a male student or male staff presence influencing classroom dynamics? How do we plan to cope with that, and what kind of support should we be giving to the male student minority?

- Should we ask male students to fulfil the role that female students seem to expect of them, and encourage them to take an explicitly oppositional 'male' stance in debate? What problems would this create for their own personal development?

- Should we ask male staff to blend in with the Women's Studies ethos, or to teach from a clearly defined 'male' position? What demands should the team be making on male staff, and what responsibilities does the team have towards its male members?

It is only by answering such questions as these that we can make our much-needed reassessment of what Women's Studies means in the mixed undergraduate classrooms of the 1990s.

One useful starting point for such a review could well be a similar survey to our own, which would gauge student opinion in a particular local situation. Our results will not apply to every course: the institutional climate, the specific syllabus, and the political and pedagogical assumptions of staff are among the important variants. Above all, the mix in the student group — of gender, age, class, ethnic background, political positioning and individual experience — will determine the spread of views on the 'men problem', as on every other issue. The sexual orientation of group members is a crucial complicating factor: one postgraduate stressed that any problems arising from male participation in the group were much less important to her than her sense of isolation as the only lesbian.

Student reaction to the involvement of men in Women's Studies forms just one area where important differences within a group are likely to emerge. Divergences of female opinion over the 'men problem', and the presence of men themselves, can be hard for a feminist teacher to handle, touching as they do on a principle so central to our concept of Women's Studies. But another principle of the Women's Movement is the recognition and celebration of difference, and our teaching must acknowledge that an uncomplicated staff/student sisterhood with shared attitudes on gender politics can no longer be assumed.

Notes

Warm thanks to all the students who have taken part in this project, and to all the Women's Studies staff who have given us their generous help and hospitality. (Spelling and punctuation are normalized in all quotations from questionnaires.)

1 But is the attitude of Women's Studies staff also changing? At the 1991 Women's Studies Network Conference in London, where we presented our findings, seventeen of the women attending our session completed an on-the-spot questionnaire. Their responses showed continuing support for all-women groups (over two-thirds saw male staff and male students as a disadvantage), but also a marked willingness to find ways of including men (half thought that *some* undergraduate and postgraduate Women's Studies courses should be open to men).
2 Over one-third of the undergraduates in our survey claimed that their attitudes to gender issues had changed 'a lot' or 'quite a bit' during their course, and less than one-fifth said that they had changed 'not much' or 'not at all'.

References and Related Reading

ACKER, S. and PIPER, D.W. (Eds) (1984) *Is Higher Education Fair to Women?*, Guildford, SRHE and NFER-Nelson.

EAGLETON, M. (1991) 'Teaching the Middle Ground of Feminism', *Pace* (SCEPCHE Newsletter), June 1991, pp. 2–5.

EVANS, M. (1991) 'The Problem of Gender for Women's Studies', in AARON, J. and WALBY, S. (Eds) *Out of the Margins: Women's Studies in the Nineties*, London, Falmer Press, pp. 67–74.

HUMM, M. (1989) 'Subjects in English', in THOMPSON, A. and WILCOX, H. (Eds) *Teaching Women: Feminism and English Studies*, Manchester, Manchester University Press, pp. 39–49.

JARDINE, A. and SMITH, P. (Eds) (1987) *Men in Feminism*, London, Methuen.

KELLY, J. (1991) 'A Study of Gender Differential Linguistic Interaction in the Adult Classroom', *Gender and Education*, 3, 2, pp. 137–45.

KLEIN, R.D. (1983) 'The "Men Problem" in Women's Studies: Experts, Ignorants and Poor Dears', *Women's Studies International Forum*, 6, 4, pp. 413–21.

KLEIN, R.D. (1991) 'Passion and Politics in Women's Studies in the 1990s', in AARON, J. and WALBY, S. (Eds) *Out of the Margins: Women's Studies in the Nineties*, London, Falmer Press, pp. 75–89.

KRAMARAE, C. and TREICHLER, P.A. (1990) 'Power Relationships in the Classroom', in GABRIEL, S.L. and SMITHSON, I. (Eds) *Gender in the Classroom: Power and Pedagogy*, Urbana and Chicago, University of Illinois Press, pp. 41–59.

LUBELSKA, C. (1991) 'Teaching Methods in Women's Studies: Challenging the Mainstream', in AARON, J. and WALBY, S. (Eds) *Out of the Margins: Women's Studies in the Nineties*, London, Falmer Press, pp. 41–8.

MORGAN, D. (1981) 'Men, Masculinity and the Process of Sociological Enquiry', in ROBERTS, H. (Ed.) *Doing Feminist Research*, London, Routledge, pp. 83–113.

SEGAL, L. (1990) *Slow Motion: Changing Masculinities, Changing Men*, London, Virago.

SPENDER, D. (1980) *Man Made Language*, London, Routledge.

STEINEM, G. (1979) 'Why Young Women are More Conservative', *Ms.*, reprinted in *Outrageous Acts and Everyday Rebellions* (1986), New York, Signet, pp. 238–46.

STONEMAN, P. (1989) 'Powerhouse or Ivory Tower?: Feminism and Postgraduate English', in THOMPSON, A. and WILCOX, H. (Eds) *Teaching Women: Feminism and English Studies*, Manchester, Manchester University Press, pp. 96–108.

THOMAS, K. (1990) *Gender and Subject in Higher Education*, Buckingham, SRHE and Open University Press.

Section II

Commonalities and Differences

Chapter 5

Difference, Power and Knowledge: Black Women in Academia

Felly Nkweto Simmonds

Prologue

In writing this chapter, I am inspired by the words of Bernice Johnson Reagon, spoken in her keynote speech at the Berkshire Conference on the History of Women, at Rutgers University, New Brunswick, NJ, in the summer of 1990, in which she claimed to speak as 'the voice of America'.[1] For a Black woman to have such daring in a world that devalues both blackness and womanhood demands a fundamental rethinking of both the personal and political. For me, it demands a rethinking of my very self and the specific position I occupy as a Black woman. I have to imagine how Reagon's voice would conduct dialogues on a global scale — with Grenada, Nicaragua, Palestine, South Africa. . . . It also demands I always locate myself at the centre of any dialogue, and not confine myself to the margins of blackness, of womanhood.

Such dialogues, however, are difficult to imagine. How will such communication occur? In whose language? What discourse? What registers? Who will speak, and for whom? It is not just a matter of who speaks and from what perspective but also of what we are able to hear, to understand, across all our differences of race, gender, culture, nationality and so on.

At the Women's Studies Network Conference (London, July 1991), a conference that explored differences between women, we were reminded, for example, by the presence of a woman with a hearing aid, that we must not take hearing for granted.[2] We also made some basic assumptions about our ability to communicate, at a psychological level, across all our isms within the conference. Confronting our ability to communicate across our differences should be an issue in itself, as should be our ability to leave our carefully constructed realities and also open them to others.[3] Dialogue is essential as we attempt the task of acknowledging difference and commonalities.

As a Black woman I have to learn to speak from a position that places me in the centre of the universe. This is a difficult position to conceptualize because of the peculiar position that I, and a growing number of Black women, occupy. We are Black feminists teaching in institutions of Higher Education. We teach white students and a few 'rare-as-gold-dust' Black students. Most of our colleagues are white men, and if we are lucky, we have white women — feminists — working in the same departments. With all these we have to have some sort of working relationship and sometimes are able to form alliances and coalitions. We also challenge not just the system, but those we come in contact with.[4] Our very existence in academia is a challenge. Much more so even than the presence of white women, because in Britain, in 1991, the idea of a Black woman as an academic is simply too outrageous. We are watched (and watch ourselves) for slips, for gaps in our knowledge. Being neither male nor white, we have no visible basis for certain kinds of knowledge. We are also presumed to have expertise in one particular field — race. It is a cycle that is difficult to break. It also means that we are placed in positions where we cannot afford to admit to a lack of knowledge in any area. Teaching in a sociology department I have to be as familiar with High Theory as with Black feminism or global politics. I cannot afford to ask someone to take a series of lectures on my course because 'you know more about it', which is what I can be asked to do, without the fear that this will show up my lack of knowledge! I have to be as familiar with Foucault as I am with Fanon or Amadiume![5]

The Whiteness of Theory

Feminist theory has given particular meanings to concepts of differences and commonalities. Commonalities between women have been more readily incorporated in feminist discourse than differences. Difference has been deemed divisive, whereas commonalities have been assumed to be the basis of unity — of a universal sisterhood. Difference has been more readily accepted in relation to men. During the 1970s and 1980s much feminist work theorized difference in terms of gender or sexual difference, assuming that women are primarily one category, the 'other', in relation to men. More recently, differences between women have been added to the feminist agenda. None the less, these differences have often been added on to existing models in which the polarity between women and men remains of primary concern. Thus basic frameworks within feminist theory have often continued unchanged by considerations of differences between women. Kum Kum Bhavnani characterizes this tendency within white feminist theory as:

> . . . this racially unselfconscious feminism which often assumes that 'woman' is a unitary and single category; that is, that there are no differences of interest amongst Black and white women. Even when the differences of interest are acknowledged by some feminists, it is rare for such differences to be actively engaged with — mere acknowledgement seems to be enough. (Bhavnani, 1992 forthcoming)

Thus much feminist theory continues to lend validity to a specific meaning of difference within feminism and, indeed, within mainstream Women's Studies. Feminists who define difference 'politically' have criticized such definitions and their underlying concepts. Radical feminists, for example, include sexuality and sexual preference in definitions of difference. Black and Third World feminists include racism, imperialism and other forms of exploitation as bases for difference. These inevitably lead to a multiplicity of definitions of difference.

Black feminists in the West, using racism as a theoretical paradigm, point out that just as women are objectified and categorized as 'other' in Eurocentric sociological frameworks, for example, so is blackness. This makes the task of theorizing

Black women's lives more complicated. Black and white women occupy different positions even in relation to men (white men, Black men). It is this that Black feminists have challenged, often without success because, as bell hooks notes,

> An example which readily comes to mind from the feminist movement centers on efforts made by women of color to call attention to white racism in the struggle as well as talking about racial identity from a standpoint which deconstructs the category 'woman'. Such discussions were part of the struggle by women of color to come to voice and also to assert new and different feminist narratives. Many white feminists responded by hearing only what was being said about race and most specifically about racism . . . white feminists could now centralize themselves by engaging in a discourse on race, 'the Other', in a manner which further marginalized women of color, whose works were often relegated to the realm of the experiential. . . . (hooks, 1991, p. 21)

Black feminism must not be relegated to marginal, or incidental, discourse within feminism. It has to be as central to the reshaping of feminism as any other feminist theory. It can be quite amusing to notice how Black feminist theory continues to be either censored or acknowledged fleetingly,[6] especially by the High Feminist Theorists of poststructural, postmodernist, postfeminist schools of thought. In her very fine book on postmodern feminism, for example, Susan Hekman asserts that 'feminism can contribute to the postmodern position by adding the dimension of gender, a dimension lacking in many postmodern accounts . . .' (Hekman, 1990, p. 3). She also acknowledges some of the critiques of postmodernism as a basis for feminist theory. In a reference to Nancy Hartsock's contribution to critiques of the relationship between postmodernism and feminism, the actual words quoted are, in fact, Audre Lorde's. Hekman states:

> [Hartsock] has argued consistently that feminists must reject all epistemologies that are formulated by male theorists and adopt an epistemology that privileges the female standpoint. Like Audre Lorde she is arguing that 'the master's tools can never dismantle the master's house'. (Hekman, 1990, p. 154)

Hekman's inability to quote Lorde directly does not surprise me. Had she done so, she would have had to rethink the implication of Hartsock's attack on the postmodernist position in relation to Audre Lorde as a Black woman. She uses, for example, Hartsock's assertion:

> that women, like colonized people, have been what she calls 'marginalized'. Like colonized people, women have always been defined as at the periphery rather than as at the centre. Following theorists who consider the problem of marginalization, Hartsock argues that in order to transcend this inferior status women must constitute themselves in a way that overcomes their marginalization: 'But to the extent that we have been constituted as Other, it is important to insist as well on a vision of the world in which we are at the centre rather than at the periphery'. (Hekman, 1990, pp. 154–5)

In fact, by placing Hartsock's arguments as 'the most central' in feminist critiques of postmodernism (Hekman, 1990, p. 155), Hekman continues to centre white feminist knowledge, in relation to Black feminist knowledge. She places Lorde at the periphery of a feminist critique of postmodernism.

As a Black woman, and a feminist, my relationship to High Theory becomes problematic. I fear feminist theory will continue to centre white women's experiences and to relegate Black women to the position of 'Other' (Collins, 1990, pp. 68–70) thus empowering white feminist theorists. In this equation Black feminists continue to be 'colonized people'. This then means that for me, the Memsahib's tools can, therefore, not dismantle the 'White' house.

Dealing with Difference

White feminist theory and Women's Studies, on the whole, ignore differences between women either through a basic reluctance to deal with the reality of difference or because difference has not been seen as adequately theorized by an Established Feminist Theorist (i.e. a white one). If we continue to see difference in feminist theory as primarily concerned with gender differences we continue to limit the use we can make of difference as a tool for analyzing the realities of *all* women. Too much time and energy has been spent theorizing difference as negative and divisive, an impediment to a universal sisterhood.[7] Even when white feminists have had to make concessions to the idea of difference between women, this has not been without reservation. Lynne Segal concludes, for example, that

> Paying more attention to the needs of Black women at a practical and descriptive level, constantly being vigilant about old assumptions that 'we' women are all white, has become an important aspect of feminism in the eighties. But it has not been easy to make theoretical connections between race, class and sex. . . . Socialist feminism might be expected to offer a fuller analysis of how oppressions of race, class and sex intersect than a feminism which analyses gender as the primary over-riding form of domination. But race was not a preoccupation of socialist feminism at its height. . . . Adrienne Rich argued eloquently that white women can and must identify with Black female experience. But she overstates her case by insisting that: 'women share suffering across the barriers of age, race, nationality, culture, sexual preference and ethnic background'. White women do not 'share' the sufferings of targets of racism, indeed many directly cause it, and they all indirectly benefit from it. (Segal, 1987, pp. 64–5)

I use this example from Segal's book *Is The Future Female?*, because this is a book that is used widely in teaching Women's Studies and general Sociology courses. It is therefore read by almost everyone who studies and teaches Women's Studies. Segal encapsulates one problem white feminist theory has in dealing with difference — the idea of 'including' Black women, of needing to 'pay more attention to the needs of Black women'. White women remain central, defining frameworks and analyzing Black women's oppressions. The other problem relates to how those women who have attempted to use difference as a tool for understanding women's realities, such as Adrienne Rich, have been criticized by those who see themselves as presenting the united face of feminism. My understanding of the quote Segal uses is a positive one. Adrienne Rich neither ignores differences between women, nor the possible links that can exist between them. Of course, white women do not 'share' Black women's experiences of racism. But racism links their lives to those of Black women *because* they benefit directly and indirectly from their whiteness (see Helen (charles), in this volume). This is what white women need to pay more attention to. They must theorize from their experience of advantage in relation to Black women. This will clarify the different positions that white women and Black women occupy in British society, for example. Whiteness gives privilege, on a global scale, be it Britain, Brazil, the USA, South Africa or Australia.

The reality is that some white women do share oppressions with some Black women: for example, those based on class, sexuality and disability — which they experience differently because they *are* white women. These other oppressions which are experienced across race have allowed Black and white women to form alliances. Such alliances should not be dismissed either because current theories cannot deal with them or even simply because they make us uncomfortable. An example of this is the way Segal has criticized revolutionary feminist literature as not being able to

> do justice to those groups of women — Black women, working class women, immigrant women — whose more general social powerlessness and vulnerability has meant that they have suffered most, and often fought hardest, against exploitative sexual behaviour from men. Nor does it mention in its theoretical analysis that western images of sex are not only sexist but also quintessentially racist. . . . And from about 1983, it was the rise of Black feminism and disputes over race which were eventually to muffle, though not resolve, the fierce debates generated by revolutionary feminism and political lesbianism in feminist gatherings and publications. (Segal, 1987, p. 102)

What is interesting about the idea in this quote is the placing of 'revolutionary' lesbians in opposition to Black women. Revolutionary, lesbian and Black are framed by difference, as separate groups of women. What Segal fails to realize is that revolutionary, lesbian and Black could also be one woman. Many of the most vocal Black feminists of the seventies (and not only since 1983) were Black lesbians (Joseph and Lewis, 1986, pp. 35–6), women such as Audre Lorde. They challenged the racism and heterosexism of the white women's movement as well as the homophobia of Black heterosexual women (Lorde, 1984, pp. 114–23). It was some of these women who began to make the significant theoretical links between race, sex, and class that even socialist feminism had failed to address (Joseph in Sargent, 1981). Black feminists identified the problem of challenging the feminist movement itself. A statement from the Combahee River Collective, written as early as 1977, identified one of their main problems:

> The major source of difficulty . . . is that we are not just trying to fight oppression on one front or even two, but instead to address a whole range of oppressions. We do not have racial, sexual, heterosexual or class privilege to rely upon, nor do we have even the minimal access to resources

and power that groups who possess any one of these types of privilege have. (Hull *et al.*, 1982, p. 18)

It is, therefore, quite baffling to me why white feminism continues to see difference as implicitly problematic and damaging to the idea of a 'potential unity about the nature, direction and goal of feminism' (Segal, 1987, p. 65). For Black women, difference is the very basis of analysis, and any idea of 'potential unity' within feminism would have to explicitly and implicitly acknowledge and work with difference between women. Feminism has to abandon its marginalization of groups of women who do not fit into whiteness, heterosexuality and middleclassness.

One of the most basic problems is that difference and commonality have been conceptualized as dichotomous and polarized positions (Lorde, 1984; Collins, 1990): either/or, *us* or *them*. What must become important for us as feminists in creating an all-inclusive feminist theory is the ability for such a theory to take for granted both our differences and our commonalities. We must recognize that our realities cannot be simplified to an essential female nature that we must rediscover or subscribe to.[8] We must analyze what creates both commonalities and difference between women. We must also recognize the reality that there are no neat lines between *us* and *them*, that sometimes we can be *us* with some groups (e.g. as a Black woman) and at other times be seen as *other* (e.g. as a teacher to my Black students). As an academic, my position immediately demands a flexibility in relating to my work, my students, my colleagues. For example, as an academic working on research on the experience of Black women in Britain, I have to be both the 'knowing self' and the 'known object' (Collins, 1990, p. 69).

Commonalities: Challenging Difference

It becomes too limiting and simplistic to privilege some forms of categorizations (and oppressions), such as race, class, gender, over others, such as age, nationality, sexuality, disability and so on. Analyzing social realities requires a more flexible framework that also challenges the very idea that there is a hierarchy of oppression, that some oppressions are more important and more valid than others! We then enter the realm of mathematics and quantification i.e. Black + woman + working-class = REALLY OPPRESSED. As Collins states:

> Additive models of oppression are firmly rooted in the either/or dichotomous thinking of Eurocentric, masculinist thought. . . . The emphasis on quantification and categorisation occurs in conjunction with the belief that either/or categories must be ranked. Privilege becomes defined in relation to its other. Replacing additive models of oppression with interlocking ones creates possibilities for new paradigms. The significance of seeing race, class and gender as interlocking systems of oppression is that such an approach fosters a paradigmatic shift of thinking inclusively about other oppressions. (Collins, 1990, p. 225)

Some of the most successful analyses which implicitly use the idea of interlocking models of oppression have been those employed by African-American feminists (Hull, Scott and Smith, 1982; hooks, 1984; Lorde, 1984) and joint work by Black and white women (Joseph and Lewis, 1986). Their works have not only attempted to theorize Black women's lives, but make relevant to feminist theory the notion of differences between women as fundamental to the creation of a feminist knowledge that can be of value to all women. It is also not such a coincidence that such theorists are mainly Black women. As Black women, the reality of our lives demands that we are constantly engaged in dialogue, debate, and negotiation with the rest of society. This does not seem to be a reality for many white women. Joseph and Lewis argue for

> the importance of Black women and White women connecting their specific understandings of oppression to an understanding of the political totality that thrives on these oppressions. Through such connections . . . both groups can re-evaluate and restructure their strategies for liberation in the most effective ways possible. (Joseph and Lewis, 1986, p. 14)

It is our otherness as Black people *and* as women which means that we have to connect and link aspects of our lives with others. Notions of hierarchies of oppression become meaningless because choice implies a fragmentation of the very self. We have to rely on the interconnectedness of our oppressions and struggles. The choice for us then becomes what alliances we make and what we use as bases for such alliances. This is what we have to offer to feminist theory and practice — an ability to use difference as a tool to analyze the reality of all women's lives, and to explore why some women are privileged over others. So far feminist theory has not challenged the privilege of white women over Black women, both in the making of feminist knowledge and in the making of a feminist practice — be it teaching Women's Studies or campaigning for women's rights.

Fears have, rightly, been expressed about romanticizing commonalities. This is a valid point. Difference is still crucial because the actual relationships between Black and white women are always framed by both difference *and* commonalities. First, Black and white women relate to power and privilege differently. Added to that, as individuals, particular relationships are further defined by class, sexuality, ethnicity, nationality and so on. Our experiences and realities can be conflictual and contradictory. This is what gives rise to conflicts within oppressed groups, in which even the naming of ourselves becomes an area of contention.[9] This must not be seen as an intrinsic inability to deal with difference, but the very fact that difference cannot, and must not, be taken for granted; neither can commonalities — both have to be negotiated.

Feminist Theory: Towards a New Model

Black women have always been suspicious about some of the bases on which global sisterhood has apparently been conceptualized. There has been a glossing over, not only of real differences, but, more importantly, of our differing access to power and privilege. Black women have insisted on separate space from which to struggle against colonialism, imperialism, patriarchy, racism. In such struggles we not only rely on other Black women, but also form alliances with many who share our political goals, if not our particular oppressions. We have constantly to remind ourselves that we are always engaged in a process of negotiating the positions that we occupy — even such seemingly absolute positions as race, ethnicity and sexuality.

Black feminist theory must enable feminism as a whole to challenge itself. This also means as Black feminists — and other feminists — we must not rely on the trap of quantifying oppressions, thus oppressing others with our own oppressions. We must acknowledge real points of contact and share real life experiences, however painful. In acknowledging commonalities, I still believe we must retain the idea that oppressions can be autonomous. Autonomy is not such a negative concept. In any relationship — especially personal ones — as feminists we demand a certain amount of individual autonomy. It shouldn't be too difficult to translate this idea into the broader framework of feminist practice and the relationships we have or choose to have with other women. This framework allows for a more flexible way of conceptualizing the kind of relationships we have with not just other women but society as a whole.

Black feminists argue that there is a need to 'connect . . . specific understandings of oppression . . . re-evaluate and restructure strategies for liberation' (Joseph and Lewis, 1986, p. 14) and that 'while Black feminist thought may originate with Black feminist intellectuals, it cannot flourish isolated from the experiences and ideas of other groups' (Collins, 1990, p. 35). As Black women and feminists we are well aware that using models that privilege one oppression over others has not necessarily given us (or others) any deeper understanding, or automatic empathy with other oppressed people, sometimes even other Black women who have different political priorities from our own.

Feminist theory, in all its forms, will only survive and continue to be a force in academia if we acknowledge our own shortcomings, help create new theoretical paradigms and use both difference and commonality as tools of analysis. We have constantly to challenge ourselves and our positions, our access to power vis-à-vis others who have less access to privilege and power. It is not simply a matter of *us*, who are oppressed, against *them*, who oppress us. As academics we can simultaneously occupy positions of power (as teachers) and powerlessness (as women, Black women, lesbians and so on). It is only recognizing our own power, powerlessness, advantages and disadvantages that helps us create new meanings in our own lives, and affects our relationship with others.

Within Women's Studies, this recognition has to extend to who in reality has access to teaching Women's Studies in Britain today. How does this reflect what is taught, how it is taught, what books/theories are put forward, who is left out, in both the teaching and learning?

When Black and white women teach Women's Studies we have to work out what relationship we have not just to each other, but also with the institutions we teach in, and even with our students. Our contact with our students can give us some of the clearest indicators about how to create alliances and locate commonalities. In my own experience, it is my position as an outsider — by gender, race, nationality (even hairstyle!) that links me with students who perceive themselves (and are often seen by others) as outsiders. It is not always for the most obvious reasons (gender and race), even though these create a solid base, it is this state of 'otherness', a recognition that I could accommodate other realities, other oppressions, other struggles. The biggest lesson for me has been the learning to do so, both in my teaching and in my own life. I have constantly to locate commonalities, clarify differences and confront inherent dangers and pitfalls that arise.

Within Women's Studies the locating of commonalities and differences will sharpen, for us, the power positions we occupy in academia, not only in relation to each other, but also to our colleagues and students. At the same time white feminists cannot continue to occupy central positions at the expense of all other women without challenging their own position and power in the making of feminist knowledge and the teaching of Women's Studies. The task of creating a feminist theory and practice has to be undertaken by all women. Black women, on the other hand, must not only engage with Women's Studies from the margins, nor be limited only to particular bodies of knowledge. Sisterhood cannot be based on a unity that devalues some women's experiences and privileges others.

Feminism is about challenging ourselves, not just others, challenging ourselves as women, as Black women and as white women. In this way we will develop the ability to work with differences and commonalities in our many struggles.[10]

Notes

1 I write Bernice Johnson Reagon's words from memory since I have no access to her speech, and in doing so, I continue our oral tradition.
2 The reality of a hearing aid must remind us to have better facilities for those with impaired hearing at all meetings, seminars, conferences and even our lecture rooms.
3 Gill Dunne's conference seminar 'Difference at Work: Interweaving Work Role, Gender Role and Relationships in the Lesbian Lifestyle' left me with the feeling that what was being put forward as a lesbian lifestyle — self-preservation and economic independence — has, in fact, a lot in common with a Black woman's lifestyle in Britain today. Black women in this society cannot afford to wait for the 'Knight in Shining Armour' for survival!
4 I am often asked how I cope with teaching nearly all white students. My reply is that I do it, that IS my job. However, my students are the ones that have to cope with being taught by a Black woman. They have had no experience of that.
5 See especially Frantz Fanon (1986), which was first published in France in 1952, and Ifi Amadiume (1987).
6 Black women are increasingly being 'added' into feminist texts — often at a level which is only made possible by the ability to manipulate a word processor!
7 This universal sisterhood, in whose celebrations I am invited to participate, has not been negotiated yet. Only those who are privileged by race, class and sexuality can afford to celebrate.
8 Power enables some of us to acknowledge differences and commonalities. White women, for example, can more readily have Black women as 'sisters' to add to politically correct agendas. For Black women, sisterhood with white women is no such asset. It can mean the crossing of a very shaky bridge.
9 I use Black as a political category to name myself, and all who are oppressed by white racism.
10 As a Black woman, I share the legacy of struggle with women worldwide who live by struggle. I dedicate this chapter to the women of South Africa. A lutta continua.

References

AMADIUME, I. (1987) *Male Daughters, Female Husbands: Gender and Sex in an African Society*, London, Zed Books.

BHAVNANI, Kum Kum (1992 forthcoming) 'Talking Racisim and the Editing of Women's Studies', in RICHARDSON, D. and ROBINSON, V. (Eds) *Introducing Women's Studies*, London, MacMillan.

COLLINS, P.H. (1990) *Black Feminist Thought: Knowledge, Consciousness, and the Politics of Empowerment*, London, Unwin Hyman.

FANON, F. (1986) *Black Skins, White Masks*, London, Pluto Press.

HEKMAN, S.J. (1990) *Gender and Knowledge: Elements of a Postmodern Feminism*, London, Polity Press.

HOOKS, B. (1984) *Feminist Theory: From Margin to Center*, Boston, South End Press.

HOOKS, B. (1991) *Yearning: Race, Gender and Cultural Politics*, London, Turnaround.

HULL, G.T. *et al.* (Eds) (1982) *All The Women are White, All The Blacks are Men, But Some of Us are Brave: Black Women's Studies*, New York, The Feminist Press.

JOSEPH, G.I. and LEWIS, G. (1986) *Common Differences: Conflicts in Black and White Feminist Perspectives*, Boston, South End Press.

LORDE, A. (1984) *Sister Outsider: Essays and Speeches*, Freedom, The Crossing Press.

SARGENT, L. (1981) *The Unhappy Marriage of Marxism and Feminism*, London and Sydney, Pluto Press.

SEGAL, L. (1987) *Is The Future Female? Troubled Thoughts on Contemporary Feminism*, London, Virago Press.

Chapter 6

Disabled Women and the Feminist Agenda

Nasa Begum

Introduction

Traditionally there has been a tendency to view disabled people as one homogeneous group with no gender distinctions. The reality of being a disabled woman and having a physical disability has, to a large extent, been overlooked by both the disability and feminist movements. However, there is little doubt that the dual oppression of sexism and handicapism places disabled women in an extremely marginalized position.

Writing as an Asian disabled woman, I want to open up a debate about the position of disabled women and demand that a concerted effort is made to ensure that our needs, wishes and aspirations are incorporated in all feminist debates. I will argue that the experiences of disabled women must be seen as an integral part of the social, economic and political structures which serve to control our daily lives. I recognize that disabled women cannot be treated as a unitary group; factors such as types of disability, race, sexuality, class and so on will influence our individual experiences and these may differ from the experiences of other disabled women. However, it is essential that we use our common experiences to develop a political analysis which creates bonds and forges positive strengths.

By drawing together literature on disability and gender, I intend to demonstrate that the concerns of disabled women strike at the core of both the disability rights and feminist movements. After a brief analysis of the concept of disability, certain feminist tools will be used to provide an analysis of the experiences of disabled women. Particular emphasis will be given to three factors which have had a crucial role in understanding the lives of women: gender roles, self-image, and sexuality.

The triple oppression of being a black disabled woman has not been overlooked. I shall suggest that all the issues affecting disabled women also apply to black disabled women. However the way in which we experience and interpret these issues is likely to differ as the dimension of race interacts to shape our lives.

Disability: What does it Mean?

It is essential to clarify at the outset exactly what is meant by the words disability and handicap. The terms used and their implicit politics within the disability rights movement are subject to ongoing debate. Throughout this article the Union of Physically Impaired Against Society (UPIAS) definition of disability will be adopted:

> Disability: the disadvantage or restriction of activity caused by a contemporary social organisation which takes no or little account of people who have physical impairments and thus excludes them from participation in the mainstream of social activities. Physical disability is therefore a particular form of social oppression. (cited in UPIAS, 1981, p. 14)

The word handicap is used to describe the social ramifications of having a disability; it is not the biological condition but the societal barriers which restrict our lives as disabled people.

There are essentially two theoretical frameworks for understanding the concept of disability. The first may be described as the individualistic perspective, in which disability is interpreted as a deviation from accepted or expected notions of normality; the 'differentness' is regarded as a personal tragedy which the individual must seek to 'come to terms with'. Stereotypes of passivity and childlike dependency are created for members of the 'disabled' and, at the same time, roles are prescribed which render us powerless. To avoid embarrassment and inconvenience to the non-disabled world, an emphasis is placed on accepting the goal of normality:

> There's a tremendous emphasis . . . to be as able-bodied as possible. It's like standing up is considered infinitely better than sitting down, even if you're standing up by standing in a total frame . . . that you can't move in, which hurts and takes hours to get on and off, and looks ugly. (Sutherland, 1981, p. 73)

The individual perspective of disability makes no attempt to examine the social, economic and political perspectives which influence the lives of disabled people. Therefore an alternative framework redefining disability as a form of social oppression has been put forward by disabled people: disability is a form of social oppression which is articulated through prevailing ideological, social and political determinants, and, as a consequence of these, disabled people are socially excluded and handicapism is constructed.

An Overview of the Position of Disabled Women

Although disability may be the predominant characteristic by which a disabled person is labelled, it is essential to recognize that gender influences play an important role in determining how that person's disability is perceived and reacted to. A frequent complaint lodged by disabled women is that rehabilitation programmes place so much emphasis on 'cultivating competitive attitudes' and addressing concerns about male sexuality, that whilst they enable men to aspire to dominant notions of masculinity, the needs of disabled women are ignored or left on the periphery (Morris, 1989; Matthews, 1983; Becker, 1978; Duffy, 1981). Fine and Asch explain:

To be male in our society is to be strong, assertive and independent; to be female is to be weak, passive and dependent, the latter conforming to the social stereotypes of the disabled. For both categories the disabled woman inherits ascriptions of passivity, and weakness. (1985, p. 11)

Both disability and gender are understood as socially constructed classifications; the impact of each may be mitigated or exacerbated according to whether the individual can be identified with an alternative social group which is perceived to be inferior. Disabled men could either identify with the negative role of disability, or they could strategically choose to identify with the powerful and advantageous male role. Both roles available to disabled women label us as inferior, passive and weak. Fine and Asch write:

Disabled women are not only more likely to internalize society's rejection, but they are more likely than disabled men to identify themselves as 'disabled'. The disabled male possesses a relatively positive self image and is more likely to identify as 'male' rather than as 'disabled'. The disabled woman appears to be more likely to introject society's rejection, and to identify as disabled. (1985, p. 9)

Disabled women have become perennial outsiders. Our powerless position has not been seriously addressed by either the disability movement or the Women's Movement. This simultaneous neglect is unforgivable; the exclusion on the basis of gender or disability cannot be defended by groups which purport to express the demands of all those who are ascribed membership to them by virtue of a particular biological criterion.

Although all women are supposed to be represented in the fight for women's liberation, disabled women have drawn attention to the fact that the movement has disregarded them:

The popular view of women with disabilities has been one mixed with repugnance. Perceiving disabled women as childlike, helpless, and victimized, non-disabled feminists have severed from the sisterhood in an effort to advance more powerful, competent and appealing female icons. (Fine and Asch, 1988, p. 4)

As disabled women, we have spoken about how our experiences as women leave us in a marginal and ambiguous position. One woman explains: 'there is no arm of the movement concerned about disabled women . . . we do fit in, but only on the outside like some sort of mascot' (Duffy, 1981, p. 167).

It is interesting to note that in the request for papers for this publication there was no mention of disabled women. One may speculate about whether this was a genuine error, or whether it is a reflection of the views of one feminist academic when she asked:

Why study women with disabilities? They reinforce traditional stereotypes of women being dependent, passive and needy. (cited in Fine and Asch, 1988, p. 4)

It must not be assumed that disabled women are silent observers of feminist issues. The contribution to be made by disabled women is substantial:

> Able-bodied women can learn from the disabled, who have had to learn this before they can truly cope, that the physical body is not as important as the person that lives inside; that one is first a person, and second a female; that sex is less important than these two; and that every woman who is honestly involved in her own personal growth is making a contribution to the women's movement whether she is aware of it or not. (Duffy, 1981, p. 168)

There are certain aspects of women's oppression which highlight the parallels and the differences between disabled women and non-disabled women. The basic issues may be the same for both groups but the impact of disability means that the implications or effects may differ. I have chosen to examine some of the areas which have played a crucial role in developing a feminist understanding of the position of women. These are gender roles, body image and sexuality. The division into three distinct areas is an artificial one created for the purposes of writing; in reality our experiences in relation to gender roles, self-image and sexuality are inextricably linked, they interweave together to determine our experiences, and thus cannot be regarded as separate aspects of our lives.

Gender Roles

A woman's role is traditionally one of nurturer: throughout her life she is to a large extent defined by her capacity as a daughter, wife or mother. Women have criticized the concept of the family as an oppressive institution through which socially constructed feminine roles have been established and maintained. It can represent the power struggle between men and women in its starkest form (see Barrett and McIntosh, 1982). Despite the fact that women have fought hard to challenge traditional sex roles, the influence of such roles still remains strong and therefore their significance should not be underestimated. Graham explains:

> caring — whether for husbands and children, or for those outside the nuclear family — is far from trivial and insignificant. It is moreover, an activity where questions of success are constantly raised, and women can indeed feel 'unsexed' by failure. (1983, p. 21)

For disabled women, there may be an automatic assumption that our disabilities will prevent us from ever taking up such traditionally-defined roles.

To many women, the absence of rigidly prescribed gender roles would be a source of great relief and a sense of liberation, but for those of us who have been constantly denied access to what could be construed as the 'goals of womanhood', the attainment of such goals can mean a real sense of achievement:

> . . . I pushed myself to have the very things my parents said I could not have. I was determined to prove I was a 'normal' woman. I deliberately sought the most handsome man to parade around. And although I did

not consciously intend to do it, I became pregnant out of wedlock at 17, which was extremely affirming for me. One of my proud moments was parading around the supermarket with my belly sticking out for all to see that I was indeed a woman, and that my body worked like a normal woman's body. (Rousso, 1988, p. 159)

Occupying a position in 'no woman's land' may either (a) push disabled women into choosing very traditional feminine roles to aspire to notions of 'normality', or (b) lead disabled women to select non-traditional feminine roles as a process of default rather than personal choice. However, one must be wary of assuming that non-traditional roles are adopted as the only option available. There are some disabled women who do not wish to be confined by the prescriptions of femininity and a decision to be a single parent, a career woman, a partner in a lesbian relationship, or a lesbian mother, is a positive choice.

Women who have been married before the onset of disability often find that the perceived threat to the traditional role of wife and housekeeper can cause irreparable damage.

If, as disabled women, we do not conform to conventional gender roles, then the fight to gain access to institutions such as the family becomes extremely difficult, if not impossible. Although these institutions are considered oppressive by many feminists, the struggle against the family may be different for those of us who are excluded from the outset.

As disabled women our experiences of institutions such as the family are significantly influenced by the pressure of conventional gender role distinctions. We either make a positive decision for political or personal reasons not to ascribe to traditional roles, or we fight very hard to conform to the ascriptions which classify us as a 'real woman'. Alternatively, we recognize society's rejection, and in realizing that the socially-sanctioned roles are prohibited, we acquire a sense of worthlessness and a negative self-image.

Self-Image

Self-image is the internal concept we have of ourselves. Our self-image as women is significantly influenced by our body image. Indeed for many women self-image is synonymous with body image. This is a direct consequence of the fact that women are primarily defined by physical appearances. Body image is determined by the messages we receive about how our bodies should look and behave. It is a gendered concept which has been constructed by men to endorse the view of women as ornamental objects put on this planet for the gratification of men. The dominant image of women does not incorporate the diverse and individual characteristics of women. Instead it suggests that an attractive woman is young, medium height, slim, non-disabled and white. Consequently black women, older women, fat women, women who are too short or too tall and disabled women are not attractive because they do not not conform to the dominant body image in Western society.

The term 'disabled women' can quickly and easily be replaced with the words 'defective women'. In a society which places substantial emphasis on 'feminine' attractiveness and the ability to take care of one's own basic bodily functions, disabled women are dealt a severe blow. One disabled woman writes 'I had this image of myself as a big blob, no shape just dead meat' (Carrillo *et al.*, 1982, p. 26).

Disabled women live in bodies which do not always work and often defy the dominant notion of 'normal' appearance. This can be particularly difficult to reconcile with the pervasive myth of perfection:

> I try hard to accept my body and improve on it but it's a losing battle.
> I'm bombarded with pictures of beautiful bodies and I just cannot compete, so I try to hide my flaws. . . . (Morris, 1989, p. 61)

Through the countless images of beauty that find their way into the daily lives of women, the message that they must have a certain appearance to be admired and loved, particularly by men, is internalized. Certain aspects of disability can make it difficult for a woman to incorporate her physical characteristics and her daily needs into this concept of attractiveness:

> Most disabilities come equipped with drooping breasts, a thin rib-cage and a lax tum, due to lack of muscle-tone. . . . The inability of the disabled person to be purely physical, showing body movement, posture . . . can be a great disadvantage within the 'market place' of relationships. (Campling, 1981, pp. 17–18)

In view of the fact that disabled women may challenge societal perceptions of accepted, or expected, standards of appearance, our differences may be labelled as 'defects':

> Specialists trained to treat one or other of our body parts have contributed to our dismembered body image. Value judgements are assigned to our 'good' parts and 'bad' parts. Health is seen as a virtue, disease as evil and ugly. (Browne *et al.*, 1985, p. 246)

With very little attention given to the positive aspects of a person's appearance and a tendency to reduce the body to a sexual object, disabled women learn very early on that their bodies can be objects which are manipulated and controlled by others:

> Having a disability made me very aware at an early age of the messages I was receiving from the larger society about how I was supposed to look and how you're supposed to be. Also as the doctors poked and studied me endlessly, I learnt more quickly than some non-disabled women that I'm seen as an object. (Campling, 1981, p. 10)

If a woman loses respect for her own body, and internalizes the negative messages that hang the label 'defective and undesirable' around her neck, then it is not surprising that her body becomes a source of pain, embarrassment and guilt. This can subsequently lead her to believing that her body is the enemy and she has no control over it:

One of the results of considering your body to be the enemy is a sort of disassociation. The disassociation manifests itself in a feeling of not owning one's body. . . . Consequently we see a mind-body split which has major implications for self-concept and sexuality. (Bogle *et al.*, 1981, p. 92)

Body image has a profound impact on the way in which we perceive ourselves. A positive body image can help to build confidence and promote self-esteem, and a negative image can affirm feelings of inferiority, worthlessness and inadequacy.

Sexuality

Sexuality refers to the whole span of personality related to sexual behaviour. To challenge male supremacy and object to the sexual objectification of women by men, the Women's Movement has demanded the right for women to define their own sexuality and an end to all discrimination against lesbians.

Disabled women are entitled to the same rights as other women; however, we may be a long way behind in trying to reach the same goals. One woman explains the dilemma she faces by saying:

It has been rare in my life that I have feared men getting sexual with me, because most men don't see me as a sex object in the same way as they see most women. For THAT I am profoundly grateful! . . . But if only more women had made me feel like a woman. (Campling, 1981, p. 32)

Until recently disabled people have been seen as asexual. The non-disabled world has found it difficult to grapple with the idea that these 'damaged' bodies could have sexual feelings, and the mere thought that they may engage in sexual behaviour is considered 'unwholesome, repulsive and comical' (Greengross, 1976, p. 2).

Usually during adolescence children develop an understanding of their own sexuality and anticipate or explore relationships with others. Body image and self-esteem often significantly influence a child's sexual development. For a disabled daughter who has acquired a negative self-concept, the control and manipulation of her body by others may leave her feeling ambivalent and confused about her own sexuality. One woman talks about her turmoil:

It was difficult enough to be feeling so confused about my sexual identity. Not to be able to experiment with boys only added to my confusion and growing self doubts. (Rousso, 1988, p. 146)

Despite the moves to push for the recognition of women's sexual needs, there is still a notion that the disabled woman's needs are either nonexistent or inferior. One young adolescent woman with spina bifida who asked her gynaecologist whether she would be able to have satisfying sexual relations received the following response: 'Don't worry honey, your vagina will be tight enough to satisfy any man' (Fine and Asch, 1988, p. 21). Greengross seems to endorse the notion that the sexual needs of disabled women are either nonexistent or inferior by writing:

'there is no doubt that women suffer the same pains of loneliness as men; and their sexual needs, though usually not as great, certainly exist' (Greengross, 1976, p. 110). Such an approach seriously undermines the sexuality of disabled women. There is no evidence to suggest that the sexual needs of women are any less than those of men (Coveney *et al.*, 1984).

The reality for many disabled women is that the lack of social and employment opportunities may exacerbate the difficulties of establishing and maintaining relationships, particularly if a woman is living in her parental home:

> The situation can be frustrating if you are at the age, as I am, when you would be living independently, working and travelling. Parents can be over-protective. (Campling, 1981, p. 17)

Given that many parents find it hard to come to terms with the fact their children are sexual beings, it is not surprising that, where the daughter has a disability, parents find it particularly difficult to accept their child's sexuality. If a daughter appears to have a 'damaged' body or mind then parents might not be able to see why anybody else would be attracted to her. Consequently they often convey negative attitudes to their disabled daughter and try to discourage any sexual development. One disabled woman describes her experience:

> as an adolescent I realised that boys do not react in the same way to a girl in a wheelchair as they do to other girls. . . . My mother did not help me during this period, telling me . . . to look for spiritual relationships, because any man who appeared to be attracted to me must be perverted. (Campling, 1981, p. 80)

Sometimes men might be attracted to disabled women because they perceive disabled women as passive and more likely to respond to their sexual advances. Men who are threatened or intimidated by women who define their own sexual needs or appear as equals in a relationship may choose to focus their attentions on those women who seem to be in a less powerful position. Thus men might choose to assert their power by establishing relations with the least powerful sections of the community such as disabled women, black women or single mothers.

Disabled women can challenge orthodox notions of the way people are expected to gain sexual satisfaction. For example, the traditional missionary position adopted in heterosexual relations may be totally inappropriate for many disabled women (as well as non-disabled women). Kirsten Hearn writes:

> Different women with different disabilities have different needs and abilities, before, during and after sex. Some of us can only lie in certain positions or may have to use different parts of our bodies. Some of us have more strength and energy than others. (Hearn in McEwan and O'Sullivan, 1988, p. 50)

The diverse range of methods used to gain sexual satisfaction by disabled women must be seen as a positive step for all women as it enables us to decide how our sexual needs can be met sensitively.

There are sometimes distinct rules relating to the type of men that disabled women are allowed to have a relationship with or marry:

> The invalid may marry another of his kind, and live happily or unhappily ever after. Society doesn't greatly care whether he is happy or unhappy as long as society isn't troubled. A wall is raised between the 'normal' world and the world of the disabled — a wall invisible and hard and cold as unbreakable glass. (Judith Thunem, cited in Shearer, 1981, p. 84)

Greengross argues:

> The principal problem for a marriage between an able-bodied person and someone handicapped is one of motivation. It begs the cruel and unavoidable question: 'What normal person would saddle him/herself with someone who probably will need a lifetime of care?' Many 'normal' people when they enter a marriage of this nature are not marrying an equal but someone they want to treat like a child. (1976, p. 29)

This type of attitude is not only patronizing but also very insulting. It wrongly assumes that a disabled woman is passive, helpless and a burden. The persistent undermining of disabled women in such a way means that if we have a relationship with a non-disabled person then we are constantly subjected to the negative responses of other people:

> I am told how wonderful he is, and how lucky I am. It's great for the self-esteem. . . . Implicit implication. . . . You (disabled) are lucky not to be alone, unwanted in an institution. No one has ever said he is lucky (unthinkable), or he obviously stays with you because you give as much as you take. But then of course, that's an unthinkable proposition, isn't it? After all I'm only one of THE DISABLED. (Campling, 1981, p. 50)

Fine and Asch (1988) argue that the fact that men want women who are not only visually attractive, but also functional in their role as a homemaker and wife means that disabled women are perceived as being incapable of fulfilling such a role.

Although society is organized and structured around heterosexual relationships, it must not be assumed that all disabled women are striving for marriage and motherhood. There are disabled women who have chosen to reject heterosexual relations and some of them will make a positive decision to be lesbian mothers. However, their experiences as lesbians can be extremely isolating:

> There's nobody here I can talk to really. I'm not telling the social worker or anyone at the centre. I'd get ostracised . . . I did tell someone years ago. . . . He told me I could get treatment for it. I don't want that, I don't want my brain interfered with, there's enough wrong with me without that. (Campling, 1981, p. 86)

> Severely able-bodied lesbians look at us and go, 'Urgh, what's *wrong* with her?' (Hearn, in McEwan and O'Sullivan, 1988, p. 50)

Some disabled lesbians argue that the lesbian community has adopted many of the values and expectations of the heterosexual community. Kirsten Hearn writes: 'You only have to go to a disco to realise to what extent lesbians have bought the image of the slim, agile, symmetrical body' (McEwan and O'Sullivan, 1988, p. 50).

Both within the homosexual and heterosexual communities disabled women have struggled to gain access to the same options as our non-disabled contemporaries. Unfortunately, our denied sexuality and exclusion from traditional gender roles has not exempted us from the threat or actuality of male sexual violence:

> Maria was twelve when her brother's closest friend began raping her regularly. He attacked her when she was in bed, unable to get to her wheelchair. He was eighteen, and powerful; she didn't stand a chance. (Matthews, 1983, p. 72)

As disabled women we can be much more vulnerable to sexual abuse and victimization, particularly if we have been bombarded with ideas that our bodies are a neutered object which is repulsive and inferior. A failure to recognize sexual development leaves us open to exploitation, one disabled woman explains:

> My first sexual experience was coercion, but I figured that nobody was ever going to do it with me again, so I'd better get it now. I now feel that was rape. (Bogle *et al.*, 1981, p. 102)

The perception that a disabled woman may never have sexual relations has been used as a justification for rape. One rapist said, 'I wanted to give her something that nobody else wanted to give' (Bogle *et al.*, 1981, p. 102).

Disability Rag (1986) and Galler (1984) report instances where women with cerebral palsy have been ignored when they have reported rape. The effects of sexual violence can cause serious psychological and social problems for all women. However, as disabled women the problems we encounter can be magnified if we are perceived as asexual and not believed when we report rape. It is harder for us to leave exploitative or abusive relationships when we are trapped by our physical and financial dependence.

Conclusion

When talking about disabled women we are talking about women who have the same hopes, differences, anxieties, fears and other emotions as non-disabled women. The oppression we experience is similar to that encountered by our non-disabled sisters, but certain aspects are magnified in our daily lives, and others are altered to fit into the position that we hold as disabled people in society. There can be no doubt that for disabled women 'it is not difference which immobilizes us, but silence. And there are many silences to be broken' (Lorde, 1985, p. 15).

By applying the feminist principle, 'the personal is political', I have shown how disabled women have become misplaced and tolerated in a society which is both sexist and handicapist. Certain aspects of feminist analysis, particularly the concepts of gender roles, self-image, sexuality and socialization, have been used to highlight our experiences. Through such an analysis it has been possible to demonstrate how the concerns, needs, wishes and aspirations of disabled women strike at the core of the feminist movement, yet our voices usually remain unheard.

The feminist movement has restricted its thinking to the needs of non-disabled women. It has had difficulty tackling diversity among women. Consequently, many women, particularly those of us who have disabilities, have been left out in the cold. Feminism urgently needs to address the issue of diversity and in the process of doing this it must learn from the experiences of disabled women. It is crucial that 'the personal is political' is not simply used to provide an analysis of the experiences of a select group of women, namely white, non-disabled, heterosexual women, and that it goes beyond understanding immediate experiences to incorporate the needs and wishes of a diverse group of women. Charlotte Bunch explains: 'We cannot . . . depend on our perceptions alone as the basis for political analysis and action — much less for coalition. Feminists must stretch beyond, challenging the limits of our own personal experiences by learning from the diversity of women's lives' (in McEwan and O'Sullivan, 1988, p. 290).

In this article I have tried to break some of the silences surrounding the experiences of disabled women. Now the feminist movement needs to engage in an open dialogue with disabled women to learn from our experiences and develop a movement which reflects the diversity of the sisterhood. It is crucial that non-disabled feminists acknowledge our experiences and recognize our needs, wishes and aspirations as being a fundamental part of feminist experience and a key component of the feminist movement.

Writing from the perspective of a disabled woman I can only conclude by emphasizing that the feminist movement has to accept the fact that disabled women have a right to full and equal participation. However, 'by this we don't mean just pity or embarrassment, or just plain access as outlined by us in the past, but an acceptance that we are viable, lovable, and totally worthy members of the . . . sisterhood' (Kirsten Hearn, in McEwan and O'Sullivan, 1988, p. 52).

Note

This chapter was first published as an article in *Feminist Review* No. 40 (Spring 1992).

References

BARRETT, M. and McINTOSH, M. (1982) *The Anti-Social Family*, London, Verso.
BECKER, E.F. (1978) *Female Sexuality after Spinal Cord Injury*, Illinois, Accent Special Publications.
BEGUM, N. (1990) *The Burden of Gratitude*, University of Warwick and SCA (Education).
BOGLE, J., DANIELS, S., SHAUL, S., WAXMAN, B. and WYSOCKI, J. (1981) 'Women's Issues: A Panel Discussion', in BULLARD, D. and KNIGHT, S. (Eds) *Sexuality and Physical Disability*, St Louis, C.V. Mosby Co.
BOSTON WOMEN'S HEALTH COLLECTIVE (1984) *The New Our Bodies Ourselves*, New York, Simon and Schuster.
BROWNE, S. *et al.* (Eds) (1985) *With the Power of Each Breath*, San Francisco, Cleis Press.

BULLARD, D. and KNIGHT, S. (Eds) (1981) *Sexuality and Physical Disability*, St Louis, C.V. Mosby Co.

CAMPLING, J. (Ed.) (1981) *Images of Ourselves*, London, Routledge and Kegan Paul.

CARRILLO, A., CORBETT, K. and LEWIS, V. (1982) *No More Stares*, Berkeley, Disability Rights Educational Defences Fund Inc.

COOK, L. and ROSSETT, A. (1975) 'The Sex Role Attitudes of Deaf Adolescent Women and Their Implications for Vocational Choice', *American Annals of the Deaf*, Vol. 20, pp. 341–5.

COOTE, A. and CAMPBELL, B. (1987) *Sweet Freedom*, Oxford, Basil Blackwell.

COVENEY, L., JACKSON, M., JEFFREYS, S., KAYE, L. and MAHONY, P. (1984) *The Sexuality Papers*, London, Hutchinson.

CREEK, M. *et al.* (1987) *Personal and Social Implications of Spinal Cord Injury*, Eltham, Thames Polytechnic.

DEEGAN, M. and BROOKS, N. (Eds) (1985) *Women and Disability: The Double Handicap*, New Brunswick, Transaction Books.

DISABILITY RAG (1986) 'Care that Kills', *Disability Rag*, Vol. 7, No. 6, pp. 9–10.

DUFFY, Y. (1981) . . . *All Things are Possible*, MI, A.J. Garvin and Associates.

FINE, M. and ASCH, A. (1985) 'Disabled Women: Sexism Without the Pedestal', in DEEGAN, M. and BROOKS, N. (Eds) *Women and Disability: The Double Handicap*, New Brunswick, Transaction Books.

FINE, M. and ASCH, A. (Eds) (1988) *Women with Disabilities — Essays in Psychology, Culture and Politics*, Philadelphia, Temple University Press.

FINKEL, P., FISHWICK, M., NESSEL, K. and SOLIZ, D. (1981) 'Sexuality and Attendant Care: A Panel Discussion', in BULLARD, D. and KNIGHT, S. (Eds) *Sexuality and Physical Disability*, St Louis, C.V. Mosby Co.

FISHER, S. (1973) *Body Consciousness*, Englewood Cliffs, Prentice Hall.

FOX, G. (1980) 'The Mother-Adolescent Daughter Relationship as a Sexual Socialization Structure: A Research Review', *Family Relations*, Vol. 29, pp. 21–8.

FRIEDMAN, G. (1980) 'The Mother-Daughter Bond', *Contemporary Psychoanalysis*, Vol. 16, No. 1, pp. 90–7.

GALLER, R. (1984) 'The Myth of the Perfect Body', in VANCE, C. (Ed.) *Pleasure and Danger*, Boston, Routledge and Kegan Paul.

GEMMA (1979) *Newsletter*, No. 7, London, Gemma.

GEMMA (1989) *What's the Use of Her Coming, She Can't Dance*, London, Gemma.

GRAHAM, H. (1983) 'Caring: A Labour of Love', in FINCH, J. and GROVES, D. (Eds) *A Labour of Love: Women, Work and Caring*, London, Routledge and Kegan Paul.

GREENGROSS, W. (1976) *Entitled to Love*, Guildford, National Marriage Guidance Council in association with National Fund for Research into Crippling Diseases.

GROTHAUS, R. (1985) 'Abuse of Women with Disabilities', in BROWNE, S. *et al.* (Eds) *With the Power of Each Breath*, San Francisco, Cleis Press.

HANNAFORD, S. (1985) *Living Outside Inside*, Berkeley, Canterbury Press.

LANCASTER-GAYE, D. (Ed.) (1972) *Personal Relationships, the Handicapped and the Community*, London, Routledge and Kegan Paul.

LANDIS, C. and BOLLES, M. (1942) *Personality and Sexuality of the Physically Handicapped Woman*, New York, Hoeber.

LORDE, A. (1985) *The Cancer Journals*, London, Sheba Feminist Publishers.

McEWAN, C. and O'SULLIVAN, S. (1988) *Out the Other Side: Contemporary Lesbian Writing*, London, Virago.

MATTHEWS, G. (1983) *Voices From the Shadows — Women with Disabilities Speak Out*, Toronto, The Women's Press.

MORGAN, M. (1972) 'Attitudes of Society Towards Sex and the Handicapped', in LANCASTER-GAYE, D. (Ed.) *Personal Relationships, the Handicapped and the Community*, London, Routledge and Kegan Paul.

MORRIS, J. (Ed.) (1989) *Able Lives*, London, The Women's Press.

ROMANO, M. (1978) 'Sexuality and the Disabled Female', *Sexuality and Disability*, Vol. 1, No. 1, pp. 27–33.

ROUSSO, H. (1988) 'Daughters with Disabilities: Defective Women or Minority Women?', in FINE, M. and ASCH, A. (Eds) *Women with Disabilities — Essays in Psychology, Culture and Politics*, Philadelphia, Temple University Press.

SHARPE, S. (1976) *'Just Like a Girl': How Girls Learn to be Women*, Harmondsworth, Penguin.

SHEARER, A. (1981) *Disability: Whose Handicap?*, Oxford, Basil Blackwell.

SMART, C. and SMART, B. (1976) *Women, Sexuality and Social Control*, London, Routledge and Kegan Paul.

SUTHERLAND, A. (1981) *Disabled We Stand*, London, Souvenir Press.

UNION OF PHYSICALLY IMPAIRED AGAINST SOCIETY (1981) 'Editorial', *Disability Challenge*, No. 1, May.

Chapter 7

Desire and the Politics of Representation: Issues for Lesbians and Heterosexual Women

Tamsin Wilton

Feminism is a politics, it is about power and the way in which power is embodied, expressed and negotiated. Specifically, it is about the inequitable power relations of two groups, men and women. However, it is abundantly obvious that sex is not the only axis across which power is differentially assigned, rather, there are many such axes. White has more power than black, male than female, heterosexual than homosexual, adult than child, able-bodied than disabled, and so on. Black, gay and feminist theories have challenged the notion that such binarism is 'natural', a transparent taxonomic practice merely reflecting a pre-existing 'reality', insisting rather that such attributes as health, sanity, intelligence or strength are discursively *allocated* to one or other of each set rather than being essentially inherent in masculinity, whiteness or heterosexuality.

Both feminism and poststructuralism, indeed, recognize that this process of discursive allocation socially constructs concepts such as gender, race, adolescence or sexuality itself (that most privileged signifier of the natural). As such, they are culturally and historically specific and amenable to deconstruction and reconstruction (Weedon, 1987). Deconstructing the taxonomic categories upon which oppressions are predicated is clearly problematic on many levels for those who fight the oppression (Gatens, 1991). If 'woman' is merely a social construct, then what price women's liberation? A politics structured around binarism is, however, politically and intellectually straitjacketed. A feminism predicated upon the binary power-struggle of gender has, for example, no intellectual place for the demands of women of colour that it respond to racism. When gender is the privileged category of signification, considerations of race, sexuality, age, disability etc. can at best be merely 'tacked on', at worst become a source of conflict and contradiction. We urgently need an analysis which, rather than confronting us with a simple linear hierarchy in which white, middle-class, heterosexual, able-bodied adult men are positioned at the apex of substrata of oppression, offers a way of understanding the complex web of often contradictory relations of power (Wilton, 1990).

In this paper I suggest an alternative model for understanding the relations of power of heteropatriarchal[1] culture, a model structured around questions of sexuality, of desire, acts and identities. I have focused on the central question of the representation of the sexual, since I believe that it is by analyzing sexualized representational practices that the political nature of sex and the sexual nature of power may best be identified and subverted.

An Alternative Model of Power

In contemporary European culture, 'sex' is positively over-charged with significance; indeed one marvels at the massive burden of signification assigned to such
a tiny word. Clearly, size is not everything when it comes to sexual semiotics!
Not only has sex become, as Jeffrey Weeks (1985) puts it, 'a contested zone . . . a
moral and political battlefield', it is also, as feminist and Foucauldian analyses
assert, the paradigmatic privileged site for the contestation of meaning and of
power (Foucault, 1976; Gavey, 1989).

Sex is clearly the site of negotiation of meaning on a grand scale. This be-
wildering multiplicity of meanings is ironic, given that sex is the one area of
human activity whose 'naturalness' is most stubbornly defended. The great discursive lie of romance tells us that sex is natural, spontaneous, primal, irresistible;
involving the whole person, mind, body and soul, in communion with another,
a moment of relief from the anxieties of existential isolation. In a culture still
processing the Judaeo-Christian legacy of sin and guilt, sex is also seen as essentially subversive and anti-authoritarian. Additionally, as in Orwell's *1984*, sex
represents the ultimate act of individualistic self-assertion set against the anonymity
of late capitalist urban angst. For the sexual libertarian, then, sexual activity is
intrinsically radical, discursively constituted as it is in diametric opposition to the
repressive influences of Church and State. 'Make love, not war' is the slogan of
an era when radical (male) political analysis had claimed that 'sex, more sex, and
sex the powers didn't like would bring the house down' (Lederer, 1979).

The libertarian assertion that sexual desire and activity are somehow intrinsically 'good' and 'natural', to be defended against attack from an erotophobic
political Right is as problematic as the assertion that the heterosexual nuclear
family is intrinsically 'good' and 'natural', to be defended against attack from sexual
libertarians. Both positions polemically elide individualist/psychological notions
such as 'promiscuity' or 'erotophobia' and socio/political notions such as 'freedom'
and 'repression' in ways which serve only to muddle analysis. The politics of the
sexual have no clear relationship to sexual politics, rather, they are riddled with
competing meanings, many of them profoundly contradictory ones competing
for the label of radicalism.

The cottaging of gay men, for example, once interpreted as the painfully
limited sexual outlet of an oppressed and hunted minority, is now proudly proclaimed as intrinsically radical behaviour, asserting a deviant and oppositional
identity against the stagnant familial norms of heterosexuality. As feminists, we
are ideologically in opposition to the stagnant familial norms of heterosexuality.
We are also ideologically in opposition to the sexual commandeering of public
space by men, carrying as it does a familiar subtext whereby women and children
are relegated to the 'safety' (read 'containment') of the home, while the wide
world is colonized by the sexually predatory male (Brownmiller, 1975). Equally,
the feminist debate on pornography is thoroughly polarized, and hence dis-
empowered, by the simplistic assertion that to be against pornography is to be
against sex. 'The pornographic "sickness"', as one gay man asserts, 'doesn't reside
in the works of pornography, but in the minds of erotophobes' (Witomski, 1985,
cited in Watney, 1987, p. 63). Even the struggle to empower children to resist
sexual abuse is countered by those who see 'intergenerational sex' as a valid minority sexual 'taste' (Jeffreys, 1990).

What sense can feminism make of this complex and contradictory set of assertions? I suggest it is helpful to consider the current historical model of sexual power in classical Athens. The classical Athenians, according to David Halperin, also constructed a binary divide around sex. It was, however, apparently very different from our own primary divisions into male and female, heterosexual and homosexual. 'Sexual penetration and sexual "activity"', Halperin tells us, 'are thematized as domination'. Put simply, the one who fucked was dominant, and his pleasure was utterly privileged; the one who was fucked was passive and his/ her pleasure was of no consequence. Additionally:

> 'Active' and 'passive' sexual roles are . . . necessarily isomorphic with superordinate and subordinate social status; hence, an adult, male citizen of Athens can have legitimate sexual relations only with statutory minors (his inferiors not in age but in social and political status): The proper targets of his sexual desire include, specifically, women, boys, foreigners, and slaves — all of them persons who do not enjoy the same legal and political rights and privileges that he does. (Halperin, 1983, p. 49)

Women, boys, foreigners and slaves. Sound familiar? Reading this I was immediately struck by the parallels between this historical model of sexuality-as-power and the radical feminist analysis of male sexuality as eroticized dominance (Jeffreys, 1990; MacKinnon, 1989; Dworkin, 1988). There is not space here to follow through the threads of this interesting analogy, to offer an analysis of such phenomena as sex tourism, child sexual abuse, racist rape, male rape, prostitution, sexual harassment, the sexualization of au pairs, pornography (including the growing field of 'exotic' or 'ethnic' porn), sex slavery, etc., etc., but there is much to suggest that our own culture is organized along very similar lines to that of classical Athens. It is not simply that masculinity is discursively constituted as sexually active (Spender, 1985), though that is undoubtedly the case. It is not simply that femininity is constituted as sexually passive and responsive (Gavey, 1989; Jackson, 1988), although that, too, is undoubtedly and demonstrably so. It is not simply that male sexuality is culturally constructed as a powerful, often irresistible force (what Jeffrey Weeks describes as the 'hydraulic model'), while women's sexual feelings are weaker and more subject to control (Scully and Bart, 1973).

My suggestion is that relations of power in Western late capitalist society are structured around the right to penetrate. It is not so much 'kill or be killed' as 'fuck or be fucked'. It is by asserting penetrative rights over others that political power is asserted, and this has been as true of so-called 'radicals' as of the establishment. The slogan of the radical European student movement of the 60s, 'Fuck the establishment — never fuck the same woman twice' (cited in Haug, 1987, p. 188), nicely illustrates the elision of sexual penetration and political power.

There are many historical pointers which indicate the symbolic significance of penetration. Lesbianism, for example, was punished in mediaeval Europe much more severely if the male privilege of penetration had been usurped by use of a dildo (Brown, 1991), and in many cultures right up to the present day, the penetrative partner in anal intercourse between men is understood not to have compromised his masculine status, while the receptive partner is anathematized (Katz, 1983; Weeks, 1985). 'Masculinity' is certainly a social construct, but as such, it nonetheless derives its dominant status precisely from its attachment to *biological* maleness. 'It is not masculinity *per se* which is valorised in our culture but the *masculine male*' (Gatens, 1991, p. 151 — emphasis in original).

The socio-political significance of penile penetration is the dominant text of hegemonic discourses of the sexual, taking precedence over pleasure, over the practicalities of family planning, indeed, over health and, potentially, over life itself. For example, the staggering obtuseness of HIV/AIDS safer sex promotional material for heterosexuals makes sense only in the light of an analysis of the politics of penetration. Penetration with the penis is the single most risky sexual activity for the transmission of HIV. By adopting alternative, non-penetrative activities, the risk of acquiring HIV sexually may be almost completely avoided (Richardson, 1989; Patton and Kelly, 1987). Yet HIV/AIDS health promotion has insisted on restricting the discussion of safe sex largely to condom use during penetrative intercourse, thus effectively side-stepping the sexual-political issues inherent in promoting the (much safer) alternatives and leading one feminist commentator to dismiss official safer sex materials as 'penetration propaganda' (Campbell, 1987). Viewed physiologically, it should be a simple matter to stop the HIV/AIDS epidemic in its tracks. Yet, as I have argued elsewhere, the widespread adoption of safe sex, although physiologically straightforward, intellectually simple and arguably more pleasurable, especially for women (Gavey, 1990; Holland *et al.*, 1990), by de-prioritizing the act of penetration, by which male power is signified, is ideologically intolerable to the heteropatriarchy, and hence unlikely to be either promoted or practised widely (Wilton, 1991). Ideology will be the death of us!

Once active sexual penetration is identified as both the prerogative and the assertion of political power, rather than a personal sexual choice, it becomes clear why women are so stubbornly constituted as the objects rather than the agents of desire. To grant women sexual agency would be to threaten not merely socially constructed gender norms but the discursive matrix of power itself. If to be powerful is to assume sexual rights over the powerless, then sexual power in women represents not only a challenge to existing gendered relations of power, but a rupture with the discursive constitution of power itself. It is significant that, as Dorothy Hage observed, 'there is no word for normal sexual power in women' (cited in Spender, 1985, p. 175). It is abundantly clear that hegemonic definitions of 'normal', 'sex' and 'power' render the notion of 'normal sexual power in women' oxymoronic. As John Berger (1972, p. 55) recognized, 'Women are there to feed an appetite, not to have any of their own'.

Representational Practices

I have argued that power in our society is predicated upon and asserted through sexual agency. I now want to consider how representational practices may re-produce, reflect or challenge heteropatriarchal relations of power. Feminist and Foucauldian analyses suggest that dominant discourses of femininity and masculinity construct the female body as the paradigmatic site for establishing and perpetuating gendered relations of power (Bartky, 1988). Since it is through representations of the specifically and overtly sexual that the cultural construction of sexuality and the sexualized body may be most clearly identified, I will consider one set of sexualized representational practices which focuses on sex itself.

Post-Freudian cultural analysis suggests, of course, that there is widespread sexualization of visual imagery. Film studies have been influential in revealing (some would say, constructing) the conscious and unconscious elements of sexual pleasure implicit in the voyeuristic cinematic 'gaze' (Mulvey, 1975; Dyer, 1990), and feminist cultural theory has explored the links between consumerism and the objectification of women's bodies in 'high' and 'ordinary' art and, pre-eminently, in advertising (Winship, 1987; Pollock, 1987; Williamson, 1987). It seems that every visual artifact, from *Neighbours* to Judy Chicago's 'Dinner Party' installation, from the Nescafe adverts to the Sistine Chapel ceiling, has a sexual message. There are however, sets of representational practices in which sex is the message as well as the medium, the text and context as well as the subtext. Pre-eminent among these is, of course, pornography, where highly sexualized imagery is used to sell sex itself. A second, and rather startling, addition to pornography in this context is health promotion, specifically (although not exclusively) HIV/AIDS health promotion, and it is this which I have chosen to focus on here. This is partly because pornography, although widely available, still lacks the official sanction and conviction of moral rectitude accorded to HIV/AIDS health promotion. Additionally, and importantly, most pornography, whether gay or straight, is produced for a male audience, while the promotion of safer sex obliges the producer to recognize women, both lesbian and heterosexual, as sexual constituencies. The representational practices of HIV/AIDS health promotion, then, offer a unique insight into the discursive construction of gender and sexual identities outside the 'deviant' discourse of pornography.

It is a largely unquestioned assumption in HIV/AIDS safer sex promotion that people will only respond to information if they can 'identify with it' (Frutchey, 1990). Since sexual identity is assumed to be a major and key component of individual identity, this has resulted in a strategy of 'targeting' specific *sexual* groups, that is, groups of people identified by means of an assumed shared sexual identity, or set of sexual behaviours. So, for example, we have the bizarre situation where advice about using dental dams as protection during cunnilingus is limited to material aimed at lesbians — as though this were under no circumstances a heterosexual practice.

The gravest problem consequent on the practice of 'targeting' safer sex materials, and the one germane to this paper, is that targeting, together with all other discursive or representational practices, does not simply 'reflect' a pre-existing social reality in an unproblematic, transparent fashion. Rather, it establishes discursive boundaries for those very groups it is seeking to target, *'identificating'* them, in the sense of making an identity for them, rather than merely identifying them as pre-existing groups. A key part of the activity of targeting is the process of deciding on the relationship which a particular group has to sex, and reproducing that relationship semiotically. If we consider some materials aimed at gay men, it becomes clear what relationship is assumed and constructed between them and sex.

Gay Men

The (in)famous Terrence Higgins Trust[2] 'Sex' leaflet (see figure 7.1) is paradigmatic of the genre. On its cover is a naked figure of a male sex object, young, white, hunky and abundantly able-bodied (you can just about make out how able-

bodied he is by peering behind the typography). Gay men are culturally defined as sexually proactive, by reason of their masculine gender, and in addition are constructed as essentially sexual, by reason of their allocation to a social group defined precisely by its sexuality. There are apparent contradictions at work in this image, since this male body is presented as an object of scrutiny, thus apparently disrupting the configuration of male = powerful/subject, female = powerless/object. Indeed, in this image the male body is presented as a sign signifying sex, in what appears to be a direct parallel with the customary semiotic loading of the female body. Does this sexualized image, then, indicate a radical, oppositional set of signifying practices which challenge and disrupt dominant relations of power? An analysis with binary tendencies, which privileges alternately a division into homo/heterosexual or into male/female might argue that such an image is indeed a radical cultural/political statement. However, an analysis predicated upon the recognition that 'boys, women, foreigners and slaves' form the legitimate objects of masculine sexual desire would clearly assert that an image objectifying a young, beautiful male body merely colluded with and reproduced dominant relations of power, *as long as the intended audience was male.* Since all the erotic richness of gay male safer sex material is aimed at men, no radical rupture of dominant relations of power can occur, and the discursive and semiotic boundaries of masculinity and male superordination remain intact.

Heterosexual Women

How does safer sex promotional material aimed at heterosexual women construct the relationship between women and sex? Typical of the genre is a leaflet

This leaflet is produced to help women to understand the ways in which they can reduce the risk of acquiring the human immuno deficiency virus (the virus which can cause AIDS) and other sexually-transmitted diseases.

THE ADVICE IN THIS LEAFLET IS EXPLICIT PLEASE DO NOT READ IT IF YOU ARE EASILY OFFENDED

Don't exchange body fluids with your partner. Make love by doing

produced by Frenchay Health Authority in Bristol (see figure 7.2), which has a cover entirely devoid of graphic titillation, unless you happen to have a fetish for large type! Additionally, it bears a conspicuous warning, 'Advice in this leaflet is explicit. Please do not read it if you are easily offended'. There is an influential gay male lobby which insists that, in order to be effective, safer sex material must be sexually arousing, functioning as what Simon Watney (1987) refers to as 'a pornographic healing'. After all, Watney argues, 'If sex were not pleasurable, people would not be at risk'. Whose pleasure is at issue here? Much feminist research has indicated that, far from being pleasurable, heterosexual sex is problematic for the vast majority of women, being often unpleasant, painful or downright dangerous (Gavey, 1989; Hite, 1987; Chapman, 1988).

Additionally, the dominant discursive structuration of heterosexuality differentially assigns sexual subjectivity to men and women. To men are allocated, as we have seen, sexual desire, the power to choose or reject sexual partners, the power to insist on sexual gratification, ownership of sexual 'drive'. To women are allocated the responsibility for sexual attractiveness, the responsibility for male sexual gratification, the responsibility for sexual responsiveness, and the responsibility to *defend themselves against sex* on many levels (Wilton, 1991). It is this construction of sex as a male activity, foisted on women both because of our subordination, and in order to ensure the continuance of that subordination, which constitutes pornography. Ironically, safer sex promotion targeted at heterosexual women, by constructing women as sexually passive, indeed, as threatened by sex, functions pornographically, according to the radical feminist critique of pornography.

The feminist critique of pornography is frequently wilfully misrepresented as prudery (Cole, 1989; Watney, 1987), most recently by libertarian gay men who have gone so far as to accuse anti-pornography feminists of posing a serious threat to the lives of gay men who, it is claimed, need pornographic safer sex material if they are to be saved from HIV/AIDS (Watney, 1987). In fact, the feminist critique of pornography is based quite overtly on an analysis of power, rather than sexual explicitness or sexual arousal. The idea that sexually explicit imagery is *per se* exploitative of women is widely rejected (MacKinnon, 1989; Brownmiller, 1975; Cole, 1989; Jeffreys, 1990), the focus being rather on the degradation of women, the pornographic construction of sex as something done *by* men *to* women (or to boys, slaves and foreigners!) in order to demonstrate and reinforce male domination. In fact, the cultural construction of women as *innocent* of sexual desire, as evidenced in most safer sex promotional material, parallels and makes logically necessary the image of women as *victims* in pornography (Stimpson, 1988).

Lesbians

There has been little safer sex material targeted at lesbians. Using the classical Athenian model of socio-sexual power, it becomes evident that the taxonomic division into 'dominant male' and 'everyone else' has no place for the lesbian. Women who reject their legitimate positioning as sexual object, either by choosing celibacy or by demanding the right to sexual agency, are punished in hetero-patriarchal culture by a variety of strategies, commonly focusing on notions of deviance and stigma (Faderman, 1985; Jackson, 1988). Women who choose other women as their sexual partners comprise the one group most threatening to the privilege and demonstration of male power. Not only do we refuse to be the objects of male sexuality, but we transgress still further by usurping the male privilege of having sex with women. Hence, to admit the existence of lesbianism is quite simply ideologically intolerable, with the result that lesbians are histori-cally and culturally 'invisible'. This invisibility is striking in HIV/AIDS health promotion, with little or no material available for lesbians. There is a demonstrable tendency for information for lesbians to be included in material aimed at the generic group 'women', the anxious subtext being that women's sexuality is of so little consequence that who cares, really, whether you are lesbian or straight. An interesting exception is the poster produced by the Terrence Higgins Trust in 1990 (see figure 7.3) as part of a series aimed at promoting safer sex to young people. The series is glossy, professionally photographed, pleasurable to the eye, and represents a range of sexual couplings. Of the six images, four show hetero-sexual couples, one a gay male couple and one a lesbian couple. There has been an obvious effort to challenge dominant readings of sexualized imagery, yet it is, on the whole, women's bodies which are most on display, and it is the treatment of the lesbian couple which most clearly reflects pornographic imagery, with its seductive glimpse of a breast and a flawless, peachy bottom, together with the most explicit piece of sexual innuendo of the series, 'Wet [sic] your appetite for safer sex', and the traditional pornographic trappings of wet hair, the shower/bathroom scenario etc. This use of pornographic cliché directly colludes with the cultural practice of invalidating lesbianism by 'capturing' lesbian sexual imagery as sexual titillation for a male audience.

Tamsin Wilton

ET

YOUR APPETITE FOR

SAFER SEX.

Heterosexual Men

What about safer sex materials targeting heterosexual men? There are not many of them, and those there are tend to straightforwardly reproduce oppressive relations of power by representing women not only as objects of desire, but as deadly seductresses; the old, offensive line about sex = woman = death (Treichler, 1989). An interesting alternative is demonstrated in one leaflet produced in London (there is no indication of who exactly produced and published it), which, by showing three suitably unattractive men on a front cover printed a rather nasty brown colour (no danger of inadvertent homosexual response here), manages to avoid troublesome issues of sexual desire altogether.

HIV/AIDS health promotion, then, colludes with dominant discourses of gender and sexual identity in important ways. It constructs women, whether lesbian or heterosexual, as the objects of masculine desire, and denies us sexual agency. We are there, in health promotion as in the National Gallery, to feed an appetite, not to have any of our own. The erotic gaze is constructed as male, and men as objects of desire only for other men. Masculine sexual agency is, therefore, never challenged, and dominant heteropatriarchal relations of power are powerfully reinforced.

Sexualized Representation and Subjectivity

The iconographic strategies of pornography or safer sex promotion are not transparent practices, merely reflecting a pre-existing sexual 'reality' elsewhere constructed. They are signifying practices, 'discourses through which material power is exercised, and through which the gendered relations of power which inhere in sex are reflected, re-established and perpetuated' (Gavey, 1990, p. 3). 'The pornographers,' Sheila Jeffreys (1987, p. 79) reminds us, 'are involved in the construction of sexuality'. Nor is the private, personal experience of sexual desire merely the embodiment of 'natural' or 'instinctive' drives and appetites. Rather, as Foucault (1976, p. 105) insists, 'Sex is always historically and socially specific, and its meaning is a site of constant struggle'.

It is one of the strengths of feminist analysis that we recognize what Nicola Gavey (1990) calls 'the importance of language/representation as a *constitutive* process'. The social discourses available to women and men not only reproduce or challenge existing gender relations, they also constitute our subjectivities, our sense of identity, our sexuality, our desire.

With an analysis which identifies representation as a political practice, and a recognition that power is mediated through sexuality, it is clear that questions of the representation of the sexual are of key importance in either maintaining or disrupting male power and the subordination of women. Current representational practices construct desire as male, desirability as female (Berger, 1972). If, as I have suggested, the power of dominant masculinity is both predicated upon and expressed through sexual agency (the privilege of sexual access to women, boys, slaves and foreigners), then a self-defined, autonomous female desire must be reclaimed and represented.

There are complexities and contradictions inherent in any such profoundly radical project. The erotic gaze has been so firmly established as male that sexualized imagery is always open to the threat of 'capture' into the seemingly boundless semiotics of male pornography. The perceived omnipotence (sic) of the male gaze leads us to police ourselves mercilessly. It is a struggle to re-construct the female body outside the boundaries of the male gaze. Lesbian artists, photographers and film-makers who work towards a non-oppressive representation of lesbian desire risk less from the moral majority's outraged censorship than from outraged feminist accusations of 'pornography'. This leads to the sad situation where lesbian-made films such as *She Must Be Seeing Things* or *Kamikaze Hearts* become the focus of greater feminist anger than *Emanuelles I, II, III* or *IV* ever were (Ardill and O'Sullivan, 1989).

Women's autonomous sexual desire has been denied for centuries, forcing us as feminists to recognize the need for what will probably be a long, slow, painful process of reclaiming, owning, indeed, *identifying* our desire and our pleasure. Intrinsic to this process is the debate on how we may most effectively disrupt those discursive and representational practices which represent and reproduce sexual desire and activity as essentially male, whilst asserting our own sexual autonomy. Questions of desire, consent and sexual pleasure are deeply problematic for women, intimately interwoven as they are with economic, religious, cultural and political threads. Women, after all, 'live in the world pornography creates' (MacKinnon, 1989, p. 155). It is unrealistic to expect pure, politically sound feminist desire to rise uncontaminated from out of the white heat of sound ideology, but by beginning the process of deconstructing dominant discourses of the sexual, and their constitutive role in the oppression of women, we start to refuse that oppression. Feminist representations of the sexual are, then, a crucial strategy to empower women and challenge the dominance of masculinity. Reclaiming the erotic, identifying and embodying female desire, validating female sexual pleasure, are politically radical processes. As Catharine MacKinnon (1989, p. 162) writes, 'The question for pornography is what eroticism *is* as distinct from the subordination of women'. It is a question which we, as women, must begin to answer.

Notes

1 I use 'heteropatriarchy' rather than 'patriarchy' to denote the role which compulsory heterosexuality plays in enforcing male dominance and patriarchal rule, and to recognize the hegemonic status of both heterosexuality and masculinity.
2 The Terrence Higgins Trust produced this leaflet in 1985; it is now no longer used, and is unrepresentative of their current materials.

References

ARDILL, SUSAN and O'SULLIVAN, SUE (1989) 'Sex in the Summer of '88', *Feminist Review*, No. 31, Spring, pp. 126–33.

BARTKY, SANDRA LEE (1988) 'Foucault, Femininity and the Modernization of Patriarchal Power', in DIAMOND, IRENE and QUINBY, LEE (Eds) *Feminism and Foucault: Reflections on Resistance*, Boston, Northeastern University Press, pp. 61–86.

BERGER, JOHN (1972) *Ways of Seeing*, Harmondsworth, Penguin.

BROWN, JUDITH C. (1991) 'Lesbian Sexuality in Medieval and Early Modern Europe', in DUBERMAN, MARTIN BAUML, VICINUS, MARTHA and CHAUNCEY, GEORGE, JR. (Eds) *Hidden from History — Reclaiming the Gay and Lesbian Past*, London, Penguin.

BROWNMILLER, SUSAN (1975) *Against Our Will: Men, Women and Rape*, New York, Simon and Schuster.

CAMPBELL, BEA (1987) 'Bealine', *Marxism Today*, December, p. 9.

CHAPMAN, KAREN (1988) 'Safer Sex for Some', *Lib Ed*, Summer, pp. 4–6.

COLE, SUSAN G. (1989) *Pornography and the Sex Crisis*, Toronto, Amanita.

DWORKIN, ANDREA (1988) *Letters from a War Zone*, London, Secker and Warburg.

DYER, RICHARD (1990) *Now You See It: Studies on Lesbian and Gay Film*, London, Routledge.

FADERMAN, LILLIAN (1985) *Surpassing the Love of Men*, London, Women's Press.

FOUCAULT, MICHEL (1976) *Histoire de la Sexualité: La Volonté de Savoir*, Paris, Editions Gallimard (translation *The History of Sexuality: Vol. 1: An Introduction*, Harmondsworth, Penguin).

FRUTCHEY, CHUCK (1990) 'The Role of Community-Based Organisations in AIDS and STD Prevention', in PAALMAN, MARIA (Ed.) *Promoting Safer Sex*, Amsterdam, Swets and Zeitlinger.

GATENS, MOIRA (1991) 'A Critique of the Sex/Gender Distinction', in GUNEW, SNEJA (Ed.) *A Reader in Feminist Knowledge*, London, Routledge.

GAVEY, NICOLA (1989) 'Feminist Poststructuralism and Discourse Analysis', *Psychology of Women Quarterly*, No. 13, pp. 459–75.

GAVEY, NICOLA (1990) *Technologies and Effects of Heterosexual Subjugation*, Department of Psychology, University of Auckland.

HALPERIN, DAVID (1983) 'Sex Before Sexuality: Pederasty, Politics and Power in Classical Athens', in DUBERMAN, MARTIN BAUML, VICINUS, MARTHA and CHAUNCEY, GEORGE, JR. (Eds) (1991) *Hidden from History: Reclaiming the Gay and Lesbian Past*, London, Penguin.

HAUG, FRIGGA (Ed.) (1987) *Female Sexualization: A Collective Work of Memory*, London, Verso.

HITE, SHERE (1987) *Women and Love: A Cultural Revolution in Progress*, Harmondsworth, Penguin.

HOLLAND, JANET, RAMAZANOGLU, CAROLINE, SCOTT, SUE, SHARPE, SUE and THOMPSON, RACHEL (1990) 'Don't Die of Ignorance — I Nearly Died of Embarassment: Condoms in Context', in AGGLETON, PETER, DAVIES, PETER and HART, GRAHAM (Eds) *AIDS: Responses, Interventions and Care*, London, Falmer Press.

JACKSON, GAIL (1988) *Promotion of Safer Sex: Or the Patriarch, Misogyny and the Condom*, unpublished paper, London, Terrence Higgins Trust.

JEFFREYS, SHEILA (1987) 'The Body Politic — the Campaign Against Pornography', in DAVIES, KATH, DICKEY, JULIENNE and STRATFORD, TERESA (Eds) *Out of Focus: Writings on Women and the Media*, London, Women's Press.

JEFFREYS, SHEILA (1990) *Anticlimax: A Feminist Perspective on the Sexual Revolution*, London, Women's Press.

KATZ, JONATHAN NED (1983) *A Gay and Lesbian Almanac*, New York, Harper/Colophon.

KITZINGER, SHEILA (1982) *Woman's Experience of Sex*, London, Dorling Kindersley.

LEDERER, LAURA (1979) 'Introduction', in LEDERER, LAURA (Ed.) *Take Back the Night*, London, Women's Press.

MACKINNON, CATHARINE (1989) 'Pornography: Not a Moral Issue', in KLEIN, RENATE D. and STEINBERG, DEBORAH LYNN (Eds) *Radical Voices — a Decade of Resistance from Women's Studies International Forum*, Oxford, Pergamon.

MULVEY, LAURA (1975) 'Visual Pleasure and Narrative Cinema', in MULVEY, LAURA, (1989) *Visual and Other Pleasures*, London, Macmillan.

PATTON, CINDY (1989) 'Safer Sex, Community and Porn', *Rites*, April, p. 10.

PATTON, CINDY and KELLY, JANIS (1987) *Making It: A Woman's Guide to Sex in the Age of AIDS*, New York, Firebrand.

POLLOCK, GRISELDA (1987) 'What's Wrong with Images of Women', in BETTERTON, ROSEMARY (Ed.) *Looking On: Images of Femininity in the Visual Arts and the Media*, London, Pandora.

RICHARDSON, DIANE (1989) *Women and the AIDS Crisis*, revised ed., London, Pandora.

RICHARDSON, DIANE (1990) *Safer Sex: The Guide for Women Today*, London, Pandora.

ROBINSON, HILARY (Ed.) (1989) *Visibly Female: Feminism and Art Today*, London, Camden Press.

SCULLY, DIANA and BART, PAULINE (1973) 'A Funny Thing Happened on the Way to the Orifice: Women in Gynecology Textbooks', in HUBER, JOAN (Ed.) *Changing Women in a Changing Society*, Chicago, University of Chicago Press.

SPENDER, DALE (1985) *Man Made Language*, 2nd ed., London, Routledge and Kegan Paul.

STIMPSON, CATHARINE R. (1988) *Where the Meanings Are: Feminism and Cultural Spaces*, London, Routledge.

TREICHLER, PAULA (1989) 'AIDS, Gender and Biomedical Discourse', in FEE, ELIZABETH and FOX, DANIEL (Eds) *AIDS: The Burdens of History*, Berkeley, University of California Press.

WATNEY, SIMON (1987) *Policing Desire: Pornography, AIDS and the Media*, London, Methuen.

WEEDON, CHRIS (1987) *Feminist Practice and Poststructuralist Theory*, Oxford, Blackwell.

WEEKS, JEFFREY (1985) *Sexuality and its Discontents*, London, Routledge and Kegan Paul.

WILLIAMSON, JUDITH (1987) 'Decoding Advertisements', in BETTERTON, ROSEMARY (Ed.) *Looking On: Images of Femininity in the Visual Arts and the Media*, London, Pandora.

WILTON, TAMSIN (with AGGLETON, PETER) (1990) *Young People and Safer Sex*, paper given at the first Scandinavian Conference on Safer Sex, Stockholm, March.

WILTON, TAMSIN (1991) *Feminism and the Erotics of Health Promotion*, paper given at the fifth Social Aspects of AIDS Conference, South Bank Polytechnic, London, May.

WINSHIP, JANICE (1987) 'Handling Sex', in BETTERTON, ROSEMARY, (Ed.) *Looking On: Images of Femininity in the Visual Arts and the Media*, London, Pandora.

WITOMSKI, T.R. (1985) 'The "Sickness" of Pornography', *New York Native*, No. 121, 29 July–11 August.

Chapter 8

Difference at Work: Perceptions of Work from a Non-Heterosexual Perspective[1]

Gill Dunne

Introduction

Heterosexuality may be usefully conceptualized as a *social practice*, amongst many, which reproduces social inequality. It shapes the very meanings that we attach to being women and men, and thus the social conditions under which women and men may relate within and across 'gender boundaries'. It provides powerful legitimation for marriage — or at least heterosexual cohabitation — as the common-sense, 'normal' goal for adult living. Consequently, the heterosexual practice is central to 'taken-for-granted' patterns of living. The 'naturalness' of heterosexuality conceals the arbitrary nature of gender-specific experiences and patterns of living.

In this paper I will explore ways that a young woman's interpretation of her sexuality may contribute to the formation of an agenda that sets goals and perceives solutions with particular reference to occupational strategies. Using ethnographic material from my research on sixty non-heterosexual women, I will focus particularly on their *remembered* secondary schooling years. I will briefly consider several interrelated questions. First, how far did these women question 'taken-for-granted' patterns of adult living, i.e. marriage? Second, how did they perceive their future working lives? Finally, were anticipated outcomes translated into approaches to skill development and work role? To do this, I shall compare those in my sample who anticipated marriage with those who did not. By contrasting the perceptions of work of these groups, I will show that their interpretation of sexuality often had an impact on approaches to skill development, and on how future work roles were perceived. I conclude that ideologies, which serve to legitimate the heterosexual practice, have very real material consequences for women (see Dunne (1991) for a more detailed discussion).

The Research

The research is based on life-history interviews with sixty non-heterosexual women. It was carried out in a county located in the south of England. Most of the respondents lived within fifteen miles of a university town. This area was chosen because of its established 'lesbian community'. Furthermore, my own participation in that community provided me with important 'insider knowledge' and helped establish the necessary trust required to carry out sensitive research. My being known for many years by members of the 'community' contributed, I think, to the enthusiasm that the research project met.

The Sample

The lesbian community is very much divided into those whose experience centred upon the university, and those whose experience centred upon the wider town economy. As I wished to draw on as broad a range of lesbian experience as possible, and talk to women from a variety of class and ethnic backgrounds, I was careful to avoid drawing on a sample of university women. The sample, there-fore, comprised women who frequented the local lesbian and gay bar and various discos; a young lesbian group; a 'Lesbian Line' discussion group; and an 'Older Lesbian Discussion Group'. A snowball technique was used to reach those who were not regular participants in the 'scene'. The ages of the women interviewed ranged from 17 to 59, with a median age of 30.

The importance of this sample is that it is fairly representative of a population of lesbians, who make up a loose collection of interconnecting satellite networks, which together constitute a community. Few of the women interviewed came from particularly privileged social backgrounds and there were very few 'high-powered' professional women in the sample. Twenty-seven were from middle-class origins and thirty-three from working-class origins.[2] Their average approximate annual salary in April/May 1990, excluding the effects of overtime, was £10,700, with a median annual salary of £9,360. Only six earned over £15,000 a year. For a general breakdown of occupations of the sample see table 8.1.

The sample included women from Scotland, Wales and England — three of whom were women of colour.[3] To aid continuity all the women interviewed had to have been educated within the British schooling system.[4] As is shown in table 8.2, thirty-seven held higher qualifications, such as degrees, higher national diplo-mas, and professional qualifications.

Women who Questioned Marriage as a 'Taken-for-Granted'

Almost two-thirds of the sample reported never holding marriage as an expecta-tion. The median age of these thirty-eight women was 30 years. A further five changed their position on marriage at some point during schooling; the median age of this group was 25 years. The rest, seventeen, assumed that they would marry. The median age of this group was the highest, at 35 years.

Non-Marriage-Orientated Women's Experience of Romantic Heterosexuality

Their experience of adolescent heterosexuality was often fairly limited during the schooling years. Twenty-eight had very limited or no dating relationships with boys. Although they often took pleasure in the company of boys, many felt uncomfortable with the roles that they felt underpinned teenage romantic attach-ments. Heavy involvement in sport, school work, and/or discomfort with these

Gill Dunne

Table 8.1   Occupations of the Sample*

	Number
Professions (including trainees) such as: legal, accountancy-related, religion-related, nursing-related professions	5
Qualified (Higher National Diploma/degree) science and technical occupations: biologists, industrial chemists, computing, electronics, engineering, agriculture	6
Technicians (below degree level): agriculture, floristry, animal welfare	1
Senior management and professional management: generally related to the 'caring professions'	3
Sundry management, and trainee managers	5
Owners of small businesses, the self-employed and freelance workers	2
Occupations within national government, local government, civil service	3
Caring occupations: nursing and technical auxiliaries, porters, support workers — handicapped, children, elderly	3
Paid workers in women's organizations, lesbian and gay organizations	4
Teachers: school, 'A' level and colleges of further education	3
Culture and arts-related occupations: administrators, marketing, sales, library assistants, literary editors and writers	5
The motor trade	1
Transport and deliveries: passenger, goods and mail	4
Sports and recreation-related occupations: managers, trainee managers, instructors	2
Receptionists, typists, telephonists, clerks and administrators	3
Temporary unskilled catering	1
University/college undergraduates	2
Women returners to education: YTS training, 'O' levels, 'A' levels, degree, HND and Access courses	6
Unemployed, sickness, disability	1
Total	60

* Unfortunately, the need for confidentiality requires that I cannot be more specific about the sample's jobs.

roles were generally the reasons cited for lack of romantic interest in boys. Seven of those who did date reported an egalitarian approach to their relationships, which were often an extension of friendship. Only one dated in a 'taken-for-granted' manner. The group's standpoint on marriage, and their problematizing of relations within heterosexuality, was often reinforced at some point during schooling by a conscious or less conscious questioning of their own sexuality.[5]

Non-Marriage-Oriented Women's Perceptions of Work

For the non-marriage-orientated women, college and/or future work role was more usually the focus of their anticipation. Eighteen women in this group looked

Table 8.2 Qualifications of respondents

	Number	Percentage
Higher	37	62
Other	20	33
None	3	5

Categories as defined by the Department of Employment.

N.B. Higher: includes three respondents working towards higher qualifications.

forward to work in terms of a professional career or a job that offered career possibilities. The ability to be economically independent was a strong motivation. As many as sixteen of these career-orientated women had to some extent been questioning their sexuality. Importantly, these career-orientated women were just as likely to have come from working-class as from middle-class backgrounds. The following extract was fairly typical of those women who had been questioning their sexuality at a young age. Future work role was seen as long-term. As such, thoughts centred on entering work that offered challenge and prospects. This 43-year-old working-class woman had been singled out from her peers, and placed in the 'O' level stream at a secondary modern school. She spent all her working life in male-dominated occupations.

> *Did you get the impression that work would be central in your future?* Oh yes, for a long time, whatever I did I would have to enjoy, because I'd be doing it for an awful long time. *Did that influence you?* I think it did, in as much as wanting to be a school teacher, to know that was a job for life.

Similarly, the knowledge that work would be long-term was consequential for this 33-year-old woman from a working-class background. She had been educated in a grammar school, and had the opportunity to go on to college. She had been questioning her sexuality while at school, and finally 'came out' at college. She has spent all of her working life in a science-related occupation.

> *Did you have a sense that work would be something that would be part of your adult life?* Yes, I suppose as I knew that I wasn't getting married, I felt that it would be something that I would be doing, all my life. . . . *Do you think that influenced you in the area of work you went into?* . . . yes I suppose if I thought I was going to get married, I wouldn't have pursued, wouldn't even have thought of going to college, or agricultural college.

Another example of this career-orientation comes from this 25-year-old woman from a working-class background. She was educated in a secondary modern school. She has reached a management position in a more male-dominated occupation.

> *When you were at school how did you see the role of work in your future?* I think I knew that really I was going to work for a good few years, and it was going to be a big part of my life . . . I wanted a job that I couldn't let go of . . . I knew that I had to get something that I was really quite happy in doing, 'cos I would be doing it for a long time. . . .

A further nine women spoke of feeling a strong desire to enter work that would offer economic independence. All but two were from working-class backgrounds. These women were generally in the lower streams at school. Significantly, six may have had their desire for independence reinforced by their questioning of sexuality. An example of this desire for independence comes from a 52-year-old woman from a middle-class background. Her early rupture with heterosexuality was an important factor in her thinking in terms of economic self-sufficiency. After leaving school, she attended evening classes, and has achieved a very senior position in a non-sex-typed occupation.

> *Did you expect to marry?* No. I knew I was a lesbian. One of the things that I never felt was expected, was that I would grow up and get married. *Did you have any idea of what you wanted to do when you grew up?* I wanted to be financially independent, but that was without thinking about what I might like to do, want to do.

The non-marriage-orientated women also had some fairly strong ideas about the type of work to be avoided. Just under a third felt negatively towards traditional low-paid areas of women's work. This was often inspired by their feelings that it required emphasis of a particularly narrow definition of femininity which they were unwilling to conform to. This sometimes stimulated a desire, in academically borderline students, to stay on after school-leaving age to acquire more qualifications. This was the case for this 26-year-old woman, from a middle-class background, who 'came out' while at school. She had been a fairly average student at school; however, her reluctance to enter the more 'taken-for-granted' options available to women school-leavers was an important contributing factor in her decision to stay on at school and take 'A' levels. She went on to college, and is now working in a sports-related occupation.

> I went into the sixth form not for intellectual reasons but to postpone the need to work. *How did you view work?* Just, I've always had that thing of people trying to make me conform . . . I mean if you left school with a few 'O' levels, you know, you're going to be sort of shoved along and pushed into what you didn't want to do . . . into the stereotype roles.

For this 23-year-old woman from a working-class background, 'taken-for-granted' areas of women's work did not appeal because she found them to be too confining. Consequently, she considered more traditional 'male' areas of work, such as the police force. In the meantime, she stayed on at school, and gained a place at college. She is now working in management in a sports-related occupation.

> *What about clerical work — did that appeal?* I didn't want to be in an office stuck behind a desk all day, I had spent all of my life out and about, so there was areas of work . . . I couldn't see myself in a nine-to-five job, which left me a bit lost because a lot of people, well everybody that you knew, your mum's and dad's friends and that, were in nine-to-five jobs. So I thought, police force, that's shifts so that gets you out of that.

Slightly under half reported a desire to enter occupations that were more traditionally 'male preserves'. This 38-year-old woman from a working-class background was in the top stream at a secondary modern school. Given the options that she felt were available to young women like herself, access to a career meant entry into a 'male' occupation which offered the opportunity to develop 'craft' skills.

> *Did you see work as a major feature of your life when you grew up?* Yes, I realized that I was probably going to have to work to support myself, obviously for the rest of my working days, rather than opting out and getting married and letting someone else support me, that was out. . . . *What appealed to you about apprenticeships?* I wanted to be good at the job, I wanted a career rather than just a job, I wanted to be a qualified sign writer. I didn't want to be just working in the local Co-op, I wanted to actually have a career rather than just a job.

Twenty-four of the non-marriage-orientated women went on to higher education. For many, college life provided an opportunity to more fully explore their sexuality. Another three women later returned to higher education, to gain qualifications that would broaden their options. A further six went straight into areas of work that offered career prospects, such as the armed forces.

Three women did in fact marry; however, only one married in the conventional sense. One was a marriage of convenience to enable a lesbian relationship to be conducted without suspicion; the other was to a gay man and was non-sexual.

Women who Changed their Perspective on Marriage

The five women within this group changed their standpoint on marriage at some point during schooling. Three were from working-class backgrounds. None of these women had any romantic attachments with boys. While at school, two had been consciously questioning their sexuality, and another may have been questioning her sexuality.

Perceptions of Work

Four had held positive attitudes towards their future work role. Two were thinking forward to work in terms of developing a career. Two others saw work as important, believing it would offer them a more independent life-style. The fifth woman held more of a contradictory position on her future work role. Even after 'coming out', she had been reluctant to make any plans regarding career strategies. After a period in low-paid 'women's' work, she did, however, return to education as a mature student. Three of these women went straight from school to university and within this context, were able to make a positive identification with lesbianism.

Women who Expected to Marry

Of the seventeen women who reported holding an expectation of marriage during adolescence, eleven looked forward to marriage uncritically. These women were more likely to be over the age of 35. The others held more ambiguous thoughts on marriage and perceived it to be inevitable rather than desirable.

Marriage-Orientated Women's Experience of Romantic Relationships with Boys

Women in this group were more likely than those in the other two groups to have experienced relationships with boys during their schooling. Seven dated in a non-questioning way. Four reported a critical standpoint on roles within heterosexual relationships, and consequently held an egalitarian approach to them. Three women in this group reported that, in retrospect, they may have been questioning their sexuality during schooling; however, this did not immediately bring about a change in standpoint towards marriage.

A Questioning Standpoint on the Social Relations within Marriage

In terms of questioning 'taken-for-granted patterns' of living for women, we have seen that some in this group held egalitarian views about the social relations within heterosexuality. Some also held strong views about the desirability of a degree of economic independence within marriage. Four women, from both working-class and middle-class backgrounds, spoke of this desire. This 48-year-old woman, divorced with children, held an egalitarian approach to her marriage. Like many of these independent-minded women, she had been critical of her mother's domestic role. She saw work as offering her an identity beyond that of wife and mother, and consequently worked for almost all of her married life.

> Looking back it was ridiculous that I ever got married anyway. Right from the start, 17 or 18, I was determined I wasn't going to be a housewife. I was going to have a job, and that was very difficult to be taken seriously . . . I saw work as a means of being independent, and I didn't want to be a housewife stuck at home looking after children, and cleaning the house, and cooking. And I thought that housewives were second-class people, I know I thought that, why I thought it I don't know, but I defiantly did think that.

There were five women who reported thinking about future work roles in career terms: in this case four were from middle-class backgrounds and all but one was in the top stream at school. These ten 'work-orientated' women, who reported a desire for economic independence within marriage and/or the pursuit of a career, include four of the six women who held a reluctant expectation of marriage.

An Uncritical Standpoint on Marriage and Perceptions of Work

Often those women with an expectation of marriage held rather contradictory perceptions of future work roles. Overall, thirteen women had not questioned the 'taken-for-granted' notion that a woman's job would be secondary to that of her husband, or, significantly, short-term until marriage. This position was held by those educated at selective or non-selective schools alike.

Seven of the 'work-orientated' women also reported holding this position. Although they desired a good job, they believed that their future work role would be short-term, or would necessarily have to fit in with a husband's job.

Importantly, the remaining six women adhered to very traditional perceptions of their role in marriage, and consequently their work role. Their 'taken-for-granted' understanding was that their future work role would be of little consequence. Work was seen as short-term until marriage. Consequently, putting effort into school work was seen as superfluous; they felt that skill development was incompatible with their anticipated future role of wife and mother. An example of this kind of thinking comes from a 38-year-old woman from a working-class background. After leaving school she entered low-paid, clerical work for a short period. A re-evaluation of her sexuality stimulated her move into a series of better-paid, male-dominated occupations. She has recently started a job in a caring occupation.

> *Did you have any ideas of what you wanted to do when you grew up?* . . . because I come from where I do, all the girls that I knew, all the people that I knew, they just went and worked in a shop or factory, and then got married and had kids, that's all I ever thought there was to life (laughter) that's what I saw my life. My education . . . I never pushed myself or anything because I thought, what's the point — I just go and work for a couple of years until I get married and have kids and that's it. 'Cos I didn't know I was going to be gay or anything like that, so if I could turn the clock back on life, I would have done things differently. . . .

A similar perspective comes from this 32-year-old, grammar-school-educated woman, from a working-class background, who entered low-paid women's work. She moved out of this work when she reinterpreted her sexuality. She is now in a management position in traditional 'male' work.

> *How about the idea of marriage?* I just assumed it was the normal thing to do . . . because everyone around me was getting married and having babies. I think [my parents] would have liked me to have got myself into university, got some qualifications, and then got married. It seems a total, not a waste, but I can't see the point of it. In their view I can't see the point of it, because once I got married, having the qualifications and just giving it up, as they would have expected me to have done. Get married and have children and look after them, 'cos that's what we did . . . at that particular time I didn't think married women ever got back into a career. They just did part-time work, or just filled the shelves at Tesco's, I didn't see them as having a serious job . . . I thought once you got married at that particular time, then really that was it, and after that your family came first and your job came second.

Furthermore, those in serious relationships with boys spoke of the relationship taking priority over their schooling. This point is illustrated by this 32-year-old woman from a working-class background, who was educated at a grammar school. She initially entered low-paid clerical work, and after the re-evaluation of her sexuality has reached a well-paid supervisory position in traditional 'male' work.

> It [school work] suffered quite a bit, I just wasn't concentrating on it — for that sort of period of a year. It went down quite a lot. I basically wasn't bothered. I couldn't see the point of it because I was going to leave school and get married to Kevin and that was it. *Did his school work suffer?* It didn't seem to actually when I think about it.

Significantly, serious relationships led to several giving up their 'A' level studies. The following extract is from a 43-year-old divorced woman with children from a working-class background. She was educated at a grammar school. She left school before completing her 'A' level studies and entered traditional low-paid women's work, which she saw as short-term until marriage. She later returned to full-time education as a mature student with the support and encouragement of her woman lover:

> . . . when I met John, this is the bloke I married, I threw myself entirely into that. But no, it wasn't an equal relationship by any means and that's where it went wrong I think — far from it. *You threw yourself into it?* Well, it became the most important thing. I mean I skived off school. I really mucked up my 'A' levels completely, not that I was interested in the subjects I was taking anyway (laughter) . . . it became very important, I saw him all the time, every evening.

Seven of these women entered low-paid women's work, and two a women's profession, with the understanding that it would be a short-term commitment until marriage. This kind of approach to work is illustrated by a 40-year-old woman from a middle-class background. She entered clerical work thinking it would be short-term until marriage. She did not marry and has ended up in a more senior position in a non-sex-typed profession. She deeply regrets the limitations she experienced through her earlier occupational 'choice'.

> *Did you have any ideas about what the future involved for you?* No, I don't think I saw it as a long-term thing. I suppose I assumed I would get married twentyish I suppose, and therefore be rescued from this dreadful thing called work. I suppose I feel a bit cheated, in that you are brought up as a woman to think that a man's going to look after you, and nobody's looking after me. And I have had this hard fight through life, and it's very hard being single — as you must know.

Overall, eight marriage-orientated women went on to higher education on leaving school. Like the non-marriage-orientated women a re-evaluation of sexuality often occurred within the college environment. A further two entered traditionally 'male' work which offered career prospects: the armed forces. Both these women reported that the satisfaction and challenge they found in their jobs contributed to their feeling increasingly less interested in marriage.

Seven did indeed marry. However, for those who entered low-paid women's work and did not marry, the re-evaluation of their sexuality often led to their movement into higher education, or jobs that offered better prospects.

Conclusion

From this brief exploration of my sample's early standpoint on marriage and heterosexuality we have seen some interesting patterns. Many held an unquestioning standpoint on heterosexuality, together with a 'taken-for-granted' expectation of marriage. This often had consequences for their approaches to skill development and occupational 'choice'. The structural limitations on, particularly, women of colour and working-class women who have not had the chance to experience social mobility in education may provide little in the way of occupational 'choice'. However, we have seen that involvement in an important heterosexual relationship and/or the expectation of marriage contributed to some of my sample thinking that educational 'achievement' was incompatible with their future role of wife and mother. These women often followed traditional pathways into routine, low-paid women's work. Importantly, their experience of this work was made bearable by the assumption that marriage would offer an 'escape'. Although this is a small-scale study, I suggest that ideologies that romanticize marriage and stress dependency have been shown here as influential for many in my sample, whilst they were being constructed as heterosexual.

Lesbianism as a Source of Empowerment

There are many ways in which experience may give rise to the evaluation of, and a rupture with, heterosexuality as 'taken-for-granted', not the least being the recognition that one has fallen in love with a woman. Regardless of the form in which rupture occurred for my sample — as a result of greater self-exploration through education, religion, or feminism — the economic consequences were evident. A positioning of the self outside of heterosexuality invariably leads to problematizing a range of other 'taken-for-granted' life patterns for women. For women who wish to follow the lesbian life-style, the 'rewards' associated with the heterosexual practice — such as the maintenance or raising of standards of living through marriage or cohabitation with a man — are no longer available. Thus, a rejection of the heterosexual practice places wage-earning onto the centre of the stage. Recognition of this may consequently stimulate the need to take responsibility and control over various important aspects of life.

An early rupture with heterosexuality was described as empowering, and enlightening, by many in my sample. As work was perceived as long-term and inescapable, these women could make an early start in developing their occupational strategies. This knowledge was particularly important for the working-class women interviewed. Low-paid women's work was seen as unsuitable because it could provide neither the wages nor the stimulation required to sustain an independent life-style. Where possible they developed skills that would provide entry into areas of work that would be more intrinsically and extrinsically rewarding. However, there were women in my sample who, while at school, felt they did not have the necessary power to attain independence. For them, the lesbian life-style had to be ruled out (although achieved later) and marriage was entered.

Those in my sample who had been following the more traditional pattern available to women, and had viewed work as short-term or secondary to a male breadwinner, were forced to rethink the role of paid work in their lives when they questioned their sexuality. In most cases this resulted in a move out of work that provided a 'component wage' into work that provided a 'full wage', or a return to education.[6] Ten women returned to education in order to broaden their options. The uncharacteristic spread of occupations of the sample (see table 8.1 above) partly reflects this need for a 'full' wage. By their own reckoning, only a third of the sample are in areas of work, or levels in an occupational hierarchy, occupied traditionally by women.

I conclude that a more adequate understanding of women's economic position must take into account the ideological processes that inform women's perceptions of work. Many of these ideologies are deeply implicated in the legitimation process that constructs the 'taken-for-grantedness' of the heterosexual practice (see Dunne, 1991). Furthermore, I believe that, through a better understanding of the lives of non-heterosexual women, we may find alternative visions of practice. Through an exploration of 'difference' we may discover signposts directed towards change.

Notes

1 I would like to thank my friend Dr Jennifer Jarman, my supervisor Dr Henrietta Moore, and Dr Bob Blackburn for their helpful comments on this paper. As always I am indebted to the women in the 'attic' for all their intellectual encouragement and emotional support. Last but not least, a big thank-you to the sixty women who shared with me their wisdom and insights.
2 Class of parents was measured using the Goldthorpe Scale (1980). In order to simplify references to their class origins, I have grouped together those coming from Class I and II origins as 'middle-class', and those from Class III to VII as 'working-class'.
3 As far as I am aware, these three women were the only women of colour living the lesbian life-style in the area. Neither they, nor other lesbian contacts, could think of any others still living in the area.
4 The schools that they spent the bulk of their time in were: secondary modern (in thirteen cases); comprehensive (in nineteen cases); grammar (in thirteen cases); private (in twelve cases); and other (in two cases). Twenty-five had some experience of single-sex education.
5 The process of 'coming out' was often of long duration for women in my sample. It is therefore difficult to pinpoint when exactly a woman was consciously aware of questioning her sexuality. In retrospect, thirty-seven women saw the process extending back into adolescence. Of these, twenty women reported a conscious questioning of sexuality or having 'come out' at some time during their schooling.
6 Here I am drawing upon the concept of 'component' and 'full' wages as developed by Siltanen (1986, p. 110). 'Full' wages enable a person to support a household while 'component' wages do not.

References

AGASSI, J.B. (1982) *Comparing the Work Attitudes of Women and Men*, Lexington, MA, D.C. Heath and Company.

BRYAN, B., DADZIE, S. and SCAFE, S. (1987) 'Learning to Resist: Black Women and Education', in WEINER, G. and ARNOT, M. (Eds) *Gender Under Scrutiny: New Inquiries in Education*, Milton Keynes, The Open University.

CHRISTIAN-SMITH, L. (1988) 'Romancing the Girl: Adolescent Romance Novels and the Construction of Femininity', in ROMAN, L., CHRISTIAN-SMITH, L. and ELLSWORTH, E. (Eds) *Becoming Feminine: The Politics of Popular Culture*, London, Falmer Press.

COCKBURN, C. (1987) *Two-Track Training: Sex Inequalities and the Y.T.S.*, Basingstoke, Macmillan Education.

CONNELL, R.W. (1987) *Gender and Power*, Cambridge, Polity.

DEX, S. (1988) *Women's Attitudes Towards Work*, Basingstoke, Macmillan Press.

DUGGER, K. (1991) 'Social Location and Gender-Role Attitudes: A Comparison of Black and White Women', in LUBER, J. *et al.* (Eds) *The Social Construction of Gender*, California, Sage.

DUNNE, G.A. (1991) 'The Contagion of Difference: Difference in Sexuality, Difference at Work', Cambridge University, Sociological Research Group Working Paper Series.

FOUCAULT, M. (1979) *The History of Sexuality, Vol. 1*, London, Allen Lane.

GERSON, K. (1985) *Hard Choices: How Women Decide about Work, Career, and Motherhood*, Berkeley, University of California Press.

GOLDTHORPE, J.H. (1980) *Social Mobility and Class Structure in Modern Britain*, Oxford, Clarendon Press.

GRIFFIN, C. (1985) *Typical Girls?: Young Women from School to the Job Market*, London, Routledge and Kegan Paul.

LEES, S. (1986) *Losing Out: Sexuality and Adolescent Girls*, London: Hutchinson Education.

LEONARD, D. (1980) *Sex and Generation: A Study of Courtship and Weddings*, London, Tavistock.

MACHUNG, A. (1989) 'Talking Careers, Thinking Job: Gender Differences in Career and Family Expectations of Berkeley Seniors', *Feminist Studies*, No. 1 (Spring).

McROBBIE, A. (1978) 'Working-Class Girls and the Culture of Femininity', in WOMEN'S STUDIES GROUP (Eds) *Women Take Issue*, London, Hutchinson.

McROBBIE, A. (1990) *Feminism and Youth Culture*, London, Macmillan.

RICH, A. (1980) 'Compulsory Heterosexuality and Lesbian Existence', *Signs*, 5, 4.

RUBIN, G. (1975) 'The Traffic in Women: Notes on the "Political Economy" of Sex', in REITER, R. (Ed.) *Towards an Anthropology of Women*, London, Monthly Review Press.

SHARPE, S. (1976) *'Just Like a Girl': How Girls Learn to be Women*, Harmondsworth, Penguin.

SILTANEN, J. (1986) 'Domestic Responsibilities and the Structuring of Employment', in CROMPTON, R. and MANN, M. (Eds) *Gender and Stratification*, Cambridge, Polity.

WALKERDINE, V. (1990) *School Girl Fictions*, London, Verso.

Section III

International Feminisms

Chapter 9

Feminist Perspectives in Development: A Critical Review

Naila Kabeer

Introduction

This chapter presents a selective look at feminist interventions in the field of development research and policy. It traces the emergence of Women in Development (WID) as a distinctive constituency in the field, offers a critique of its main theoretical underpinnings, and draws out its lessons for an alternative feminist perspective for development.

The Early Years of WID

In its narrow sense, development refers to the planned process by which resources, techniques and expertise are brought together to expedite economic growth in an area of the world which is designated in different ways in different discourses (the South, underdeveloped, less developed, developing, the periphery), but which I will call the Third World.

There is another, more inclusive, way of talking about development; still as a managed process, but with unacknowledged assumptions and unanticipated implications. Development then becomes the processes of social transformation unleashed by the often conflicting attempts of development agents, local, national and international, to achieve their intended goals. Obviously, socio-economic transformations have existed as long as human history, but since my story has to begin somewhere, I will begin with the 1960s, since it was officially declared by the UN to be the First Decade of Development.

It was not, however, until the early seventies that the idea of 'women' as a distinctive, rather than residual, category made its appearance in development thinking. In fact, most accounts of the emergence of WID customarily cite a book published by Ester Boserup in 1970 as the watershed (Tinker, 1990; Maguire, 1984). Indeed it has been called 'the fundamental text for the UN Decade for Women' (Tinker, 1990, p. 8).

However, as Maguire (1984) suggests, the international climate would not have been as receptive to Boserup's critique if certain social movements had not been gathering momentum during that period. The 1960s and 1970s were a time of social struggle — in the South against colonialism and in the North against the deadening effects of class and race privilege in the universities and factories. Particularly critical was the international women's movement which emerged out of the questioning mood of that period and which mounted a challenge to the basic axioms underlying and compartmentalizing the social sciences, policy discourse and personal experience. This challenge pervaded development thinking at a time when it was itself undergoing a change of direction, a phase of reassessment and rethinking. Previously-held convictions that increases in a country's Gross National Product would 'trickle down' the income hierarchy to its poorest groups had been invalidated by evidence that economic growth was frequently accompanied by increases in unemployment and poverty. A growing concern with basic needs and poverty alleviation became the hallmarks of the Second Decade of Development.

Linked with this changing agenda, research highlighting women's critical role in food production and basic needs, women's predominance in the ranks of the poor and the links between women's status and fertility decline helped to give legitimacy to the idea that 'women's issues have development policy implications' (Buvinic, 1983, p. 23). The stage was cleared to allow women's status to take on increasing instrumental importance in the achievement of a variety of development-related objectives and for a UN Decade for Women to be declared with the full integration of women into the development effort as its stated goal.

As a result of policy and research during the Women's Decade, a great deal has been accomplished. Earlier cultural stereotypes have been scrutinized, anti-discriminatory legislation passed and national machineries for women's affairs set up in a large number of countries. Yet today as large sections of the Third World undergo a painful process of debt repayment and structural adjustment, it seems that some of the basic gains won by women are being clawed back. A Commonwealth Secretariat Expert Group, reviewing this period, concluded:

> Women have been at the epicentre of the crisis and have borne the brunt of the adjustment efforts. They have been most affected by the deteriorating balance between incomes and prices, by the cuts in social services, and by the rising morbidity and child deaths. It is women who have had to find the means for families to survive. To achieve this, they have had to work longer and harder. (Commonwealth Secretariat, 1989, p. 5)

Changing Agendas in WID Policy: From Welfare to Efficiency

To understand the limits to WID advocacy, we need to consider first of all what it set out to achieve. A WID agenda emerged in the 1970s, not because women had been totally ignored by policy-makers in the early years of development, but rather because they had been brought into development policy in very gender-specific ways. In other words, men entered the policy process primarily as household heads and breadwinners, while women were viewed primarily in their capacity as mothers and dependents.

'Development' efforts were targeted mainly at the male population, while women were relegated to the 'welfare' sector (Buvinic, 1983). However, welfare spending remains a residual category in national and international budgets, and the first to be cut back in times of economic downturn. It is perceived as assistance for those who have failed to be self-reliant through more socially acceptable mechanisms of the market-place (Moser, 1989). The 'dependency' connotations of welfare expenditures were further exacerbated where women were concerned by deep-rooted and normative assumptions about 'sex roles' which circulated among elitist national and international agencies.

The result of these cross-cutting exclusions was that women were considered only in connection with welfare efforts, within which interventions were further narrowed to address the 'primary' roles assigned to them in official discourse — as mothers, wives and 'at-risk' reproducers. Women were consequently concentrated in programmes delivering nutritional training, home economics, maternal and child health care and family planning programmes.

Against this background, Boserup's (1970) analysis came as a startling revelation. Writing in language familiar to planners, she made a strong case for women's productive roles, in direct challenge to previous orthodoxies equating women and domesticity. Her argument was that colonial and post-colonial governments had systematically bypassed women in the diffusion of new technologies and skills because of their preconceptions about women's roles. She pointed to the number of countries where, despite women's critical roles in farming systems, planners had continually operated with stereotyped assumptions about female dependency. Her insights were picked up and built upon by various scholars who documented the various ways in which planners had overlooked women's productive potential for development (Tinker and Bramsen, 1976; Rogers, 1980).

Although this new thinking filtered into the development agencies, it was not immediately translated into measures giving women equal access to the benefits of development. As Buvinic (1983) points out, the official Decade rhetoric of equity was slow to translate into policy because its redistributive implications were as relevant to the development agencies themselves as they were to communities they planned for. In the face of resistance from the predominantly male staff of most development agencies to redistributionist concerns, equal opportunities programmes presented high political and economic costs which undermined their chances of implementation (Buvinic, 1983).

Instead, a transitional phase occurred during which the new focus on women was accommodated within the new focus in mainstream development thinking on poverty alleviation and basic needs. Conceptualizing women as managers of low-income households and providers of basic family needs retained a continuity with earlier welfare approaches, in that it focused on women's responsibilities for family and child welfare. However, it also incorporated the WID concern with women's productive roles by recognizing that these responsibilities had an economic component and called for income-enhancing measures.

Ironically, it was with the deterioration in the world economy in the 1980s that there emerged a growing emphasis on women as economic agents in their own right. The overriding concern of the major donors, under the aegis of the International Monetary Fund and the World Bank, became the recovery of Third World debt and resolution of chronic balance-of-payments crises. Assistance was made conditional on countries adopting programmes of economic austerity, privatization and trade liberalization. Behind these programmes was a neo-liberal ideology which maintained that the dismantling of bureaucratic controls and greater reliance on market forces was the most efficient route to economic recovery.

A version of efficiency had been an important strand in WID thinking: the idea that women were productive agents whose potential had been under-utilized under welfare-oriented approaches. With the ascendancy of the free-market philosophy in donor agendas, there has been increased emphasis on this argument. Competitive market forces, free of the prejudices and biases of development planners, it was argued, would generate gender-free incentives to women and men alike. Women were given increasing recognition as key agents in the development process — as micro-entrepreneurs and parallel marketeers, as the 'nimble fingers' behind the export successes of global market factories and the food farmers who would solve sub-Saharan Africa's food crisis. It appeared that Boserup's plea that women's economic agency be recognized had finally been taken to heart by international development agencies.

In practice, however, the neo-liberal definition of efficiency is often at odds with some of the objectives of WID advocacy. The stress on women's economic agency, juxtaposed with cut-backs in public provision of various services through structural adjustment programmes, has led to the shifting of responsibility for welfare service delivery from the paid to the unpaid economy, usually through the intensification of women's labour time and effort. The recognition of women's productive potential appears to have been achieved at the expense of recognition for their unpaid reproductive work within the household.

This has uncovered a basic contradiction between the mainstream concern with market-led efficiency and the WID stress on women's economic agency. If the market is to be primary allocator of economic resources, then women who generally have lower purchasing power are unlikely to be able to demand the support services which would help them cut down on their domestic/reproductive labour overheads. And if women are unable to find these labour-replacing services, then they will be unable to pursue the kinds of economic activities which would help to increase their purchasing power.

Ironically, some of those calling for a 'human face' to structural adjustment appear to be falling back once again on women's family roles. UNICEF's Socio-Economic Advisor, for instance, argues for decentralization of health care in favour of self-provision within the community or family: 'This decentralisation is not costless. . . . While such an approach will increase time costs for women, it will place extremely modest monetary costs on the households; and will lead to substantial savings in the public sector' (Cornea, 1987, p. 174, cited in Elson, 1991, p. 178). As Elson points out, 'The implication is that increased time-costs for women do not matter, a result perhaps of the belief that women have lots of spare time' (Elson, 1991, p. 178).

We seem to be going round in circles. Somehow, it appears, over a decade of WID has not educated policy-makers to fully appreciate the interconnected nature of material and human production and women's vital role in both. However, critiques of integrationist WID strategies have existed as long as WID itself and they help us to understand some of the critical omissions and assumptions in WID thinking which have rendered the nature of this attempt at 'integration' so problematic.

Limitations of WID

Gender: Difference or Power?

A number of writers have described WID as liberal feminism writ global (Bandarage, 1984; Maguire, 1984). As such, it shares many of the limitations of liberal feminist thinking identified by Jagger (1983). WID analysis identified irrationality and prejudice on the part of planners as responsible for women's marginalization in development. The limitations of such analysis became apparent in the course of evaluations of various agencies involved in WID policy (Staudt, 1982; Gordon, 1984). These studies uncovered an important dimension which had hitherto been missing from WID analysis. In place of WID's theory of irrationality, they suggested the need for a theory of power which could explain deep-seated resistance within institutions to attempts at redistributive gender equity.

A revealing study by Staudt (1982) into the continuing poor performance of WID policy in the United States Agency for International Development (USAID) identified the institutionalized hierarchy of interests which had prevented its WID unit from carrying out what appeared to be a clear mandate to integrate women into AID programmes and projects:

- a limited budget ($1 million out of $4 billion) and a handful of staff (in an agency with around 6,000 employees in the late 1970s).
- ideological resistance from male colleagues, in the form of trivializing comments and personalized attacks on WID advocates' personal appearance and characters; accusations of 'exporting women's lib' and destroying the family; tedious jokes about 'developing a woman' or 'what about men in development'; frequent tendency to discuss women's income-earning or agricultural activities with reference to their own wives; outright hostility.
- lack of veto power or formal authority in the decision-making process.

These were not problems peculiar to donor agencies. As Staudt (1986) pointed out, the institutionalization of male privilege was also a feature of the 'bloated' bureaucracies characteristic of many Third World states whose officials were as threatened by gender redistribution as they might be by 'politically provocative' class redistribution. However, such gender conflicts were often disguised because they occurred 'behind the closed doors of bureaucracy, as threatened officials personalize such prospects and resist, deflect and/or undermine those policies' (Staudt, 1986, p. 329).

Rational Individualism and Gender Equality

A second limitation in the WID problematic appears more abstract, but has far-reaching and concrete implications. As Jagger (1983) points out, a central tenet of liberal thinking is the belief that the essential human characteristic, distinguishing humans from animals, is the mental faculty for reason. Jagger describes this thinking as 'normative metaphysical dualism', in that the mind is seen as separate from, and higher than, the body because it is the site of what is essentially human. Unlike animals, which instinctively utilize available resources to meet their sole objective of survival, human beings have the faculty to choose between different means to attain their goals.

Binary oppositions flowing from such a framework are repeated in a variety of forms in liberal thinking — mind/body; human/animal; nature/culture; manual/

mental; rational/instinctual — and permeate the ways in which value is given to labour and production. Thus work which requires the exercise of intellectual faculties is given precedence over manual labour, and work which is guided by instrumentalist criteria is given precedence over caring and nurturing.

It has been the claim of liberal theory that all men are equal because they possess this essentially human ability to reason. By extension, liberal feminists have claimed that women are equal to men because they too are rational individuals who have been prevented from realizing their full potential by the persistence of irrational prejudices and outmoded practices. WID advocates extended the logic of this argument for equality to women globally, and blamed the prejudices and preconceptions of planners for the absence of equal opportunities in the development process.

However, in accepting the liberal feminist argument for equal opportunities in development, WID advocates were also bound into its normative dualisms. In ignoring the social significance of biologically-derived activities — the physical needs of the human species and how they are met — liberal (and other) philosophies have helped to make invisible the labour, time and energy of those who carry them out. Since a near-universal feature of the social division of labour is that women are primarily responsible for the labour necessary to reproduce healthy, active human life on a daily and generational basis, the devaluation of this labour has powerful gender implications.

It relegates a great deal of women's time and energy in their mothering and caring activities to instincts rather than institutions, natural process rather than productive effort. It overlooks the fact that the gender division of labour in production and reproduction may differentiate women's and men's needs, interests and priorities. And it ignores the implications of interdependence in the gender division of labour for agency and rational behaviour. If men respond to market incentives and exercise instrumentalist rationality more readily than women in given contexts, the explanation must be sought in the social constitution of agency and rationality. Women's labour in the satisfaction of men's daily biological needs — and the needs of dependent family members — allow men the appearance of free, rational agents. Rephrasing Butler (1987, p. 133), the fiction of disembodied male rationality can only be sustained on the precondition that women are given monopoly of the bodily sphere. In the specific context of development planning, the consequences of these cumulative oversights is that significant aspects of women's labour are denied policy recognition and the incentives and resources that go with it.

Rational Individualism and Global Sisterhood

The argument for gender equality on the basis of universal rational individualism, which led to the stress on similarities between women and men, also led to an initial tendency among WID advocates to stress similarities between women. While recognizing, and indeed highlighting, differences in gender roles across the world, WID researchers were keen to point out the similarities in the ways in which women had been denied the fruits of modernization in both modern and premodern societies. The identification of 'Western-malestream' theories and policies as key factors in the worldwide domestication of women served to simultaneously 'name' the common enemy and emphasize the global basis of sisterhood.

It is, of course, true that many aspects of women's exclusion from the development process can be laid at the door of the Western and Western-educated men who dominate the policy and research institutions in both First and Third Worlds. However, focusing on the commonalities of women's subordination in the context of an unequal world order simply served to disguise and deny material differences in power, resources and interests between women. As an African women's research and development network (AAWORD) pointed out, most research on women in Africa before and during the Decade was carried out by Western academic women who sought to challenge the sexist assumptions of the social sciences and planning discourses, and to recommend ways of integrating women in development (AAWORD, 1982). While acknowledging the useful contributions of such research, AAWORD disputed that this sufficed to constitute a global constituency for women in development:

> While patriarchal views and structures oppress women all over the world, women are also members of classes and countries that dominate others and enjoy privileges in terms of access to resources. Hence, contrary to the best intentions of 'sisterhood', not all women share identical interests. (AAWORD, 1982, p. 105)

On the contrary, the unequal world order ensured that WID interventions too were distorted by the politics of development and reflected the divergent experiences, interests, needs and orientations of women from the North. WID scholarship had rarely acknowledged that the distortions brought about by colonial penetration in the global distribution of power, privilege and resources also extended to the terms on which First and Third World women entered the field of development.

Nor did the WID agenda offer any challenge to the *kind* of development that was being promoted by the international agencies and their national representatives:

> African women have begun to ask what exactly is the nature of this 'development' from which they alone have been excluded and into which they now should be integrated. Have colonialism in the past and the asymmetrical world economy and political reality been so generous as to put all males in structurally dominant and skilled positions? (AAWORD, 1982, p. 106)

The problem of development was, therefore, not that its benefits had been dichotomously distributed, with uniform benefits for all men and uniform disbenefits for all women. The problem was rather that the development model on offer was itself inherently asymmetrical. Third World countries had little autonomy in determining their own development trajectories as long as power and resources were concentrated in the hands of a few countries of the North. Consequently, most of its women and many of its men had been integrated into the international economic order on structurally disadvantaged terms.

Rethinking Development

Reversing the Hierarchy of Interests

These critiques of WID have thus helped to uncover some of the omissions of its early analysis: the intersection of women's subordination with other structures of global and local power; the devaluation of women's reproductive labour in a philosophy which privileges the rationality of the market-place; and, finally, the underestimation of male power as an integral aspect in shaping development thinking and practice.

Hartsock (1990, p. 36) has pointed out that in systems of domination, those in power have a very partial understanding of social relations, and one which reverses the real order of things. We need therefore to carry out our own conceptual reversals in order to understand the political economy of gender in development from an alternative feminist standpoint to that offered by WID.

One such reversal was suggested by a network of Third World activists, policy-makers and researchers (Development Alternatives with Women for a New Era). They pointed out that feminism could not be monolithic and homogeneous in its issues, goals and strategies, since it constituted the political expression of the concerns and interests of women from different regions, classes, nationalities and ethnic backgrounds (Sen, with Grown, 1985, p. 13). They proposed instead that it was from the vantage point of the most oppressed — women who are disenfranchised by class, race and nationality — that the complexities of subordination could be grasped and strategies devised for a more equitable development. This should not be taken to justify a single-minded focus on poor women, but rather to assert that without a structural transformation of the lives of the poorest, most oppressed sections of all societies, there could be neither development nor gender equity.

From 'Women' to 'Gender': A Relational Approach

In order to work towards such a goal, socialist feminists have sought to shift the focus from 'women' as an analytical category to 'gender relations'. Focusing on women appears to suggest that the problem — and hence the solution — is confined to women. A focus on social relations extends the analysis from women and men as isolated categories to the interconnecting structures which construct gender divisions in attributes and capabilities, tasks and responsibilities, resources and power.

It also serves as a constant reminder that gender relations are not the only form of social relations governing the lives of women and men. 'Gender', as Whitehead (1979) pointed out, 'is never absent'. But neither is it ever present in pure form. It is always interwoven with other social relations and processes, both within the domestic and larger economy, and has to be analyzed in this holistic framework if the concrete conditions of women's — and men's — lives are to be understood.

Reversing the Hierarchy of Production

Concerned primarily with a notion of production which stresses instrumental rationality, development thinking ignores any production which is deemed to be governed by affective criteria. Consequently, its concern is entirely with the measurement, evaluation and promotion of marketed goods and services. These are, however, only the tip of the economic iceberg, the visible segment of an indivisible whole. Below the surface are other kinds of production — household subsistence, informal-sector and community-based activities which complement marketed activities in ensuring the survival of families and households. Finally, since all these activities entail human labour, the broad base of the iceberg is the production, care and reproduction of human resources.

The skewed representation of the economy in conventional thinking becomes comprehensible once it is juxtaposed with the following facts: that women are under-represented at the tip of the iceberg, where development resources are concentrated; they are less so in subsistence and informal-sector production; and they dominate in the reproduction and care of human resources, the neglected sectors in the policy-making domain. It neatly illustrates, in other words, the point made earlier about the way in which systems of domination reverse the real order of things in the interests of those in power.

Another perspective becomes possible if we step back to ask once again what exactly the goals of development are supposed to be. The stark suffering of the 1980s has provided a fresh reminder that development is about the well-being and creativity of *all* members of society, regardless of where they are located in the hierarchy of production. It is, of course, true that economic recovery is not possible without increased economic growth; but economic growth requires — and is intended to achieve — the health and well-being of all people.

A human perspective on development — and one which promotes gender equity — requires that activities which contribute to the health, well-being and reproduction of people are seen as productive labour, to be counted as pluses in national balance sheets, regardless of whether they are carried out through families, markets or bureaucratic agencies. Such recognition will ensure that planners take account of these activities — and their interlinkages — in allocating their priorities and resources. Expenditures in public provision of health and maternal and child care services will be seen, not as an unproductive drain on the national budget, but as productive investments in the nation's 'human capital'. They will also be seen as the necessary precondition for freeing women from routine domestic chores to pursue alternative forms of productive activities, should they wish to do so.

Welfare, Efficiency and Equity: A Gender Perspective

Reversing the hierarchy of production also gives us the basis for rethinking the relationship between welfare, efficiency and equity. Although welfare is ultimately about human well-being, the conceptual confusion between 'welfare' and 'welfarism' has resulted in an unnecessary and unfortunate polarization between the concepts of 'welfare' and 'efficiency'.

While the early WID advocates were instrumental in revising the policy pre-occupation with women in their roles as mothers and wives, the new emphasis on efficiency which constructs women as economic agents has tended to ignore their greater embeddedness in familial and domestic responsibilities. If gender equity is to be grounded in concrete arguments about social justice rather than formal ones about equality of opportunity, it has to recognize the social significance of biological difference and the different priorities, needs and interests that it gives rise to.

I noted earlier the basic paradox in the notion of market equity for women: without effective purchasing power, they cannot acquire support services to alleviate the burden of reproductive work, while without alleviating the burden of reproductive work, they cannot acquire greater purchasing power. Equality of opportunity is meaningless without equality of agency. As Elson (1991) has pointed out, there is a complementarity between state provision of services required for human resource development, and women's ability to gain from market participation. Equality of agency, in other words, requires that the relationship between welfare and efficiency be seen as complementary, rather than competitive.

But welfare provision takes resources. Entrenched spending priorities have to be shifted before the necessary funds are made available and that will require alliances and networks between those working within the development institutions and their grass-roots constituencies. If knowledge was the terrain of struggle in the first decades of development, feminists must now extend the struggle to the new and difficult terrain of the development budget.

Towards Empowerment

Although development with gender equity entails recognition that men and women have different needs arising from their different situations in society, there is a tension between meeting needs in ways which preserve these differences and meeting them in ways which attempt to transform the underlying structures of inequalities which created them. Here, Molyneux's important analysis of these questions has made a valuable contribution (Molyneux, 1985). Molyneux makes the point that there is no such thing as women's needs since this assumes an unproblematic unity among all women, based on their common biology. Different groups of women have different needs and interests depending on their positioning within the social structures of their societies. Women's practical gender needs are those which emerge out of their location in concrete and pre-existing social relations. Thus women's roles as family carers in specific contexts give them a practical need for flexible health services or for childcare centres.

The notion of strategic gender interests, on the other hand, stems from an analysis of the mechanisms of women's subordination and a vision of an alternative, less oppressive society. It shifts the focus from what *is* to what *could be*, from planning for practical needs to strategies for empowerment. While there are no blueprints for empowerment, the victories, defeats, mistakes and struggles of women around the world become the raw material from which new strategies are constantly evolving.

What is most striking and specific about the power dimension of gender is the extent to which ideologies about gender difference and gender inequalities are internalized as a natural state of affairs by women as much as by men. Consequently, it is with the individual that the process of change begins. The empowerment of women is the process by which they develop the tools with which to identify and analyze the structures of their oppression and construct alternative ways of being, living and relating.

Since such a process is unlikely to be effective if women's practical needs for food, shelter, health for themselves and their families are not met, the provision of various services can also be a way of bridging the gap between practical and strategic. 'Subverting welfare for equity'[1] is one way of describing the strategy of various grass-roots development organizations who combine 'conscientization' with welfare service delivery; we now need to subvert the new discourse of efficiency to win resources which serve the strategic interests of women.

Concluding Comments

This paper has been about feminist interventions in shaping the development process. Clearly, the development context also intervenes to shape feminist contributions in the field. On the positive side, it exerts a constant pressure to engage in a practical feminism. The debates within development have far-reaching repercussions for the lives of women and men throughout the world. To influence the terms in which it is conducted means that feminist researchers in development cannot simply address each other, but have to take their arguments into forums where the strategic gender interests of men still permeate the vocabulary and politics of the debate. On the negative side, therefore, there is a constant potential within these forums for defusing, dissipating and subverting feminist contributions even in the process of appearing to incorporate them into policy.

Thus what began as a challenge by the advocates of WID to the narrow and outmoded equation between women-and-welfare appears to have ended by substituting another, equally narrow one between women-and-efficiency. If there are apparent convergences between the WID orthodoxy and the new orthodoxies about market-led efficiencies, the reason has to be sought in their common roots in a rational individualism which devalues the interdependencies of human society and the biological dimensions of human existence. What is necessary now is the displacement of the WID paradigm by alternative perspectives which appreciate the social significance of biological difference, which recognize the concrete circumstances out of which gendered needs and interests arise and which therefore offer the possibility of a situated, rather than abstract, politics of sisterhood.

Note

1 The phrase was coined by Dorienne Wilson-Smilie, the first Director of the Women and Development Programme, Commonwealth Secretariat.

References

AAWORD (1982) 'The Experience of the Association of African Women for Research and Development (AAWORD)', *Development Dialogue*, 1–2, pp. 101–13.
BANDARAGE, A. (1984) 'Women in Development: Liberalism, Marxism and Marxist-Feminism', *Development and Change*, 15, 3, pp. 495–515.
BOSERUP, E. (1970) *Women's Role in Economic Development*, New York, St Martin's Press.
BUTLER, J. (1987) 'Variations on Sex and Gender: Beauvoir, Wittig and Foucault', in BENHABIB, S. and CORNELL, D. (Eds) *Feminism as Critique*, Cambridge, Polity, pp. 128–42.

BUVINIC, M. (1983) 'Women's Issues in Third World Poverty: A Policy Analysis', in BUVINIC, M., LYCETTE, M. and McGREEVEY, W.P. (Eds) *Women and Poverty in the Third World,* Baltimore, Johns Hopkins Press, pp. 15–31.

COMMONWEALTH SECRETARIAT (1989) *Engendering Adjustment for the 1990s,* London, Commonwealth Secretariat.

CORNEA, G.A. (1987) 'Social Policymaking: Restructuring, Targeting, Efficiency', in CORNEA, G.A., JOLLY, R. and STEWART, F. (Eds) *Adjustment with a Human Face,* Vol. 1, Oxford, Oxford University Press, pp. 165–82.

ELSON, D. (1991) 'Male Bias in Macro-Economics: The Case of Structural Adjustment', in ELSON, D. (Ed.) *Male Bias in the Development Process,* Manchester, Manchester University Press, pp. 164–90.

HARTSOCK, N. (1990) 'Rethinking Modernism: Minority vs. Majority Theories', in JANMOHAMMED, A.R. and LLOYD, D. (Eds) *The Nature and Context of Minority Discourse,* New York, Oxford University Press, pp. 17–36.

JAGGER, A. (1983) *Feminist Politics and Human Nature,* Brighton, Harvester Press.

MAGUIRE, P. (1984) *Women in Development: An Alternative Analysis,* Amherst, MA, Centre for International Education.

MOLYNEUX, M. (1985) 'Mobilization without Emancipation: Women's Interests, State and Revolution in Nicaragua', *Feminist Studies,* 11, 2, pp. 227–54.

MOSER, C. (1989) 'Gender Planning in the Third World: Meeting Practical and Strategic Gender Needs', *World Development,* 17, 11.

ROGERS, B. (1980) *The Domestication of Women: Discrimination in Developing Societies,* London, Kogan Page.

SEN, G. and GROWN, K. (1985) *Development, Crisis and Alternative Visions: Third World Women's Perspectives,* New Delhi: DAWN Secretariat.

SHIRLEY, G. (1984) *Ladies in Limbo,* London: Commonwealth Secretariat.

STAUDT, K. (1982) 'Bureaucratic Resistance to Women's Programs: The Case of Women in Development', in BONEPARTH, E. (Ed.) *Women, Power and Policy,* New York, Pergamon Press, pp. 263–81.

STAUDT, K. (1986) 'Women, Development and the State: On the Theoretical Impasse', *Development and Change,* 17, pp. 325–33.

TINKER, I. (1990) 'The Making of a Field: Advocates, Practitioners, and Scholars', in TINKER, I. (Ed.) *Persistent Inequalities,* Oxford, Oxford University Press, pp. 27–53.

TINKER, I. and BRAMSEN, M.B. (Eds.) (1976) *Women and World Development,* Washington, DC, Overseas Development Council.

WHITEHEAD, A. (1979) 'Some Preliminary Notes on the Subordination of Women', *IDS Bulletin,* 10, pp. 10–13.

Chapter 10

Women's Rights and Human Rights in Muslim Countries: A Case Study

Shaheen Sardar-Ali and Siobhan Mullally

Introduction

The Convention on the Elimination of All Forms of Discrimination Against Women, adopted by the United Nations in 1979, represents the first significant challenge to a vision of human rights which has traditionally excluded much of women's experience. Although in modern human rights discourse 'rights of man' has been said to include women, this has not been reflected in human rights theory or in its application. Women's human rights have been marginalized, both institutionally and conceptually, from national and international human rights movements. Abuse of women's rights has been perceived as a cultural, private, or individual issue and not a political matter requiring state action (Bunch, 1990, p. 489). The main international organs established for the promotion and protection of human rights have dealt with violations of women's human rights only in a marginal way. The Convention is an attempt to ensure that women's rights are placed firmly on the mainstream human rights agenda.

In this article, we will be looking at some of the implications of the Convention for Muslim countries, and examining, in particular, the assertion by a number of Muslim states that the requirements of the Convention conflict with Sharia (Islamic Law). We will be arguing that the concept of equality between the sexes is not necessarily in conflict with Sharia, but is so mainly because of the political biases and prejudices that have been brought to bear in its interpretation and application.

The Provisions of the Convention

The adoption of the Convention was one of the main achievements of the UN Decade for Women (1976–1985). It is the culmination of work begun in 1974 by the UN Commission on the Status of Women. Dissatisfaction with the impact of existing instruments led from the mid-1960s to increasing efforts to develop international instruments providing a global conceptualization of the human rights of women and containing concrete measures of implementation and supervision. These efforts led in 1967 to the adoption of the Declaration on the Elimination of All Forms of Discrimination Against Women and resulted in 1979 in the adoption by the UN General Assembly of the Convention on the Elimination of All Forms of Discrimination Against Women (hereinafter the Convention).

The Preamble to the Convention is unusual both in its length and in its scope. While referring to the equal rights of men and women as proclaimed in various international legal instruments, the preamble recognizes the need to go beyond these documents to address factors which will help to eradicate *de facto* inequality between men and women. The establishment of a New International Economic Order; the eradication of apartheid, racism, foreign occupation and domination; and the strengthening of international peace and security, including nuclear disarmament: these are all urged as being essential to the equality of men and women.

Part I outlines the obligations undertaken by States Parties (i.e. states who are party) to the Convention. Article 1 defines discrimination against women. This definition is important as it expressly addresses the traditional distinction between public and private spheres. It transcends this dichotomy by calling for the international recognition of women's human rights both inside and outside the private or familial sphere. Article 1 should be read together with Article 4, which provides for the possibility of affirmative action aimed at accelerating *de facto* equality between men and women. Under Article 4, however, any special measures taken may be temporary only and must be discontinued 'when the objectives of equality of opportunity and treatment have been achieved'. Article 5 is perhaps one of the most ambitious provisions in the Convention in that it obligates States Parties to do no less than to modify the behaviour patterns of its citizens. Paragraph (b), for example, stresses the need for 'family education' to recognize the common responsibility of men and women in the upbringing and development of their children. The traditional justification of denying human rights to women on the basis of established customs and practices is thus directly challenged and rendered unacceptable.

Part II deals with the political rights of women and includes within it the obligation on States Parties to grant men and women equal rights to acquire, retain or change their nationality.

Part III of the Convention covers economic, social and cultural rights. Of particular interest is Article 14 which deals with the special problems of rural women. This was the first time that an international legal instrument had dealt with the problems facing such women.

Part IV deals with matters of civil law. Article 15 obligates States Parties to ensure equality before the law. Article 16 concerns issues of family law, in particular, the right to choose a spouse and enter into marriage, and equal rights and responsibilities for the parenting of children. The inclusion of provisions on family law, even in the most general terms, represents a step towards transcending the traditional public/private dichotomies of international human rights law.

The implications for States Parties are potentially very far-reaching indeed. Not only must they abolish all existing legislation and practices that are discriminatory, they are also under a positive obligation to eliminate stereotyped concepts of male and female roles in society. The possibility of hiding behind 'traditional customs and practices' no longer remains. The language throughout the Convention is essentially non-discriminatory, representing a significant advance on previous legislation which was usually 'protective' in tone, and, at best, 'corrective' (Hevener, 1983). The possibility of discriminatory practices creeping in, in the guise of 'protective' legislation, is no longer acceptable.

If effectively implemented, the Convention has the potential to touch on many aspects of daily life previously outside the domain of international human rights law. The next part of this article examines the implementation provisions contained in the Convention.

Enforcement of the Convention

The Convention established the Committee on the Elimination of All Forms of Discrimination Against Women (CEDAW), a body of twenty-three experts, elected by States Parties to serve in their personal capacity. The Committee is established 'for the purpose of considering the progress made in the implementation of the Convention' (Article 17(1)). The main part of this task is to be carried out through the examination of reports submitted by States Parties. These reports are to be submitted every four years or whenever the Committee requests them.

However, unlike the Convention on the Elimination of All Forms of Racial Discrimination (on which the Women's Convention is closely modelled), no provision is made for one State to complain of a violation of the Convention carried out by another State. Neither is there any provision for an individual who claims to have suffered a violation of the Convention to submit a complaint against a State Party. The approach taken to enforcement of the Convention is one of 'progressive implementation' rather than a requirement of immediate action on the part of States Parties. Rather than formally pronouncing a State Party to be in violation of the Convention, the Committee has preferred to engage in a 'constructive dialogue' with States Parties. The result of this has been that while, on the one hand, countries remain party to the Convention, and are not alienated within that system, neither do they feel under any immediate pressure to implement and conform to the requirements of the Convention.

The reporting procedure is the only enforcement mechanism established under the Convention. Unfortunately, it is perhaps the least effective method devised by international law to try to enforce human rights standards. Its success or failure is very much dependent on the goodwill of the States Parties. The Committee's ability to assess the accuracy of States' reports and comment upon them has been hampered by the lack of information on the status of women in States Parties. This problem has been compounded by the lack of any formal procedures to ensure effective consultation between NGOs (non-governmental organizations) and members of the Committee. Such consultation is essential to ensure that Committee members have access to independent information on the *de facto* status of women, thus enabling them to assess the accuracy of States Parties' reports.

One of the most serious problems encountered in implementing the Convention has been the reaction of Muslim states and the assertion by them of the supremacy of Sharia, and it is on this issue that the rest of this article will focus.

The Muslim Context

The implementation of secular human rights standards presents particular difficulties in Muslim states where most people perceive international human rights instruments as reflections of 'Western' values and norms and hence both culturally and religiously alien. The term 'secular' in most Muslim societies is seen as being synonymous not only with 'un-Islamic' but also 'Western'. At the governmental level, the degree of opposition to international human rights norms is determined to a large extent by the ideological leanings of the particular Muslim country. For example, fundamentalist Iran rejects them unequivocally and completely, whereas countries like Indonesia, Turkey and Tunisia adopt a more compromising stance. However, the majority of Muslim countries are reluctant to ratify the Women's Convention because they perceive it as a secularization of women's rights. The status of women in Islamic societies is strictly regulated by the Sharia and cannot, it is claimed, be included within the ambit of a secular human rights regime.

Sharia, however, does not form a single coherent body of law. The corpus of Sharia existing today is a collection of individual juristic opinions, and considerable differences continue to exist among jurists as to its requirements. Sharia represents the human endeavour to understand and implement the core values and principles specifically referred to in the Quran. It must be remembered, however, that although Sharia has a religious nature, it is not immutable or unchangeable as is the Quran. The true essence of the Sharia is brought out by Parwez who describes it thus:

> The Sharia refers to a straight and clear path and also to a watering place where both humans and animals come to drink water, provided the source of water is a flowing stream or spring. (Parwez, 1960, p. 941)

It is, therefore, as Hassan so forcefully argues:

> no slight irony and tragedy that the Sharia, which has the idea of mobility built into its very meaning, should have become a symbol of rigidity for so many Muslims in the world. (Hassan, 1980, p. 4)

In the commentaries on the Quran, in Hadith literature and books on Fiqh (Islamic jurisprudence), women are usually mentioned with the greatest contempt and as the cause of *fitna* (chaos) in the world. Reference is made to verses of the Quran to prove the inherent superiority of men, and to justify male dominance. Women have thus been the greatest victims of the abandonment of the Sharia as an emancipatory and creative force.

Discussion of Sharia would be incomplete without appreciating the impact of the more potent force of Islam as a cultural reality and a strong motivating force behind the rejection of international human rights obligations by Muslim states. Since its initial phenomenal expansion within the first few decades of its existence, Islam has tended to incorporate and assimilate the social customs and institutions of the various regions and communities which converted to Islam. In these societies, religion and culture interacted, creating a blend of 'cultural Islam', the manifestations of which are evident in the diverse cultural patterns of various Muslim societies. In the Kordofan and Sarfur regions of the Sudan, for example, women enjoy relative autonomy as independent agricultural producers. According to Badri, some women in these regions own land, and even act as tribal chiefs; in some communities, women also have the same inheritance rights as men. Although Muslim, these tribes do not follow the Sharia guidelines on inheritance which equate a man with two women (Badri, 1984). In contrast, however, in some areas of Pakistan women are completely debarred from inheriting, particularly land. The varying shades of interpretation of Sharia result in divergent views on what constitute 'Islamic' values and norms, thus paving the way for national governments to use religion as an escape route from domestic and international legal obligations.

With the above background of the Sharia in mind, it is now proposed to analyze the reservations entered by Muslim States Parties to the Women's Convention and to evaluate their implications for women's human rights.

Reservations to the Convention

To date ten Muslim countries[1] — Bangladesh, Democratic Yemen, Egypt, Indonesia, Iraq, Libyan Arab Jamahiriya, Mali, Senegal, Tunisia and Turkey — have ratified the Convention. Two others, Afghanistan and Jordan, have signed it. Of these countries, Bangladesh, Egypt, Iraq, Jordan, Libyan Arab Jamahiriya, Tunisia and Turkey have signed or ratified the Convention subject to substantial reservations, which have sparked off a number of controversies. Firstly, it is uncertain whether the reservations are compatible with the 'object and purpose' of the Convention as required by Article 28. The issue was raised at the 1986 session of CEDAW, causing considerable controversy and tension. Non-Muslim 'Third World' countries were also drawn into the conflict, as the issue was perceived not only as an attack on Islamic States but also as an attack on all non-Western countries. The outcome of the discussions was inconclusive and as yet no objective method of evaluating the compatibility of reservations with the 'object and purpose' of the Convention exists. Nonetheless, a number of States Parties have objected to the reservations entered by both Egypt and Bangladesh,[2] on the grounds that they are tantamount to a total negation of the 'object and purpose' of the Convention.

Four of the seven countries entering reservations — Bangladesh, Egypt, Iraq and Libya — make their reservations to the Convention on the basis of conflict with Sharia, whilst the other three — Turkey, Tunisia and Jordan — do not mention it. The reason for this lack of consistency in invoking Sharia is due to the absence of a unified interpretation of religious law, which in turn increases the discretion of individual States Parties. There is considerable scope for differing judgments as to the nature and extent of conflict between the Sharia and the requirements of the Convention. Libya, for example, has not entered reservations to specific articles of the Convention, but rather has entered a general reservation, stating that accession to the Convention

> cannot conflict with the laws on personal status derived from the Islamic Sharia. (United Nations, 1990, p. 175)

No indication is given as to which provisions it considers to be in conflict with the requirements of the Sharia, which permits a substantial degree of discretion to be retained by the state in the implementation of the Convention. Bangladesh, Iraq and Egypt have entered reservations to Article 2, which requires States Parties to take all appropriate measures including legislation to modify or abolish existing laws, regulations, customs and practices which constitute discrimination against women. (Article 2(f))

This is one of the basic obligations undertaken by States Parties to the Convention. By reserving their position regarding this article, it becomes very uncertain what obligations, if any, a State Party is undertaking. The good faith of such states must also be brought into question because, in the final analysis, they do not incur any additional obligations by becoming party to the Convention on such terms. Bangladesh has also entered reservations to Articles 13(a) (concerning economic, social and cultural rights), 16(c) and 16(f) (concerning the equality of men and women in all matters relating to marriage and family relations), invoking the requirements of Sharia 'based on the Holy Quran and Sunna' as its reason for doing so (United Nations, 1990, p. 171). Iraq and Egypt have entered reservations to Articles 9 (concerning the nationality of women and their children) and 16. In entering its reservation to Article 16, Egypt stated that under Sharia

> women are accorded rights equivalent to those of their spouses so as to ensure a just balance between them. This is out of respect for the sacrosanct nature of the firm religious beliefs which govern marital relations in Egypt and which may not be called into question and in view of the fact that one of the most important bases of these relations is an equivalency of rights and duties so as to ensure complementarity which guarantees true equality between the spouses. (United Nations, 1990, pp. 172–3)

Notions of 'complementarity' and 'equivalency' are invoked as forming the basis of 'true equality'. Egypt goes on to state that the Sharia restricts the wife's right to divorce by making it contingent on a judge's ruling, whereas no such restriction is laid down in the case of the husband. The reason for this, it is claimed, is that, in accordance with the provisions of the Sharia, the husband must pay bridal money to the wife and must maintain her fully. He must also make a payment to her upon divorce. The wife, however, retains full rights over her property and is not obliged to spend anything on her keep. No account is taken of the practice (prevalent particularly in India and Pakistan) whereby a woman brings a 'dowry' with her to the marriage. Neither is any account taken of the *de facto* contribution made by women to the maintenance of the household. The application of Sharia, moreover, with respect to marriage and family relations, is not consistent in all Muslim countries. In Pakistan, for example, the Muslim Family Laws Ordinance 1961 restricts the husband's power to declare unilaterally the dissolution of a marriage. Polygamy is legally and officially abolished in Turkey, Tunisia and Algeria, although it is permitted by the Quran. The entire premise of the argument for male dominance in marriage, during its subsistence and at its dissolution, therefore, tends to disintegrate.

Another sensitive aspect of family law is the law relating to custody and guardianship of children (see Article 16(f) of the Convention). Under classic Sharia, the mother is not entitled to guardianship of her child after the demise of the father or upon divorce. This rule, however, has been diluted considerably in its application by municipal courts in a number of Muslim countries. In Pakistan, for example, the courts have ruled that the best interests of the child should be the paramount consideration in determining custody or guardianship, and this may or may not require that s/he be awarded to the mother. The requirements of Article 16(f) are not, therefore, necessarily unacceptable to all Muslim countries.

Iraq has also entered a reservation to Article 16 on the basis that Sharia requires that the wife maintain complete control over her own personal property including her dower and that she is not required to maintain herself or her family. Therefore, it is argued, Sharia is more favourable to the woman than the provisions of the Convention. This perceived advantage conferred by Sharia, however, contributes significantly to the perpetuation of patriarchal forms of social organization and to the exclusion of women from the 'public' and 'political' spheres. This objective is achieved by marginalizing the woman in the 'private' domain where she is seen merely as a 'passive consumer', while the man is the 'provider', the 'maintainer' and the 'breadwinner'. It is also clearly in conflict with the requirements of Article 5 of the Convention which requires States Parties to take 'all appropriate measures' to eliminate stereotyped concepts of men and women.

The Struggle within Islam

The question remains as to how to proceed with the struggle to achieve equality in Muslim countries. Should we continue to struggle within the framework of Islam, or should we instead attempt to work within a secular framework?

At a strategic level, an emancipatory struggle operating entirely within a secular framework would be extremely unlikely to succeed. Islam is not only a religion, it is an all-pervasive code of economic, social and political life. As such, it permeates all aspects of a Muslim's life. The secularization of the women's rights movement would alienate and exclude many women. Furthermore, the abandonment of a struggle within Islam would leave the path clear for fundamentalist arguments, thus endangering the status of women even more. In Iran, for example, the former Shah attempted to secularize laws affecting women including the banning of the 'chadder' (the equivalent of the veil). As we all know, the fundamentalists and the 'chadder' struck back with a vengeance.

On a more theoretical level, a number of Muslim scholars have advocated the continuation of a struggle within Islam. It is felt that the in-built dynamism in the basic sources of Sharia — the Quran and Sunna (words and deeds of the prophet, Mohammad) — renders it possible to evolve an interpretation of the sacred texts compatible with equality between the sexes.

In addition to the main sources of Sharia, there is an important subsidiary source, *ijtihad*, which means 'to exert with a view to forming an independent judgment on a legal question'. With the political expansion of Islam, systematic legal thought developed to find expression in recognized schools of Sharia. This development, however, stunted the growth of independent juristic reasoning (*ijtihad*). In the early part of the twentieth century, Dr Mohammad Iqbal, the renowned Muslim poet-philosopher, urged a re-opening of the doors of *ijtihad*. He argued:

> The closing of the doors of ijtihad is pure fiction suggested partly by the crystallisation of legal thought in Islam, and partly, by that intellectual laziness which especially in a period of spiritual decay turns great thinkers

into idols. . . . The claim of the present generation of Muslim liberals to reinterpret the foundational legal principles, in the light of their own experience and altered conditions of modern life is, in my opinion, perfectly justified. (Iqbal, 1971, p. 168)

More recently, Riffat Hassan, following Iqbal's views on the use of *ijtihad*, argues in favour of a conceptual break from the artifically imposed concept of a static Sharia. She suggests that Sharia could be reformulated through *ijtihad*. Such a process could be used, she argues, to resolve the inequalities which exist between men and women within Islam (Hassan, 1980).

Other Muslim scholars, too, have taken up the challenging task of struggling for women's rights within the framework of Islam. Fatima Mernissi, a Moroccan sociologist, has undertaken extensive research on the status of women in contemporary Islamic society through an examination and reassessment of the literary sources of Islam as far back as the seventh century. In her opinion, the belief that Muslim women have to choose either equality or Islam is a grave misinterpretation of Islam. She argues that, in the Muslim context, to defend violations of women's human rights, it is necessary to go back into the shadows of the past, manipulate the sacred texts and rewrite history. Mernissi bases her arguments on the Quranic verse, '*Inna nafa'at al dhikra*' ('of use is the reminder'). By 'lifting the veils with which our contemporaries disguise the past in order to dim our present', Muslim women can, she argues, recapture the essence of the true message of Islam, which, she claims, is one of complete equality. It is contended that the message of Islam had only a limited and superficial effect on the deeply superstitious seventh-century Arabs, who failed to extend its novel approaches to the world at large and in particular to women. Hence, the liberating effect of its message was blocked by a re-assertion of pre-Islamic values and norms. The Muslim woman today then must liberate herself from the shackles of the 'male-managed' history that so far has succeeded in concealing her rightful place within Islam (Mernissi, 1991).

A more revolutionary approach was adopted by the late Sudanese reformer, Ustadh Mahmoud Mohammed Taha. He calls for the shifting of legal efficacy from one set of Quranic verses to another, in keeping with the needs of societies today. He believes that the inferior status of women and practices such as the wearing of the veil (*al-hijab*), polygamy, and the segregation of men and women are not original precepts of Islam. Rather, these discriminatory practices were imposed only for a transitional period as immediate change from the *Jahilliya* (state of ignorance) to complete equality was considered too drastic a step for seventh-century Arabian society to imbibe and adopt. The true message of Islam, according to Taha, is one of complete equality. He suggests that the fundamental and universal message of Islam is to be found in the Quran and Sunna texts of the earlier stage of Mecca. Those earlier sources were not lost forever, despite subsequent superseding texts. Their implementation, he claims, was merely postponed until such time as it would be possible to enact them in law (Taha, 1987). The specific methodology proposed by Taha seems to be one of the most viable and effective ways of achieving complete equality regardless of race, sex or religious belief. His writings therefore remain as a significant challenge to Islamic fundamentalism and to all those struggling for equality within Islam.

Taha's approach has been taken up by his followers and students, among them Professor Abdullah An-Naim. He believes that by conceding the basic premise of Taha's revolutionary thinking, a whole new era of Islamic jurisprudence, compatible with international human rights norms, can begin. The fact that 'traditional' Sharia does not treat women and non-Muslims equally with male Muslims is beyond dispute. Rather than seeking to justify such discrimination in apologetic terms, modern Muslim scholars claim that some of the objectionable rules may now be reformed by reviving the techniques of creative juristic reasoning (*ijtihad*). None of these scholars, however, claims that this method of reform can possibly remove all discrimination against women, as *ijtihad* itself is of limited use. It is not, for example, permitted with respect to any matter governed by an explicit and definite text. Some of the most blatantly discriminatory rules are based on explicit texts of the Quran and Sunna. The only way out of this dilemma according to An-Naim is to

> evolve Islamic Law on a fresh plane rather than waste time in piecemeal reform that will never achieve the moral and political objective of removing all discrimination against women in Islamic Law. (An-Naim, in Taha, 1987, p. 23)

Taha's and An-Naim's writings represent a progression beyond the approach adopted by Hassan. Whereas Hassan accepts the need for extensive 'protective' practices and legislation, both Taha and An-Naim question the need for many such practices and emphasize instead the possibility of building non-discriminatory forms of social organization, along the lines of those envisaged in the Women's Convention.

It must be remembered, however, that while proponents of human rights generally assume the universality of 'rights' and 'rights language', many moral systems throughout the world do not centre on rights at all. Rather than the crude imposition of Western concepts of rights and rights language, we must recognize the possibility of fulfilling the same needs and achieving the same aims through other forms of social organization. What is needed then is a reformulation of Sharia along the lines advocated by Taha and others. Such a reformulation could, we believe, bring about the realization, within the framework of Islam, of the fundamental norms and values contained in the Women's Convention.

Conclusion

The struggle for sexual equality in Muslim societies must come from within those societies if it is to be successful. Furthermore, any such struggle must be one which recognizes the participation of women as a productive and creative force. Women can no longer be seen merely as objects to be moulded and defined by the whims and political needs of male rhetoric. The writings of Taha and others pose a significant challenge which could be taken up by Muslim women in order to achieve the objectives articulated in the Women's Convention. Some Muslim women's organizations such as 'Women Living Under Muslim Laws' have organized Quranic interpretation meetings, both as a consciousness-raising exercise and as an attempt to bring about a feminist interpretation of the Quran and Sunna. The support and solidarity of international society in general, and international feminist movements in particular, is essential in any such struggle. A case in point is that of Safia Bibi, a blind servant girl, who, after having been raped by her employer and his son, was convicted for adultery, under the Hudood Laws of Pakistan, because she could not produce witnesses to substantiate her charge. Her punishment entailed public lashing and a prison sentence. A campaign mounted nationally and internationally by human rights activists saved her from this fate.

The Women's Convention can play a useful role, both as a political lever and as a point of reference, when attempting to articulate specific demands. Women in many Muslim countries continue to be treated merely as chattels of the male members of their households. In the words of a report by the Commission on the Status of Women in Pakistan, 'the average rural woman of Pakistan is born in near slavery, leads a life of drudgery and dies invariably in oblivion' (Commission on the Status of Women, 1986, p. 31). Women in some parts of Pakistan are even today handed over by their male relatives as peace-offerings to settle longstanding blood-feuds or vendettas, or are given in 'exchange' marriages. While such practices continue, the urgency of working towards the effective implementation of the Women's Convention cannot be overestimated.

Notes

1 Countries where Muslims constitute 70 per cent of the total population are taken to be 'Muslim countries'.
2 Upon accession to the Convention, on 6 November 1984, the government of Bangladesh entered the following reservation:

> The Government of the People's Republic of Bangladesh does not consider as binding upon itself the provisions of articles 2, 13(a), and 16.1(c) and (f) as they conflict with Sharia law based on Holy Quran and Sunna. (United Nations, 1990, p. 176)

Upon signature of the Convention on 16 July 1980, the government of Egypt entered a number of reservations, including a general reservation on Article 2 stating that:

> The Arab Republic of Egypt is willing to comply with the content of this article, provided that such compliance does not run counter to the Islamic Sharia. (United Nations, 1990, p. 176)

References

BADRI, H.K. (1984) *Women's Movement in Sudan*, Khartoum, Khartoum University Press.
BUNCH, C. (1990) 'Women's Rights as Human Rights: Towards a Re-Vision of Human Rights', *Human Rights Quarterly*, 12, pp. 486–98.
BURROWS, N. (1985) 'The 1979 Convention on the Elimination of All Forms of Discrimination Against Women', *Netherlands International Law Review*, 32, pp. 419–60.
CLARK, B. (1991) 'The Vienna Convention Reservations Regime and the Convention on Discrimination Against Women', *American Journal of International Law*, 85, pp. 281–321.

COMMISSION ON THE STATUS OF WOMEN (1986) '*Report of the Pakistan Commission on the Status of Women*', Islamabad, Government of Pakistan Press.

COOK, R. (1990) 'Reservations to the Convention on the Elimination of All Forms of Discrimination Against Women', *Virginia Journal of International Law*, 30, pp. 643–716.

HASSAN, R. (1980) 'The Role and Responsibilities of Women in the Legal and Ritual Tradition of Islam', paper presented at a biannual meeting of a Trialogue of Jewish-Christian-Muslim scholars on 14 October 1980 at the Joseph and Rose Kennedy Institute of Ethics, Washington, DC, USA.

HEVENER, N. (1983) *International Law and the Status of Women*, Boulder, Colorado, Westview Press.

IQBAL, M. (1971) *The Reconstruction of Religious Thought in Islam*, Lahore, Shaikh Mohammad Ashraf.

MERNISSI, F. (1991) *Women and Islam — An Historical and Theological Enquiry*, translated by LAKELAND, M.J., Oxford, Basil Blackwell.

AN-NAIM, A. (1984) *A Modern Approach to Human Rights in Islam: Foundations and Implications for Africa*, Albany, State University of New York Press.

AN-NAIM, A. (1987) 'The Rights of Women and International Law in the Muslim Context', *Whittier Law Review*, 9, pp. 491–516.

PARWEZ, G.A. (1960) *Lughat-ul-Quran*, Lahore.

TAHA, U.M.M. (1987) *The Second Message of Islam*, translated and with an introduction by AN-NAIM, A., Syracuse, NY, Syracuse University Press.

UNITED NATIONS (1990) *Multilateral Treaties Deposited with the Secretary General*, New York, United Nations.

Chapter 11

Women's Studies in Central and Eastern Europe

Chris Corrin

Much has been written on the dramatic developments within central and eastern Europe since 1989. These changes had not been 'prepared for' in the sense that no, or very little, policy preparation had taken place. The rejection of the previous economic and political structures entailed some rejection of social policies and legislation that had played a role in mitigating the worse excesses of women's stressful lives — support for creches, nurseries, incentives (financial and otherwise) for working mothers. Many of the ideas concerning 'free-market democracy' remain at the level of imagination and the increasing moves towards more market-oriented societies have raised fears and questions concerning the strains which will be placed on people's everyday lives. The gender-specific nature of many of these social changes is just beginning to be realized. The changing conceptualizations and perceptions of women's roles in society and consequences for gender relations will form expanding areas of research in the coming years.

This paper explores aspects of women's experience of education in East-Central Europe and its aims are threefold. Firstly, I wish to point out the different experiences of education for girls and women in East-Central Europe. Secondly, I would argue that 'Women's Studies', whether within higher, further or adult education, tends to rely upon some basic groundswell of support within academic circles and/or the broader community. This support, or lack of resistance, from within educational circles, has been markedly absent with East-Central Europe generally, and certain countries in particular. My third point concerns both the historical focus of 'research on women' and the embryonic nature of feminist theory and Women's Studies within the countries of central and eastern Europe.

As always I start with some qualifying words about considering 'women' as a collective entity.[1] In short, there can be no general grouping of women internationally, nationally or within cultures: women have never been and indeed cannot become one 'category'. In these societies there were, of course, Party women, richer women, poorer women, and their concerns were nuanced and various. Women do make up half of the world (at least) and so are involved in many different arenas of life. Yet, the important point for this study is that the Party-state systems in these countries systematically produced policies based on a specific collective entity: 'women'. This state identification of women cut across traditional social and economic divisions. Although fundamental differences exist in economic activities, household patterns and life-styles among women, and the urban/rural divide is a very important one, it can be seen that decisions and policies were made concerning 'women'. One major aspect of difference in comparison with men is women's ability to give birth, which, when neglected or relegated in importance, becomes a direct channel of social inequality. Women suffer inequalities on the basis of their ability to give birth to children and thereby are assigned gender qualities which are social, and are often officially constructed.

Background

It is important to remember that the countries under consideration in central and eastern Europe — Albania, Bulgaria, Czechoslovakia (CSFR), German Democratic Republic (former East Germany), Hungary, Poland, Romania and Yugoslavia — did not form an 'evenly coloured bloc' on the map, and that the label 'Eastern Europe' did not really exist, other than for military and political strategic purposes. These peoples have always differed in their histories, traditional activities, cultural experiences and expectations. Some countries were considered to be more 'developed' — Czechoslovakia, Hungary and East Germany — whilst others were viewed as 'developing' — Albania, Bulgaria and Romania. Yet, with the Soviet Union becoming dominant in the region from 1945, these countries did undergo a very dramatic shift in their development, from 1947/48 onwards.

The basic thrust of the 'Sovietization' of East-Central Europe was a move towards planning within the economy and society, and a shift towards favouring heavy industrial output over consumer needs. Socially, there was to be an equalization of differentials, in terms of material and hierarchical spheres. Yet the marxist aim of breaking down class and wealth divisions could not be recognized within the Stalinist bureaucracies that were created in these countries. The 'top down' approach and the centralization of power with economic needs dictating all others was not egalitarian. It was not until the 'de-Stalinization' processes which Khrushchev tentatively began in 1956 that there was any public recognition of how divergent the Soviet reality had become from the theory, especially in the countries of East-Central Europe. Moreover, for women, in terms of the vast difference between 'emancipatory rhetoric' and the real conditions of their lives, recognition has still not yet emerged. It is against this background that the development of 'Women's Studies' can be considered.

It is useful here to have a cautionary note on what statistics do not and, by their very nature, cannot tell us. In comparing the two Germanies, basic figures on student numbers illustrate nothing of the differences experienced by the student populations within these two countries — one factor being the lack of adult education available in many areas of the former GDR. One major aspect for women was the reality of discrimination, so that regardless of their educational qualifications, they could rarely work with men on an equal footing. Yet according to UNESCO statistics (*Higher Education: Statistical Report and Studies*, No. 19, (1975), Paris, Unesco Office Statistics), women in the former GDR took up 9 per cent more space within the total of students aged 20–24 in 1970 than did their neighbours in the former FRG. I note this primarily to say 'beware' particularly of the aggregated nature of 'statist' statistics which were produced in the former 'socialist' countries. As has been pointed out many times it is possible to lie with statistics and to a certain extent the statistical yearbooks regularly produced throughout central and eastern Europe until about 1989 were at best generalizations and at worst misrepresentations. Yet such comparisons can serve as a useful starting point for cross-national studies, provided all the relevant variables are also available to readers.

The term 'higher education' in East-Central Europe generally refers not only to universities and colleges of education but to other institutions offering shorter courses of professional training. The major drawback of these centralized systems of higher education, though, is the very decisive nature of the decision taken at 14 as to the type of secondary school to be chosen. This will be changing in the coming years as there is very real interest in changes in the field of secondary education to improve the quality of learning and to allow more flexibility. For women, education can be a powerful and liberating experience, yet much depends on the ways in which women gain their educational experience and how they are able to expand their opportunities after their full-time education has finished.

Women's Educational Experiences in Central and Eastern Europe

The period after 1948 was one in which educational institutions throughout central and eastern Europe became centralized. Students all over central and eastern Europe, for example, sit their entrance examinations for admission to universities in the same week in June each year. This centralization had several negative consequences. One primary consequence was an obvious lack of flexibility concerning both the content of courses and student/teacher choice within the curricula. In turn, this led in many cases to what was described to me as a 'woodenness' on the part of teachers and students alike. Learning by repetition and by memory was more 'useful' within a rigid exam system than creative, imaginative or original capabilities. Often structural considerations outweighed general developments. A failure in chemistry for a 15-year-old student could mean, in such a system, re-sitting a whole year.

Differences in exam study and marking meant that school pupils and university students were graded from 1 to 5, with 5 being the highest score. When we consider marking schemes used in Western countries, the difference between, say, 38 per cent and 52 per cent, is large, but out of five they are both, basically, 4. I would not argue for percentage grades, nor indeed for the necessity for any particular grading systems, but it was apparent that, under the 5 system, whilst the motivation to get a 5 was often high, students generally felt little sense of 'progress' or development in their work, and found it hard to assess the value of their efforts.

The contradictory nature of centralization was perhaps even more apparent at university level. Generally, studying politics meant learning the 'line' on Marxism-Leninism and dialectical materialism without any relation to everyday life, philosophy could mean the history of 'acceptable' philosophers, sociology did not include any aspects of poverty as these had been 'overcome' in the 'socialist transition', history was one of 'liberation', and so on for all social sciences and many arts subjects.

One interesting outcome of the fact that certain researchers were studying areas that were not being taught to students was the very practical division between research institutes and teaching universities. Those academics working at research institutes, often on 'sensitive' topics, did not teach students, whilst those teaching at universities were left very little time for any research activities. In this way, not only were artificial barriers set up between researchers and teachers, but practical divisions are still in place between the combination of these two activities. This has consequences for Women's Studies courses to which I shall return.

Five-year national plans were adopted in the countries of East-Central Europe after 1948, based on projected needs, like enrolment data, unit costs connected with pupil/teacher ratios, standards of buildings, equipment, and salaries. These were then translated into investment sums and budget components. In this way national plans were drawn up with some changes taking place when the plans were broken down at county or local levels. The content of educational courses was very much controlled in the early period up to the 1960s. In certain countries, such as Hungary and Yugoslavia, there was some experimentation within educational institutions, or at least a slight loosening of central ties, whereas in other countries, such as Czechoslovakia (especially after 1968) and Poland, the central control remained quite firm. It was during the 1960s that group 'education' was beginning for children at a much earlier age. Given the introduction of women into the workforce from the late 1940s, there was a perceived need for childcare services. Yet in most countries in central and eastern Europe the building of creches and kindergartens was not fully under way until the early 1960s. From this time, though, large numbers of babies and young children were cared for collectively. The extent of such services ranged widely from country to country, with Poland, say, having far fewer childcare institutions than the former GDR. Yet the content of the care was remarkably similar across the region.

How the so-called 'socialist'[2] content of the educational programmes affected children and young people is becoming a much-debated topic. From my talks with women who grew up within the 'socialist' period, it became clear that they often felt a distinct lack of explanation. There was a so-called 'socialist identity' to which they were supposed to aspire but it was never clear quite what this was, or how they were to achieve it. Many women said that the examples of their mothers' everyday lives made a very marked impression on them concerning the contradictory nature of women's achievements within their societies. The 'double burden' is pivotal here in that working women with children led very stressful and constrained lives, which meant little leisure time with their children, and next to no time 'for themselves'.[3] In addition, the vertical and horizontal gender segregation played, and still plays, large parts in pushing women into low-paid, low-skilled and monotonous jobs, often in poor conditions.

In terms of attitudes, several small-scale studies have shown that apparently 'traditional' (although this is nowhere clearly defined) gendered expectations are still very much present within young people's minds. School pupils in Hungary, for instance, who were asked how they envisioned their future lives, gave markedly different answers. The girls all expected to work outside the home but also to be the main carers within the home, and to earn less than their husbands who would (of course) be doing more important jobs. The 'education for liberation' concept within most East-Central European high-school syllabuses basically meant that girls and young women were led to expect to have to earn their living and to contribute to 'family budgets', but that caring and domestic work was something to which they would also have to aspire. The radical ideas which were present within early post-revolutionary Soviet society in the 1920s were never considered within the East-Central European context. The weight of oppressive bureaucratic structures within these countries cannot be overestimated.

In such school systems, many parents, and quite often it was mothers, passed on to their children certain forms of guidance and ways of living 'alongside' the system. One instance stands out in my mind when a young mother visited her daughter's kindergarten to find the child in tears. Her picture was not good enough to go on the wall because in drawing the 'Liberation Day' parade (commemorating the day when Soviet troops had 'liberated' the country) the child had drawn only her national (Hungarian) flag and not the Soviet flag as well. This error meant that the picture was not good. The mother assured her daughter that the picture was indeed good, and they put it on the wall at home. Small issues such as this multiply over time — whether the children wanted to join the Pioneers, what are the costs of allowing them to be different, and so on — to a point at which enjoyment of educational experience becomes devalued and a measure of cynicism tends to set in.

Support for Women and Women's Studies

There has been a fair amount written on the gap between the theory and reality of women's lives in these countries during the last four decades.[4] As with many social and political developments, many women's experiences of education in East-Central Europe has been double-edged or even contradictory. For many, the opportunity to be in compulsory, full-time, free education is in itself an obvious social good and many women feel that they have benefited from their (albeit extremely competitive) experience of university education. Yet the same women have told me how they felt constrained by the educational system with its lack of real choice, and also with their status as 'second-class' citizens. For women worldwide, there seem to be common themes in terms of how women are able, and often more able than men, in subjects across the academic spectrum, but when it comes to specialization in certain fields women hold back, or are held back by basic social attitudes. It is certainly the case that there were more women employed in less obviously 'women's work' (whatever that might be) in the countries of East-Central Europe. Women did take up positions as engineers, tram drivers, telegraphic workers, doctors, pharmacists, and dentists in larger numbers than their counterparts in Western Europe. Yet it remains the case that such professions as those of doctors and teachers became 'feminized', in that there were a majority of women working in the profession and wages and conditions deteriorated. Teaching in schools is not well paid and conditions and support are insufficient to develop women's motivation or enthusiasm. Key 'feminized' industries such as textiles generally had some of the worst working conditions.

Considering women's position vis-à-vis men's situation in some of the East-Central European societies, I risk gross generalization in stating my belief that neither men nor women have had very positive educational experiences in the last few decades. Yet it remains the case that men have been privileged over women in at least one sphere, and that is in terms of paid work — be that unskilled, semi-skilled, professional or agricultural work.

It has become a commonplace for women in central and eastern Europe to expect to gain access to education and to be able to work outside the home, yet it remains the case that women are still the primary domestic workers. Given the lack of autonomous organization of women's groups prior to the removal of the former communists from power, it has taken time for women to begin to organize various groups to represent their interests. In some countries this has developed at a much quicker pace than others and across a wider spectrum of the population. Certainly in Czechoslovakia there are now over thirty different groups of women organizing. In Hungary there are fewer groups with only one avowedly feminist grouping. The Feminist Group in Poland has been active since 1981 in their battle against the united forces of Church and State which are attempting to constrain women's rights to control their bodies and childbearing. In the former Yugoslavia there were several active feminist groups, including a Party for Women. Given the unsettled political outlook, certainly in the former Yugoslavia but to some extent in Romania and Albania also, it is not possible to make even broad comments on the likely developments in 'Women's Studies'.

The remainder of this study focuses upon gender research and Women's Studies within Poland, Czechoslovakia, the former GDR, Yugoslavia and Hungary. In most of these countries some research has focused on the relationship between women's paid work and their domestic working patterns, in terms of how much time women spend on housework, have as 'leisure' time, and are able to spend with their children. Studies have been carried out regarding gender and wages, showing that women's actual situation is one of discrimination based on gender segregation (Ladó, 1991; Siemienska, undated). In the majority of cases where women's educational opportunities and motivations have been studied, this was generally in a historical context, by educational sociologists. Sex was treated as a variable influencing the type of motives for education and the course of educational processes of young people. If women's education was considered important, this was mainly from the viewpoint of its suitability to the needs of the market. This point cannot be too highly stressed — that of research priorities, especially regarding women, being subsumed within the needs of production and labour force efficiency. In this context, women's (and men's) education was primarily directed toward labour force requirements. Yet research has been carried out concerning girls' and boys' motivations, showing that girls' selection of schools is more strongly modelled on 'sex-role expectations'. Girls more often than boys wanted to achieve a professional status higher than that of their parents (Sas, 1977; Stasinska, 1986).

   Although in all of the countries considered studies under similar rubrics have been carried out, there were specific differences which I can only begin to outline here. In Czechoslovakia, there has always been something of an emphasis on public opinion polls or enquiries often showing very different results in the Czech lands and Slovakia. Studies from Czechoslovakia have pointed out the 'misuse' of the high level of female qualifications within the CSFR, in that women were employed in the overgrown bureaucratic and administrative apparatus and the human waste, both for women and men, is only now beginning to be realized.[5] In Hungary, very little gender-specific research has been carried out at all. Usually the topics which concern women are predominantly looking at 'family' or aspects of 'socialization'. Yet, given that Hungary introduced a quite radical childcare grant (GYES) and childcare benefit (GYED) from 1967,[6] which enabled women to remain at home on a very low allowance for up to three years to care for young children, some research has focused specifically on this topic. These research studies looked at the benefits and drawbacks of the childcare allowance for mothers, children, families, employers and society generally. Within this, some, fascinating work was written about the so-called 'gyes disease' or childcare syndrome.[7] In addition, studies considering how certain social policy measures have had unintended outcomes in terms of their effects upon women's situations have also been carried out (Adamik, 1990).

In the former GDR, studies quite often had a comparative aspect with the former West Germany even if this was not always explicit. The ability to receive West German television programmes was something that was often highlighted in terms of 'socialization' studies. In addition, much empirical work focused on the higher numbers of childcare institutions available in the former GDR, and, in turn, the high proportion of women engaged in productive and professional work. Figures of women employed are notoriously difficult to compare, as in Hungary those women absent for up to three years on childcare leave but with their jobs remaining open are counted as being 'economically active'.

Given the republican differences within the former Yugoslavia which had their impact on the violent confrontations of 1991, very few joint Yugoslav research projects have been carried out and coordinated through official research institutions, certainly since the mid-1980s. Often the research projects concerning women have concentrated on the differences between birth rates in one or other republic or on differences in economic situation between the poorer and richer republics. Since the death of Tito in 1980, power-political tensions have been surfacing intermittently and causing disastrous economic decline, so that the money available for country-wide research was virtually nil.

Feminism and Women's Studies

I conclude with some considerations of the nature of feminism and Women's Studies within the countries under discussion. Certainly since the dramatic upheavals of 1989 there is much more openness in these societies, particularly in terms of being able to question, and to work towards changing, certain things. The onward drive towards more market-oriented societies is beginning to impact upon women in certain ways, especially in terms of unemployment. Partly as a consequence of this, discussions often concentrate on women being in the home. Many women are keen to leave badly paid, monotonous jobs for the chance to spend more time with their children and there are even discussions concerning a 'family wage'. The reality is already proving somewhat different, with unemployed women in the former GDR and Poland realizing that spending time frantically trying to feed and clothe their children was not something that could be imagined in advance. The strength and size of the new so-called 'pro-life' movements across these countries — although, given their attitudes towards pregnant women, it seems that their label is definitely a misunderstanding of 'life' — is indicative of an anti-woman trend which could grow in the coming years if certain women are seen to be competing too closely with men for scarce resources.

There could, potentially, be many positive aspects within the changes for those involved in education, but, as is often the case, there are also certain negative elements within the changing situation. The reintroduction of religious education in certain countries such as Hungary and Poland could add to the general conservatizing attitudes which seriously underestimate women's potential for development and change. It is fair to say, though, that there are at least three major barriers to gender research and the teaching of Women's Studies within East-Central Europe today, which centre upon:

1   a lack of interest in research concerning women and gender, not just generally but amongst scholars too;

2   a quite dramatic lack of resources and finances for such work;

3   the reorganization of higher educational institutions in terms of attempts to 'streamline and make more efficient' the teaching of higher education, and also to introduce more flexibility and relevance within courses.

These factors lead to a variety of insecurities on the part of those engaged in teaching within areas which could develop various Women's Studies courses. In addition the lack of financial support has come to mean that only 'serious' or 'useful' projects will be supported. Given the male assessment of what is considered 'serious' or 'useful', it is hardly surprising that research concentrating on women's topics is seen as relatively unimportant if not actually useless.

Yet valiant women in these countries are attempting to draw together some Women's Studies courses and research into gender questions. In Yugoslavia, such intellectuals try to keep their professional contacts and links all over the country in order to overcome informational and other barriers, but this is mostly done through personal contacts. As women can, and often do, excel in terms of networking, it was possible in the 1980s to develop quite good networks especially between the three biggest university centres in Ljubljana (Slovenia), Zagreb (Croatia) and Beograd (Serbia). It was often the feminist groupings, including those women around the Women's Parliament (set up in March 1991), who have voiced their views against militant nationalism and in favour of finding a peaceful solution to the violent break-up of the republics.

From the Polish case, it is clear that, since much research into women's situation was geared towards the prevailing needs of the regime, setting up 'Women's Studies' courses will be difficult. It is claimed that there are more important issues than 'women questions'. Even though the 'socialist systems caused many contradictions and paradoxes concerning the issues of gender and sex equality' (Gontarczyk-Wesola, 1991), women are working on establishing 'Women's Studies' in both Poznan and Warsaw.

In the former GDR the initial positive effects of Autumn 1989 could be seen in terms of the many autonomous activities of women, their active participation in political activity and the foundation of the Independent Association of Women, which were supported by women academics in various ways. Yet for many women these changes soured quickly as they lost their jobs and their hopes for a more democratic and humane future. At Humboldt University in Berlin, the scholar in charge of the (only) Centre for Women's Interdisciplinary Studies was dismissed and the Centre thereby devastated, on the grounds that she had, a number of years ago, worked at the Marxist-Leninist department (Behrend, 1991). These setbacks will certainly take time to overcome.

In Czechoslovakia there are several centres where women are attempting to implement Women's Studies courses, especially in Prague and Bratislava. At Comenius University in Bratislava there is a Club for Women's Studies and Feminist Research[8] with its primary aim to promote interdisciplinary research in 'Women's Studies' and to promote the position of women in society. At Charles University in Prague academics in the sociology department have also set up some courses on women's issues and a library section for 'Women's Studies'. These are good examples of Western women collaborating with women from East-Central Europe on joint projects.

In Hungary, in September 1990 there was an attempt to set up some Women's Studies courses in Budapest but there was very little student interest and eventually the courses were abandoned. This seems ironic in that it was the very demand and popularity of a course about women's issues in the academic year 1989–90 which set in train the forming of the Hungarian Feminist Network in June 1990. Women's Studies is unlikely to receive financial support from the state structures, unless perhaps as part of a foreign-language programme or a general social policy course.

Yet there are bright spots on the horizon, not least in the growing numbers of cross-national conferences that are being funded by Western sources. I have attended some such events which have proved fairly disastrous, because of the misunderstanding between the women involved in terms of recognizing the different histories, cultures and expectations of women from different countries. Yet, as women become more used to meeting, listening to each other, developing ways of living with, and learning from, the differences, cooperation towards overcoming some of our common difficulties will build confidence in our ability to work well together. Resources remain a major problem. There are various initiatives available at the present time such as the TEMPUS (Trans-European Mobility Programme for University Staff and Students), NOW (New Opportunities for Women) and such schemes as PALP, HALP and CZALP (British Council — Academic Links Programmes with Poland, Hungary and Czechoslovakia). There are also many bilateral connections between particular universities/ colleges in Western Europe, the USA and East-Central Europe. It is important to keep up our networking and to try to work practically towards supporting the efforts of women within the East-Central European countries.

Two material problems remain — money and resources. Recently some academics in Sofia, Bulgaria, have embarked upon fund-raising towards creating a Women's Studies Centre, yet resources remain a major drawback. Good researchers are now leaving academia in East-Central Europe for much better paid commercial jobs. In the Institutes resources such as computers, faxes and copiers are still in short supply. Feminism is still a 'dirty word' in all of these societies and the majority of women do not believe they are 'oppressed' any differently than their hard-working husbands. In such a situation, women prepared to stand up and be counted as feminists are brave and are facing multiple barriers and challenges. The first step in breaking down the isolation has been taken, but given the geo-political and economic insecurities in East-Central Europe, it is difficult to say how effectively East-West collaboration can proceed.

Notes

1   For more detailed consideration see Corrin (1990).
2   I have used so-called 'socialist' as a descriptive term for the systems in place in East-

Central Europe solely to signify that which was commonly used by those in power within these countries. Much has been written on the obvious lack of socialist theory or practice present within the regimes in place from 1948 to 1988.

3　The terms double burden/shift/day all describe how women worked outside the home in paid work during the day or doing night shifts (for extra money), and worked inside the home in unpaid work during evenings or weekends.

4　See initially Scott (1984); Heitlinger (1979); Corrin (1992a).

5　For a more detailed consideration see Mita Castle-Kanerova in Corrin (1992a).

6　This maternity allowance was increased to a parental allowance in 1982. Despite its popularity with women less than 2 per cent of take-up was from men. This was another instance in which attitudes lagged behind legislation, begging the question as to whether policy-makers felt the 'risk' of men becoming house-husbands was small enough to take.

7　This literature is detailed in Corrin (1992b).

8　Feminist research contact: Olga Plávková, Institute of Sociology of Slovak Academy of Sciences, Hviezdoslavovo nám. 10, 81364 Bratislava, CSFR.

References

ADAMIK, MÁRIA (1990) 'Women and Welfare in Hungary', unpublished paper, ELTE University, Department of Social Policy, Hungary.

BEHREND, HANNA (1991) 'Women in the Former GDR', *European Forum of Socialist Feminists Newsletter*, No. 4, Spring.

CORRIN, CHRIS (1990) 'Women's Liberation within Socialist Patriarchy', *Slovo*, Vol. 3, No. 2, November.

CORRIN, CHRIS (Ed.) (1992a) *Superwomen and the Double Burden: Women's Experiences of Change in Central and Eastern Europe and the Former Soviet Union*, London, Scarlet Press.

CORRIN, CHRIS (1992b) *Magyar Women: Hungarian Women's Lives, 1940s–1990s*, Basingstoke, Macmillan.

EBERHARDT, EVA (with SZALAI JULIA, 1991) *Women of Hungary*, Supplement to *Women of Europe*, Commission of the European Communities, Women's Information Service, Rue de la Loi, 200 B-1049 Bruxelles.

GONTARCZYK-WESOLA, EWA (1991) 'The Development of Women's Studies in Poland: Opportunities for Feminist Perspectives', paper given at the Women in a Changing Europe Conference, Aalborg, Denmark, 18–22 August.

HEITLINGER, ALENA (1979) *Women and State Socialism: Sex Inequality in the Soviet Union and Czechoslovakia*, Basingstoke, Macmillan.

LÁDÓ, MÁRIA (1991) 'Women in the Transition to a Market Economy: The Case of Hungary', United Nations Conference on the Impact of Economic Reform on the Status of Women in Eastern Europe and the USSR, Vienna, 8–12 April.

SAS, JUDIT (1977) 'Way of Life and Family Aspirations', in SZÁNTÓ, MIKLÓS (Ed.) *Ways of Life: Hungarian Sociological Studies*, Budapest, Corvina Press.

SCOTT, HILDA (1984) *Women and Socialism: Experiences from East Europe*, London, Allison and Busby.

SIEMIENSKA, RENATA (undated) 'Approaches to Gender and Women's Issues in Polish Sociology and Political Science', Mimeograph.

STASINSKA, MARIA (1986) *Influence of Status and Psycho-Social Factors on Education Paths of Polish Youth*, PhD dissertation, Institute of Sociology, Warsaw University.

Chapter 12

Does Equal Opportunity Legislation and Practice Serve the Women's Movement? A Case Study from Australian Higher Education

Christine Wieneke

Introduction

Equal opportunity and affirmative action legislation have operated in areas of the Australian public sector for over ten years and in higher education institutions for five years. The intent of the legislation is to provide equal opportunity for women (and other specified groups) in employment and other areas of public life, and to pursue affirmative action strategies to eliminate the effects of past discrimination. We must continually assess whether this legislation is producing outcomes which are in the interest of, and which benefit, women.

New South Wales (NSW) was the first Australian state to introduce a legislative requirement to undertake affirmative action for specified target groups (women, Aboriginal and Torres Strait Islanders, people of non-English-speaking background and people with a physical disability) to achieve equality of opportunity in employment. Introduced as an amendment in 1980, Part IXA of the NSW Anti-Discrimination Act 1977 required all public service departments and statutory authorities, and, in 1983, all higher education institutions, to produce an Equal Employment Opportunity (EEO) Management Plan, setting out strategies for achieving EEO for target group members. Scheduled organizations were required to report annually to the Director of Equal Opportunity in Public Employment (DEOPE) on progress made towards this goal.

The federal Affirmative Action (Equal Employment Opportunity for Women) Act 1986 requires all higher education institutions in Australia and all private companies with more than 100 employees to undertake affirmative action programmes on behalf of women. These organizations are also required to report annually to the Director of Affirmative Action on progress made in implementing their programmes.

Feminist theoretical writing in Australia is currently providing a solid framework within which to assess the effectiveness of EEO and affirmative action legislation and programmes for women (Burton, 1991; Caine *et al.*, 1988; Eisenstein,

1990, 1991; Franzway *et al.*, 1989; Pateman and Gross, 1986; Sawer, 1985; Thornton, 1985; Yeatman, 1990). In addition, feminist jurisprudence is allowing us to examine the content, intent and structure of the law, including anti-discrimination and affirmative action legislation, to unmask its gendered nature and assess whether the legislation is simply an instrument of the patriarchal system designed to contain women's demands (Graycar and Morgan, 1990; Naffine, 1990; Thornton, 1990; Scutt, 1991; Game and Pringle, 1983, 1984, 1986), or whether there is something inherently radical in the legislation which can be used to serve the needs of the Women's Movement (Game, 1984; Eisenstein, 1985). Theoretical analysis helps us to assess how far we have come, whether we have come in a direction consistent with the goals of the Women's Movement, and where we are going from here.

EEO and Feminist Jurisprudence

We need to be aware that anti-discrimination legislation has been developed within a gendered legal system and therefore, on the surface at least, necessarily supports existing patriarchal structures, processes and interests. The content of law in terms of the control it exercises over women's lives, the processes of the law in terms of its adversarial system and the partiality of the law in terms of its definition of 'the legal person' combine to produce a legal system that is deeply gendered.

Within this context, anti-discrimination and affirmative action legislation cannot but be questioned in terms of its intent and its content. EEO assumes that equality is possible and treats people as individuals and 'equal' before the law. However, women do not have equality and the law has been structured to maintain the status quo. EEO legislation, as it is currently constructed, is problematic in terms of achieving equality for women.

Anti-discrimination legislation in Australia has all the hallmarks of supporting the dominant capitalist patriarchy. It is, like the Sex Discrimination Act (1975) in England, complaints-based. It requires equal treatment of women and men in the same or similar circumstances and regards as discriminatory preferential treatment of one sex over the other. If special programmes are devised for women, *exemption* must be sought under the legislation. It fails to acknowledge that women do not start from a position of equality with men and imposes a requirement for equal treatment of both sexes which assumes a 'level playing field'. Anti-discrimination legislation thus entrenches existing inequalities by insisting that both sexes must *now* be treated the same.

In Britain, as in Australia, pursuing complaints is difficult, stressful and extremely costly. Frequently women who experience discrimination are, organizationally, in a less powerful position in the hierarchy than those against whom they are lodging complaints. If the complaint is against the employer, which many are, then the disparity in resources — both financial and physical — available to the complainant and the respondent can be very significant.

Universities and other respondents not only finance cases from the organization's resources, but have access to files (some of which are confidential), staff to assist in preparation of the case, and psychological and emotional support among the senior management who frequently close ranks to fend off a perceived unjust accusation. The complainant, on the other hand, often is isolated within her organization since colleagues do not want to be seen supporting a person who is 'upsetting' the status quo. Frequently, the complainant has extremely limited financial resources and, having already experienced the alleged discrimination, is usually already highly stressed.

Discrimination can be quite subtle and in order to demonstrate a case the discrimination has to have been frequent and/or form a pattern of events and behaviour. The cumulative effect of this alone causes considerable stress to the complainant. Adducing evidence to demonstrate that the discrimination occurred is difficult and the process of collecting evidence in itself can create further emotional harm. But the onus is on the complainant to prove the case, not on the employer or respondent to prove they did not discriminate. The legislation could be reformed to empower women who have suffered discrimination by requiring the respondent to demonstrate that he has not discriminated against the complainant!

Legal Tribunals

The number of cases reaching the Equal Opportunity Tribunal in the state jurisdiction or the Human Rights and Equal Opportunity Commission in the federal jurisdiction is small and the number successful even smaller. The price paid by those pursuing cases is very high, and I know EEO practitioners often try to discourage women complainants from pursuing complaints as far as the legal forum.

The process of lodging a complaint and pursuing it through the legal forum with its aggressive adversarial legal proceedings is, for most complainants, emotionally damaging and debilitating, as well as financially costly. Personal knowledge of cases brought to legal tribunals by complainants working in universities and the public sector in Australia reveals that complaints-based legislation is not designed to be used to great effect by powerless individuals: in this instance, women.

However, the legislation has been successfully used by men to the detriment of women. For instance, a recent case in Australia involved a senior bureaucrat in the Federal Department of Health lodging a complaint of discrimination with the Human Rights and Equal Opportunity Commission because new initiatives for women's health were not also being provided to men:

> While making no complaint against services dealing specifically with women, such as pregnancy services or mammography, he said services which were not sex-specific were not also provided for men. (Chamberlin, 1991)

The Human Rights and Equal Opportunity Commission refused to hear the complaint, arguing that the Sex Discrimination Act allowed for special measures to be taken for women to remove discrimination. However, the Federal Court upheld the appeal of the complainant and referred the matter back to the Human Rights and Equal Opportunity Commission for deliberation.

It is clear that the legislation is being used by its opponents to insist on absolute equality of treatment now, even though it can be demonstrated that women have been discriminated against in the past and would continue to be discriminated against if special measures were not taken on their behalf. The mainstream legal system interprets legislation in a supposedly 'impartial' manner and concludes that failure to provide equal treatment to women and men constitutes discrimination.

EEO as Redistributive Outcomes

Many critics of EEO have pointed out its failure to change structures to ones which encompass, reflect and acknowledge as important women's experiences, interests and aspirations. These critics regard EEO as a numbers game where the object of the exercise is to get women into senior positions, or at least on the career path to senior positions (Sobski, 1985; Poiner and Wills, 1991).

The Office of the Director of Equal Opportunity in Public Employment in NSW has specified that one of the intended outcomes of Part IXA of the Anti-Discrimination Act, and one of the measures of its success, is the redistribution of 'target group members' in public sector employment (Ziller, 1980). This implies that existing structures are acceptable to women and an appropriate outcome is simply to redistribute women in relatively equal numbers to men throughout existing organizational hierarchies. Because of the pyramid structure of organizational hierarchies, only a few women will reap the full benefits from such EEO strategies, leaving untouched the large majority of women at the bottom of the hierarchy in poorly-paid, low-status positions with poor career prospects.

The underlying theoretical assumption in the redistributive EEO or liberal reform model is that the male-constructed and male-dominated organizational structures and processes are the yardstick against which success or failure to provide 'equal employment opportunities' for women are measured. There is no questioning or analysis of the nature of the structures themselves and the contexts within which they are created, nor of the part they play in constructing and maintaining the very inequality we are attempting to eliminate.

Affirmative Action: Potential for Radical Change?

Affirmative action seems to incorporate the potential to effect structural changes within organizations. Specifically it recognizes the inequitable position of women *as a group* and seeks to identify and remove barriers to women's equitable participation in the paid workforce. It recognizes that women have suffered past disadvantage and that steps need to be taken to overcome the effects of past discrimination as well as to remove existing discrimination in organizations.

Removal of barriers can be as straightforward as advertising positions actively targeting women: for example, including a statement in an advertisement specifying that 'suitably qualified women and men are invited to apply'; or providing staff development opportunities, such as training in committee work, enabling women to participate more confidently in the sometimes opaque committee proceedings. At the other end of the spectrum, affirmative action has within its parameters the potential to remove quite significant barriers to women's equitable participation in paid work, by, for example, restructuring work relations in organizations to remove hierarchical levels and democratizing the workplace. Introduction of participative decision-making and collective work arrangements within organizations may create more opportunities for women to work in ways where they are more adept and comfortable while at the same time receiving the same rewards as other workers.

This is affirmative action at its most radical and will be difficult to achieve in the short term. Affirmative action in this form attacks too obviously the interests of the power-brokers, the overwhelming majority of whom are men. Arguably, one of the greatest structural barriers to women's equitable participation in paid work is hierarchies: a peculiarly and consciously male way of organizing so that power and rewards can be differentially distributed. There seems to be something intrinsically contradictory and incompatible between equality of opportunity and unequal distribution of rewards for work which is valued arbitrarily within an organization by those who have the power to construct the value-system.

EEO and Merit

This brings us to the issue of 'merit'. When the Affirmative Action Bill was being debated in Australia, advocates of the legislation strongly emphasized that it was firmly based on the principle of appointment and promotion on 'merit'. As with EEO, 'merit' was the cornerstone of affirmative action programmes and strategies. 'Merit', however, is defined variably depending upon who is doing the defining and upon those values and characteristics in workers which are held to be important within a particular organizational culture (Martin, 1987; Burton, 1988).

In EEO terms, the legislation is interpreted to mean that a person has the right to be considered for a job or promotion or other work-related benefit on the basis of *merit* and not on the basis of characteristics irrelevant to the effective performance of the job (Ziller, 1985). The underlying and unstated assumptions of this interpretation are that not only are the rules for determining merit impartial and neutral, but that those people competing for a position or promotion or other work-related benefit start from similar positions of advantage.

Martin disputes that merit is a neutral concept and argues instead that it is 'tied to the interests of those in positions of power, so that application of the merit principle is compatible with continued structural inequalities. In practice the concept of merit is used as a resource in organisational power struggles' (Martin, 1987, p. 436). Merit, defined in organizational terms, encapsulates what is of value to that organization and rewards are distributed accordingly.

Affirmative action strategies could be developed to enable women to participate in constructing definitions of merit which would remove barriers to their equitable participation in the paid workforce.

Accommodating Women in the Paid Workforce

Affirmative action in the workplace must be accompanied by changes outside paid work to provide real advances for women. We know that women's subordination is constructed and reproduced within the domestic or private sphere and to address this site of inequality we need to break down the artificial divisions between the public and private worlds which women straddle. Unless we deal concurrently with women's subordination in paid and unpaid work, we cannot hope to make changes sufficient to ensure women's effective participation in the public sphere.

There have been significant changes in women's workforce participation in Australia since the post-war period, and similar changes have been noted by Sylvia Walby (1986) in Britain. In Australia, for example, women now constitute 41 per cent of the workforce; over 51 per cent of women work, 60 per cent of them full-time. However, 78 per cent of the part-time workforce are women (DEET, 1991) and trade union membership is relatively low at 35 per cent (ABS, 1990).

Increased participation of women in the paid workforce relates to a range of factors, including the economic necessity for two-income families in the current recession to pay mortgages and other living costs. There is tacit recognition in Australia that women have the right, and often from economic necessity need, to work. There is less support for the views that women should have economic independence and/or a satisfying job in the paid workforce. We still have rhetoric produced by reactionaries in hard economic times about women taking men's jobs or jobs that should be going to the young unemployed.

A recent letter to the editor in the Australian press, entitled 'Affirmative Action Hurts Youth', argued:

> If the Government is fair dinkum about genuine equal opportunity, reducing youth unemployment and distributing incomes equally amongst families, then it must — as a matter of social justice — abandon the affirmative action program for women which exacerbates the gap between the 'haves' and the 'have nots'. (Barron, 1991)

Women's increasing participation in the paid workforce has produced concomitant changes in conditions of employment, particularly in the public sector. Conditions which specifically affect women's ability to participate effectively in the paid workforce include childcare, maternity leave, flexible working hours and provision of permanent part-time work with pro-rata conditions of employment. Such provisions allow women to work before and after having children and to adapt work patterns to take account of domestic responsibilities.

Ratification, by Australia, of ILO Convention 156 also requires signatories to make provision for workers with family responsibilities. The Australian Federal Industrial Relations Commission has already brought down a decision granting parents (fathers and/or mothers) up to two years unpaid leave to care for young children. This decision creates an industrial framework for men to assume more responsibility for rearing children. Whether they take up that responsibility is another question.

Conditions of employment which assist women to participate in the paid workforce with greater flexibility and independence may be regarded as affirmative action strategies and were certainly introduced into universities in this context. Their intention is to improve women's paid working lives, but we need to examine carefully what the real effects of participation in both the paid and unpaid workforce have been for women.

Sexual Harassment: A Form of Sex Discrimination

Another major affirmative action strategy for women has been action taken to eliminate sexual harassment in the workplace following its identification as a barrier to women's equitable participation at work. Both state and federal legislation in Australia render sexual harassment in employment and education unlawful. Legal precedent, through cases brought before the Equal Opportunity Tribunal and the Human Rights and Equal Opportunity Commission, confirm that sexual harassment is a form of sex discrimination and that employers are vicariously liable for the unlawful behaviour of their employees unless it can be demonstrated that all possible steps have been taken to eliminate sexual harassment and to create a working environment free from this form of sex discrimination. This appears to be comparable in large measure to the legislation in Britain (Rubenstein, 1989).

Sexual harassment, by its nature, is a relatively overt form of sex discrimination and cases have been successfully prosecuted on these grounds. Australian employers, particularly in the higher education sector, seem anxious to develop explicit policies indicating that sexual harassment will not be tolerated in the workplace and to encourage staff development seminars to inform workers of their rights and responsibilities in this regard. Having performed this duty, they would no doubt argue that they are not vicariously liable for the behaviour of their employees since they have taken reasonable steps to educate staff around the issue of sexual harassment.

At a pragmatic level, employers wish to avoid the costs involved in pursuing sexual harassment cases through legal tribunals. Moreover, demographic trends in Australia and Britain indicate an aging population and a current and future shortage of young skilled workers to supply the labour needs of industry. Employers are looking to women as the industrial reserve army. But in order to retain women workers, employers need to ensure that at least a tolerable working environment is provided, including a working environment free from sexual harassment.

Resistance to Affirmative Action

One test of affirmative action's inherent potential for radical change is the degree of resistance generated by its introduction. It was opposed by the higher education and the private sectors, both of whom argued vehemently that legislation was unnecessary since each sector was eminently capable of complying voluntarily with the spirit or principles of EEO and affirmative action. The fact that many of these institutions had been operating for decades, or for approximately one hundred years in the case of some universities, and had not yet approximated equality of opportunity for women in their organizations, strongly suggested the need for legislation and accompanying sanctions.

Because affirmative action is resisted so strongly, gains for women at work have been slow and hard-won. Women, as well as men, oppose affirmative action (Kramer, 1985), and while they may agree that women should have equality of opportunity in employment, they do not believe affirmative action is necessary. Sometimes opponents deliberately fail to understand the nature of affirmative action in Australia, arguing that it is positive discrimination and that unqualified women will be given jobs in preference to more qualified men. Opponents muster a multitude of arguments to bring affirmative action into disfavour, but I believe they intuitively or consciously know the radical potential of affirmative action and are actively trying to undermine and if possible eliminate this form of social change.

One university EEO Coordinator, interviewed in 1990, perceptively identified the nature of opposition to affirmative action:

[T]he current senior men . . . have made it through the system as it was. So what's wrong with the system. They made it. It suited them. . . . It validated them. And also in that system, prior to EEO, they had considerable power to dispense patronage. Which is wonderful. It must be very satisfying to be able to promote, to be mentor to, transfer the ones you like and dislike. And EEO takes away that power. So why would they want that? I think those senior men quite rightly, and quite quickly, realised [the] potential of EEO — and I think in many instances, much more quickly than the people that EEO is designed to help. (quoted in Wieneke and Durham, 1990, p. 6)

Many universities reluctantly comply with the letter of EEO legislation, although not necessarily the spirit. And some comply only after they have been taken to the Anti-Discrimination Board or the Equal Opportunity Tribunal. Interviews conducted with EEO Coordinators in New South Wales universities in 1990 provided evidence that in some cases management do not comply with either the spirit or the letter of the legislation. During massive restructuring of higher education in 1989/90, EEO gains which had been made in previous years were lost. Management, in many instances, took the opportunity of rapid change and greater centralization of decision-making to marginalize EEO Coordinators and their work (Wieneke and Durham, 1990).

Similarly in the New South Wales public sector, after the election of a conservative government in 1988, some EEO Units were drastically reduced, necessitating the winding down of many programmes. Threats to EEO resulting from political and organizational change highlight the precarious position of this type of social reform which challenges the dominant patriarchal system.

Ordinarily, changes introduced by management into the workplace become relatively rapidly embedded within the fabric of organizational culture. Affirmative action programmes — theoretically a management-driven enterprise — do not display the usual processes associated with organizational change (Wieneke and Durham, 1990). The implementation of affirmative action programmes in male-dominated, hierarchically-organized institutions, with their inequitable distribution of power and rewards, creates a fundamental contradiction which the organization resists incorporating into its normal practices. Given the slightest opportunity, the organization will attempt to rid itself of the source of contradiction.

It is interesting to analyze how affirmative action strategies have been introduced into the higher education sector. Because we largely work on a committee system, special committees were established to advise management and/or the governing body on how EEO and affirmative action should be implemented in the organization. These committees frequently included strong feminist women committed to changes which would improve women's position in the organization. In addition, particularly since the enactment of the Affirmative Action (Equal Employment Opportunity for Women) Act 1986, unions have been strongly represented on Affirmative Action and Equal Opportunity Committees. Many of the gains made in higher education are a consequence of agitation from women on staff and in unions.

Christine Wieneke

Affirmative Action and Unions

The Affirmative Action Act specifically requires employers to consult with unions represented at the workplace. Unions have a strong tradition and presence in the Australian public sector and there is a clear coincidence of interests between the espoused principles and goals of unions and those of affirmative action in its radical form. Alignment of interests, either overtly or implicitly, between the work of EEO practitioners and that of unions may contribute to resistance by employers to the introduction and implementation of affirmative action strategies aimed at restructuring work practices and employment conditions which would benefit women (Wieneke and Durham, 1990).

Unions have a significant say in determining wage levels and conditions of employment in many workplaces (albeit mainly those which are male-dominated), and also play a part in resolving employment-related grievances, by negotiating satisfactory outcomes of conflicts between employer and employee. To some extent, the advent of EEO and affirmative action has overlapped the role of the union, but inclusion of this requirement in the Affirmative Action Act recognizes the coincidence of interests in creating fair and equitable conditions of employment for all workers, but especially for women who have been disadvantaged in the past.

The inclusion of union consultation as a requirement of the Affirmative Action Act is interesting because of its potentially contradictory and radical nature. The Affirmative Action Agency itself has noted that of all the steps in the legislation, this is the one that causes the most problems to private sector employers (Affirmative Action Agency, 1990; Kramar, 1987), many of whom actively discourage staff from joining and becoming involved in union activities (Lewis, 1991). Others barely tolerate the presence of unions in the workplace or do not tolerate the presence of unions at all. A registered club in the hospitality/leisure industry, for instance, stated on its Annual Report Form:

> Whilst the company comes under the Liquor Trade Union Award we have very little, if any, involvement with Unions. Only a small percentage belong and this is the way we want it.

In reporting annually to the Affirmative Action Agency, many private sector employers indicated failure to consult with unions on devising and implementing affirmative action programmes. It is the step that has the lowest compliance rate of the eight steps under the legislation. In its 1989/90 Annual Report, the Affirmative Action Agency noted:

> As in previous years, there was, overall, a low level of compliance with this step. In total, only 45 per cent of companies indicated that they had consulted with all or some trade unions that were affected by the affirmative action program. (Affirmative Action Agency, 1990, p. 31)

So restrained is the legislation that private sector organizations are not even required to indicate which unions are represented in their workplace. This is in marked contrast to higher education institutions where there is a specific provision on the reporting form for us to list *all* those unions which are represented and/ or have members on campus.

Unions are charged with the responsibility of protecting the rights of workers, ensuring they are paid a fair wage for their work and that they enjoy reasonable conditions of employment. If women are not being treated equitably with their male colleagues this should be a matter for the union. Unions represented in higher education, under pressure from women members, have generally supported EEO and affirmative action, electing or appointing affirmative action officers from within to advise the union itself on these matters.

However, there is a general difficulty in many unions with lack of support for, and promotion of, women's interests and issues. The positions of power in unions, as in other areas of public life, are dominated by men. Not only do women form a minority of union members in Australia, but they are very poorly represented in policy-making and decision-making positions. The Australian Council of Trade Unions, the peak union body, has moved slowly and does not have a particularly outstanding record in the promotion of women's interests.

There is a real danger that with EEO and affirmative action in place, women will bypass unions and seek to resolve issues and grievances directly with management using EEO and affirmative action legislation (Winters, 1987, p. 168; Kramar, 1987, p. 185). This will undermine the power of unions who, taking their lead from women members, must be seen as better positioned than management to create structural changes in workplaces and work relations which will be in the interests of, and benefit, women.

Conclusion

It is doubtful whether anti-discrimination legislation in Australia, or Britain, has the capacity to create equality of opportunity for women. On the other hand, implemented in its radical form, affirmative action has the potential to create new opportunities for women in the paid workforce and to alter organizational structures and practices to address the needs of working women, including those in low-paid, low-status jobs. It is critical, however, that women's unpaid work also be examined and taken into account in creating new workplace structures so that dual responsibilities for paid and unpaid work are shared equally with men.

Unions, because of their specific responsibilities in promoting the interests of all workers, are well positioned to assist with the implementation of affirmative action programmes for women. If women workers combine forces with, and work from within, sympathetic unions and with those feminists in bureaucracies who have pushed through changes benefiting women (ILO ratifications, provision of childcare, maternity leave, permanent part-time work, and so on), then there is a possibility that we can effect significant and lasting change consistent with the goals of the Women's Movement.

It is critical to have feminists in the bureaucracy, the legal system and the political system promoting women's interests, conversant with and supporting the goals of the Women's Movement. These are the ones who will identify and push the radical potential of affirmative action and push for changes from within the system. Informed by feminist theoretical developments in the academy and feminist practice in the community, feminists in the bureaucracy (femocrats as they are called in Australia) are in a good position to effect change through affirmative action. In the hands of non-feminists, affirmative action becomes a

Christine Wieneke

PR, management exercise which can have the effect of undermining the position of women.

It is crucial for those of us who are feminists working inside the system to be able to identify, articulate and theorize the contexts and constraints we work within so we can continue to move towards creating conditions where women can engage as equal participants in constructing a world which reflects and incorporates our experiences, interests and needs.

References

AFFIRMATIVE ACTION AGENCY (1990) *Annual Report 1989–1990*, Canberra, AGPS.

AUSTRALIAN BUREAU OF STATISTICS [ABS] (1990) *Trade Union Members in Australia*, Canberra, AGPS.

BARRON, A. (1991) 'Affirmative Action Hurts Youth', *Sydney Morning Herald,* 9 May, p. 14.

BURTON, CLARE (1988) *Redefining Merit*, Affirmative Action Agency, Monograph No. 2, Canberra, AGPS.

BURTON, CLARE (1991) *The Promise and the Price: The Struggle for Equal Opportunity in Women's Employment*, Sydney, Allen and Unwin.

CAINE, BARBARA, GROSZ, E.A. and LEPERVANCHE, MARIE DE (1988) *Crossing Boundaries: Feminisms and the Critique of Knowledges*, Sydney, Allen and Unwin.

CHAMBERLIN, PAUL (1991) 'Legal Threat to Women's Health Services', *Sydney Morning Herald*, 23 March.

DEPARTMENT OF EMPLOYMENT, EDUCATION AND TRAINING [DEET] (1991) 'Women at Work — Facts and Figures', *Women and Work*, 13, 1, pp. 12–13.

EISENSTEIN, HESTER (1985) 'The Gender of the Bureaucracy: Reflections on Feminism and the State', in GOODNOW, JACQUELINE and PATEMAN, CAROLE (Eds) *Women, Social Science and Public Policy*, Sydney, Allen and Unwin, pp. 104–15.

EISENSTEIN, HESTER (1990) 'Femocrats, Official Feminism and the Uses of Power', in WATSON, SOPHIE (Ed.) *Playing the State: Australian Feminist Interventions*, Sydney, Allen and Unwin, pp. 87–103.

EISENSTEIN, HESTER (1991) *Gender Shock: Practising Feminism on Two Continents*, Sydney, Allen and Unwin.

FRANZWAY, SUZANNE, COURT, DIANNE and CONNELL, R.W. (1989) *Staking a Claim: Feminism, Bureaucracy and the State*, Sydney, Allen and Unwin.

GAME, ANN (1984) 'Affirmative Action: Liberal Rationality or Challenge to Patriarchy?', *Legal Service Bulletin*, 9, 6, pp. 253–7.

GAME, ANN and PRINGLE, ROSEMARY (1983) *Gender at Work,* Sydney, Allen and Unwin.

GAME, ANN and PRINGLE, ROSEMARY (1984) 'Production and Consumption: Public versus Private', in BROOM, DOROTHY (Ed.) *Unfinished Business: Social Justice for Women in Australia*, Sydney, Allen and Unwin, pp. 65–79.

GAME, ANN and PRINGLE, ROSEMARY (1986) 'Beyond Gender at Work: Secretaries', in GRIEVE, NORMA and BURNS, AILSA(Eds) *Australian Women: New Feminist Perspectives*, Melbourne, Oxford University Press, pp. 273–91.

GRAYCAR, REGINA and MORGAN, JENNY (1990) *The Hidden Gender of Law*, Sydney, Federation Press.

KRAMAR, ROBIN (1987) 'Affirmative Action: A Challenge to Australian Employers and Trade Unions', *Journal of Industrial Relations*, 29, 2, pp. 169–89.

KRAMER, LEONIE (1985) 'Feminism's Fantasies and Fallacies', *Sydney Morning Herald*, March 28 (reprinted in *Refractory Girl*, May 1985, p. 16).

LEWIS, JULIE (1991) 'Coke asks Staff to Quit Union', *Sydney Morning Herald*, 21 June, p. 2.

MARTIN, BRIAN (1987) 'Merit and Power', *Australian Journal of Social Issues*, 22, 2, pp. 436–51.

NAFFINE, NGAIRE (1990) *Law and the Sexes: Explorations in Feminist Jurisprudence*, Sydney, Allen and Unwin.

PATEMAN, CAROLE and GROSS, ELIZABETH (1986) *Feminist Challenges: Social and Political Theory*, Sydney, Allen and Unwin.

POINER, GRETCHEN and WILLS, SUE (1991) *The Gifthorse: A Critical Look at Equal Employment Opportunity in Australia*, Sydney, Allen and Unwin.

RUBENSTEIN, MICHAEL (1989) 'Preventing Sexual Harassment at Work', *Industrial Relations Journal*, 20, 3, pp. 226–36.

SAWER, MARIAN (Ed.) (1985) *Programme for Change: Affirmative Action in Australia*, Sydney, Allen and Unwin.

SCUTT, JOCELYNNE A. (1991) 'Feminism and the Law, the Sexes and Society', *Womanspeak*, 14, 1, pp. 22–6.

SOBSKI, JOZEFA (1985) Letter to the *Sydney Morning Herald*, reproduced in *Refractory Girl*, May, p. 18.

THORNTON, MARGARET (1985) 'Affirmative Action and Higher Education', in SAWER, MARIAN (Ed.) *Programme for Change: Affirmative Action in Australia*, Sydney, Allen and Unwin, pp. 123–32.

THORNTON, MARGARET (1990) *The Liberal Promise: Anti-Discrimination Legislation in Australia*, Melbourne, Oxford University Press.

WALBY, SYLVIA (1986) *Patriarchy at Work: Patriarchal and Capitalist Relations in Employment*, Cambridge, Polity.

WATSON, SOPHIE (Ed.) (1990) *Playing the State: Australian Feminist Interventions*, Sydney, Allen and Unwin.

WIENEKE, CHRISTINE and DURHAM, MARSHA (1990) 'EEO as a Management-Driven Enterprise: Contradictions and Consequences for EEO Practitioners', paper presented at The Australian Sociological Association Conference, University of Queensland, Brisbane, December 10–16.

WINTERS, SYLVIA (1987) 'Women and the Future of Unions', in FRENKEL, STEPHEN J. (Ed.) *Union Strategy and Industrial Change*, Kensington, UNSW Press.

YEATMAN, ANNA (1990) *Bureaucrats, Technocrats, Femocrats: Essays on the Contemporary Australian State*, Sydney, Allen and Unwin.

ZILLER, ALISON (1980) *Affirmative Action Handbook*, Sydney, NSW Government Printer.

ZILLER, ALISON (1985) Keynote Address to the Merit Conference, Macquarie University, 27 September.

Section IV

Theories and Methods

Chapter 13

Defending the Indefensible?
Quantitative Methods and
Feminist Research

Liz Kelly, Linda Regan and Sheila Burton

This paper addresses what has become something of an orthodoxy, especially in sociology: that feminist methodology, and, therefore, feminist research, draw on the qualitative tradition and involve women. In the terms set out by many writers the research project we have recently completed would not count: apart from the fact that it involved young women and young men we used traditional survey research methods. Our questioning of the view which defines this methodology as antithetical to the feminist project is not a defence of that research, but a reflection on the challenges and issues that our work has produced. Whilst other individual feminist researchers have also used survey methodology, and at least one recent text (Stanley, 1990) has argued for a more open definition of feminist research/methodology, this is not yet reflected in the majority of discussions, either in writing or teaching, on feminist research. This paper both records our changing perspectives, and reflects similar shifts taking place elsewhere.

Our original intention was to construct a dialogue between writing on feminist epistemology and the mundanity and messiness of everyday research practice. The difficulties we encountered confirmed the increasing gap that is developing between theory and practice even within academia. When extended to the connection, or more accurately lack of connection, with practice and activism 'beyond the institution', this separation raises uncomfortable questions.

The Construction of 'Feminist Method'

Our central theme is that whilst recent feminist theory has questioned binary oppositions and accompanying value hierarchies in Western patriarchal thought (see Harding, 1987), many discussions of feminist methodology have reproduced them, albeit reversing the value hierarchy. In suggesting that an 'orthodoxy' has developed we refer to definitions of feminist research which specify that studies investigate women's lives (Klein, 1983) using forms which are 'non-hierarchical, non-authoritarian and non-manipulative' (Reinharz, 1983, p. 181). Qualitative methods, particularly the face-to-face in-depth interview, have become the definitive feminist approach, marginalizing if not excluding work which is indeed feminist but the participants men, or the focus on institutions and/or written texts. In many of these discussions 'experience' is privileged as unmediated access to women's reality. Thus far where experience has been problematized the discussions have tended to focus either on one's own experience (Stanley and Wise, 1983) or more recently on the construction of experience through discourses/texts.

Whilst most discussions of method refer to Ann Oakley's (1980) classic paper on interviewing women, few explore the implications of the fact that many of the charges made in relation to quantitative methods also informed traditional views on the conduct of the research interview: being distanced, objective, keeping to the researcher's agenda — i.e. not seeing oneself as a participant in an interaction. This suggests that what makes research feminist is less the method used, and more how it is used and what it is used for.

One of the fundamental premises of feminist research has been that we locate ourselves within the questions that we ask, and the process of conducting the research. Maureen Cain (1990) argues that there is a difference between personal and theoretical reflexivity, the former being seen as the unique thoughts, feelings and experiences of the researcher, the latter a theoretical understanding of the site from which one is working, which creates the standpoint from which one works. We will use both in this chapter. It is not easy to separate them unless we take theoretical reflexivity as informing the initial design stages and personal reflexivity as reflections on the 'doing' of research.

The Research Project

Each of us comes to research through a non-traditional route: taking first degrees as 'mature' students with a prior, and continuing, involvement in activism and no clear ambition or intention to become academics/researchers. Janice Raymond has described the position of feminists in academic institutions as 'inside/outsiders' (1986). Her discussion focuses on the areas of choice we have about our location and the necessity of connection to feminism outside the institution. The extent to which women feel, and are, 'outside' involves more than choice, being amplified by identity and biography: class, race and sexuality have also functioned to exclude or marginalize, as has active political involvement. Differences in status, career prospects and visibility between full-time researchers and lecturers who also do research, amplify the 'outsider' location and have not been addressed by feminists, nor have the hierarchies that exist, or develop, within groups of feminist researchers.

The project on which our reflections are based was a study of the prevalence of sexual abuse, funded by the Economic and Social Research Council. The application resulted from discussions within the Child Abuse Studies Unit, which was established in 1987 to develop feminist theory and practice on child abuse. The context was a lack of a British knowledge base and growing debates around gender in terms of both victimization and offending. Policy and practice were developing rapidly, but in a reactive and ad hoc way, drawing on contested theoretical perspectives and generalizations drawn from small clinical samples.

The original application proposed to compare what young people chose to tell in a self-report questionnaire and what they revealed in face-to-face interviews. We wanted to explore the contention, based on US research, that face-to-face interviews encourage reporting of sexual victimization. No study has yet directly compared the two methods. Our original application to do so was turned down

Table 13.1   *Research models in contemporary sociology*

	Conventional or Patriarchal	Alternative or feminist
Units of study	Predefined, operationalized concepts stated as hypotheses.	Natural events encased in their ongoing contexts.
Sharpness of focus	Limited, specialized, specific, exclusive.	Broad, inclusive.
Data type	Reports of attitudes and actions as in questionnaires, interviews and archives.	Feelings, behavior, thoughts, insights, actions as witnessed or experienced.
Topic of study	Manageable issue derived from scholarly literature, selected for potential scholarly contribution, sometimes socially significant.	Socially significant problem sometimes related to issues discussed in scholarly literature.
Role of Research: in relation to environment	Control of environment is desired, attempt to manage research conditions.	Openness to environment, immersion, being subject to and shaped by it.
in relation to subjects	Detached.	Involved, sense of commitment, participation, sharing of fate.
as a person	Irrelevant.	Relevant, expected to change during process.
impact on researcher	Irrelevant.	Anticipated, recorded, reported, valued.
Implementation of method	As per design, decided a priori.	Method determined by unique characteristics of field setting.
Validity criteria	Proof, evidence, statistical significance: study must be replicable and yield same results to have valid findings.	Completeness, plausibility, illustrativeness, understanding, responsiveness to readers, or subjects' experience; study cannot however, be replicated.
The role of theory	Crucial as determinant of research design.	Emerges from research implementation.
Data analysis	Arranged in advance relying on deductive logic, done when all data are 'in'.	Done during the study, relying on inductive logic.
Manipulation of data	Utilization of statistical analyses.	Creation of gestalts and meaningful patterns.
Research objectives	Testing hypotheses.	Development of understanding through grounded concepts and descriptions.
Presentation format	Research report form; report of conclusions with regard to hypotheses stated in advance, or presentation of data obtained from instruments.	Story, description with emergent concepts; including documentation of process of discovery.
Failure	Statistically insignificant variance.	Pitfalls of process illustrate the subject.
Values	Researchers' attitudes not revealed, recognized or analyzed, attempts to be value free, objective.	Researchers' attitudes described and discussed, values acknowledged, revealed, labelled.
Role of reader	Scholarly community addressed; evaluation of research design, management and findings.	Scholarly and user community addressed and engaged; evaluate usefulness and responsiveness to perceived needs.

as was a subsequent one. The research eventually funded limited us to the self-report questionnaire. To have refused this restriction would not only have prompted a major crisis around the future of the Unit, but would have left the knowledge gap in place.

The structure of the rest of this paper is an engagement with the binary oppositions which construct the counterposing of quantitative/qualitative, traditional/feminist research methods. To organize the discussion we have used a table from Shulamit Reinharz's paper 'Experiential Analysis: a Contribution to Feminist Research' (1983, pp. 170–2). Our paper is not a critique of that piece, but draws on it as an explicit and systematic outline of a position which defines quantitative methods as antithetical to feminist work. The table as it appears in that paper is reproduced as table 13.1.

Units of Study

No feminist would suggest studying sexual abuse (or a range of other issues) as 'natural' events occurring within an ongoing context. We saw our project as an exploration of both method and issue. We did not know whether young people would complete the questionnaire, or tell us about experiences of abuse, and we experimented with ways of encouraging them to tell us. What counts as 'sexual abuse', both from the point of view of the young people and within analytic definitions, was part of the study. Hypothesis testing is an epistemological issue, linked to particular constructions of science. It is a use to which questionnaires and large-scale surveys have been put, but not an inherent feature of the method.

Sharpness of Focus

Our original intention was to adapt a questionnaire used in an American study, but it was constructed within the limited and specific parameters of survey research, with ease of coding a primary concern. It placed huge limitations on what participants could say and the structure was extremely complex. In our questionnaire ease of coding was subordinated to encouraging responses, using open-ended questions where it was inappropriate to offer only pre-defined options, and placing experiences in context. The forms of questions were as inclusive as possible, particularly not using pre-defined concepts of what counts as abuse.

Data Type

Here interviews are located with questionnaires, and the limitations on what can be researched, and how, within the feminist band probably excludes the majority of published work by feminists. It is true that most survey research concentrates on closed questions and attitude scales, as these are most amenable to the hypothesis testing approach. However, just as researchers have changed interview practice it is possible to change the structure and content of questionnaires. There were no attitude-scaled questions in ours, and where we gave options about, for example, the impacts of abuse or on policy issues, space was left for alternatives and/or comments. We also included questions about emotional responses.

Nor is our data restricted to the questionnaires. We kept detailed notes of the process of negotiating access, field notes for each session and notes of questions/ insights that arose during coding. As a rider to this some patterns which we noted during coding turned out to be less marked within the complete data set.

We are not disputing the breadth and depth of understanding that research which adopts Reinharz's suggested approach to data can bring. But we would argue that by only using small-scale studies we can be misled into believing that we have baseline knowledge which has not actually been collected. For example, most work on all areas of sexual violence draws on women who have in some way made their experiences public, and most work on domestic violence draws on women from refuges. The different experiences and needs of women who have not sought help, and why they haven't, have hardly been explored. Where they have, critical issues about how services for women are organized and perceived emerge (McGibbon, Cooper and Kelly, 1989; Schecter, 1989). Survey research is one way of expanding our understanding of the dimensions and complexities of the issues that concern us.

Topic of Study

This raises the vexed question about what is a 'socially significant' problem. It would be unusual to find someone who did not agree that sexual abuse is a socially significant issue about which there is also a scholarly literature. One of our motivations in doing the study was to develop a stronger knowledge base from which to take issue with some of what we have called the 'new mythology'. In developing feminist understandings as researchers we are constantly engaged in re-evaluating prior constructions of knowledge, and usually have direct connection, albeit a critical one, to scholarly literature.

Role of Research

In Relation to Environment/Implementation of Method

Our practice here is definitely a compromise between Reinharz's two positions. We did construct a protocol which we hoped to follow in each of the colleges we visited. Apart from some forms of participant observation there are practical arrangements that are necessary for research to take place; the issue must surely be how rigid one is about them. If researchers routinely provided detailed descriptions of how large-scale projects are actually conducted, we suspect that a more complex model would emerge which involves negotiation and adaption in particular settings and circumstances. The 'management and control' model is reinforced through a silence about the realities of fieldwork on larger projects.

Our 'ideal' was to have students in combined class groups of forty to fifty, meaning we could do four groups on day one, and pick up on any problems during the next two days. We wanted to do the introductions ourselves, to ensure confidentiality for the students, and so that we could observe the process. The reality was that the research environment changed from one college to the next. We suggested exam-type conditions because it could provide some privacy and decrease the likelihood of group responses. However, many students resisted our suggestion that they spread out and treat it like an exam. Rather than imposing our model, we only intervened where discussion and comments were disturbing others. Where we suspected that students had discussed their responses we marked the questionnaires and looked at this when coding.

As to immersion, again our position was a compromise. Whilst not 'hit and run', our presence for three days in each college was not immersion in the physical environment, but our study was not about the colleges. Our observations of the general atmosphere and interactions did aid our understanding of some responses. More interesting was the response of the students to our presence, some greeted or acknowledged us each time we saw them, others chose to act as if we were strangers. Amongst those who made a point of greeting us were individuals who had reported extremely painful experiences.

In Relation to Subjects

The concept and meaning of 'sharing of fate' is problematic given the increasing recognition of differences between women — unless we are to be limited to studying other (white) women sociologists/researchers! It also rules out the possibility of feminists studying men, or those more powerful than themselves. We were however not detached. One of our major concerns was whether participation might distress students. We produced resource sheets listing support services in college, in each local area and nationally for each college and one was placed in each questionnaire. We produced guidelines for staff on how to handle students telling about abuse, and conducted training with staff in three colleges.

Our field notes are full of references to behaviour and responses of students whilst they completed the questionnaires, and our own reactions and perceptions. For example:

> Strange sound of paper turning, turning . . . does it inhibit those who are writing, concentrating?

> Three boys finish first — insist on chatting to women who cover their questionnaires with their bodies.

> Why is it taking degree-level students longer to fill in than CPVE class? Literacy and ability far more complex — is it something about thinking/ reflecting and the connection to learning? Cannot tell from time taken to complete those who are answering the detailed sections — has this got something to do with how 'in control' of their experiences they feel?

> Three women holding their heads in their hands.

> Long line of young women next to one another — interesting how some feel fine close to others and some choose more privacy — doesn't seem to affect how much they say.

> Lots of questions but group appears very relaxed, comfortable. Able to spread out. Space in non-traditional settings far more conducive than formal teaching settings.

We adopted a stance of unobtrusive monitoring, shifting between reading and watching, taking note of any students who showed signs of distress/difficulty; some young people looked for reassurance and we responded through smiles and 'thank-yous' as they left.

It was impossible to be detached when we coded, and we learnt very quickly to pick up on each other's distress — tears, rage and despair were seldom far away. Sharing the accounts which distressed us was one strategy we developed. Including questions about resistance and coping, and about wider aspects of their lives, meant that we had a sense of the young people beyond their experiences of victimization.

Our concern about the issue and connection to the young people resulted in contradictory responses to students' accounts. Where there were no reports of unwanted sexual experiences, especially by young women, our initial reaction was one of disbelief and even irritation. Whilst the issues of willingness to tell, defining and remembering abuse could have affected these young women, we were resisting the possibility that they may have escaped sexual victimization. We denied ourselves the possibility of responding positively to that potential. The flip side of this was that when abuse was reported our initial response was relief, followed fairly rapidly by distress. The complexity of our reactions to the research process, and our uncomfortableness with some of them, were a source of tension and confusion, which have echoes in theoretical debates between feminists concerning sexuality and sexual violence.

As a Person

Our relationships with each other, as well as our perspective on both sexual abuse and methodology, were transformed over a two-year period. We, like many feminists, had paid relatively little attention to abuse of boys or abuse by women. Both became essential to address if we were to do justice to what we had been told. The empathy we felt for some of the boys surprised us.

We were also surprised by how much some students chose to, or felt able to tell us. We began to ponder on whether they would have been so revealing in a face-to-face interview, and are fairly certain that some of them would not have told so much, if anything at all. Young people completing the questionnaire were given the choice to complete combined with control over what and how much they told. Young people share with adults difficulties in talking about sexual experiences but we believe that the control they were given combined with our explicit permission to tell as much as they felt able gave them the security they needed. Those women who have taken part in in-depth interview studies are usually self-selected — this was a far more random group of young people. The confidentiality, not having to verbalize their experiences to someone, and the control over how much is said may enable some to tell about sexual abuse, especially those who have not told anyone thus far. It is this possibility which has led us to reassess survey research.

Impact on Researcher

We had anticipated that we would be affected by the research process, but had confidence in our ability to 'handle' the topic. However, the fact that we hired a television during the most intense period of coding which coincided with Wimbledon and the World Cup, that our humour became increasingly barbed and full of 'in jokes' tells a rather different story, as does the fact that we often seemed to spend weekends in a haze. The intensity of that period is hard to put into words, as is documenting our individual and collective coping strategies. We have attempted in different ways and at different times to write about the project, but none of us has put a word on paper until now. Whilst we talked of keeping research diaries, the fact that we did not suggests that making ourselves consciously reflect on what we were doing daily threatened the fragile balance we were maintaining.

The impacts extended into our family and friendship networks, not only in terms of our needs and actions, but also how we were 'seen' by others. We became 'safe' to tell, and for us sexual abuse was indeed everywhere. In virtually any situation, no matter how unlikely, women and men would begin telling us about their experiences. The fact that we were being paid to work on this issue, that it was in most of the rest of our lives, made it hard to maintain boundaries.

Validity Criteria

Here too our position is a compromise between these two positions, especially since what 'completeness' might mean is unclear and contested. The coding and punching of data has been meticulously checked, and mistakes or inconsistencies explored. Contradictions within detailed accounts or observed behaviour are not considered problematic, but they are within numeric data sets. Where coding is conducted as a routine task inconsistent responses are ignored, since they 'even out' in the data. Since we coded for meaning and were building a sense of each young person in the process contradictions were a source of concern. Did we leave them in, thus faithfully keeping to what was in each questionnaire, or did we attempt to create some kind of coherence and consistency? How should you code where individuals answer 'no' to the first question in a section and then proceed as if they had said 'yes'? Can you presume that the first response was a mistake, or is something more complex being communicated?

The idea that all studies must be not only replicable but produce the same results derives from a simplistic model of the physical sciences. Even experiments in the most controlled environments do not necessarily produce the same findings. It is extremely unlikely that any study in social science could be replicated in this way, even if it was desired. What does, and should, occur is that we build upon, adapt and extend previous work.

The Role of Theory

As feminists we cannot argue that theory emerges from research, since we start from a theoretical perspective that takes gender as a fundamental organizer of social life. Moreover, any piece of research refers to what has gone before either by adding in levels of complexity or challenging previous perspectives. What research should produce is modifications, re-workings, extensions and/or critiques of existing theory, and the creation of new concepts.

Data Analysis and Manipulation of Data

Analysis was not determined beforehand, indeed if it had been we would have saved ourselves a great deal of work. By structuring the questionnaire in order to encourage telling, not imposing our definition of abuse, giving students the option to tell very little or much more, analysis was extremely complex. There were eight places on the questionnaire where students could tell us about their experiences of abuse. There is no question that this resulted in experiences being reported, but it also created the danger of double counting. The only way of preventing this was to recode every questionnaire.

We have already pointed to the danger of relying solely on subjective perceptions of meaningful patterns. It is clear that the logic and meaning of an individual account cannot be translated into large-scale numeric data sets. But what we have are coexisting forms of information, and each can add meaning to the other. It is possible to recontextualize from numeric data — to move between quantitative statistics and the complexity and immediacy of individual experience. In working with two women film-makers for a feature on the research, we began with the figures. They decided which areas they wanted to focus on and we constructed young people's stories from their questionnaires as illustrative examples.

Research Objectives

Our aim was not to test hypotheses but to build a knowledge base on sexual abuse. The concepts we developed through coding and recoding did not simply emerge from the accounts of the young people, but drew on previous work. Since one of our concerns was to enable 'telling' and to limit any distress, we abandoned the most useful quantitative way of asking about forms of abuse — providing an explicit list of sexual acts. Our pilot groups said the list was too 'stark' and 'terrifying'. This meant that whilst we gave control to the young people in terms of what level of detail they gave us, in some circumstances we do not know what forms the abuse took — in others we have to work with responses such as 'interfered with'. We face the critical issue of whether we use less detailed information from more individuals or more detailed from fewer. That is one of the difficulties of attempting to balance researchers' desire for particular information with giving participants control over their responses.

Presentation Format

Our research report does present the data, but is not a technical description of statistical methods or hypothesis testing. We attempted to make it accessible to a non-academic audience and included a shortened summary for practitioners. We are also publishing short pieces in practitioner journals, using our work in training, and writing a book where the words of the young people will be integrated with quantitative analysis.

Failure

The notion of failure is in many ways inappropriate in relation to social research. The issue is not simply use of variant analysis or illustrating the pitfalls but rather what methods and projects enable and limit and what is learnt both about the topic and about research.

Values

Our values informed our choice of topic, our research design and the ways we interpret, conceptualize and extrapolate from it. Our research was about being committed to reflecting, and attempting to explain/account for what participants say, including allowing for findings which don't 'fit', and have not been addressed thus far by feminist perspectives. Both research and feminism are about discovery which requires being open to surprises, contradiction and challenge.

Role of Reader

Clearly this study has a number of overlapping audiences — academics, practitioners, feminists. One of the challenges is finding ways to speak simultaneously to different knowledges and interests. We hope that our work will be useful within current debates, but as researchers we cannot assess the usefulness of our work to others; that will emerge only in time and through feedback.

One of the core features of much large-scale survey research is that it is not the same individuals who design the study, conduct it, code and punch the data, do the analysis, make sense of the data and write up the project. The fieldwork is usually done either by research assistants or by contract research companies. In a very real sense what they deal with are decontextualized numeric values and the relationships between them. This is not an inevitable part of the method, however. Immersion in the data is possible, as other researchers have found and as the many months we spent coding are testimony to. Our practice was one of creating numeric values for complex responses and then once we began analysis needing to recontextualize, to check for data errors and to explore specific areas. Each new piece of work we do involves going back to the questionnaires. This has far more in common with the ways sociologists work with qualitative data.

Relationships in Research Teams

There are key areas that Reinharz's conceptualization of feminist method does not include, and the most critical for us are the relationships between researchers in terms of hierarchies of status and division of labour. We came to this project with different skills and statuses. Our skills were complementary, but the status division structural. The funding provided for two research fellows, in order that there be no structural inequality between the two full-time workers, and a part-time administrator. Whilst our aim was to cooperate collectively, the pressure of work meant that it was impossible to develop the skill-sharing we had hoped. However, a strong sense of collective responsibility for our work developed during the project.

A major factor affecting our working relationships is that one of us had a history and status as a feminist researcher. For the other two this was their first job after graduating. Deference to experience, knowledge and status has been something we have struggled with from our different positions. 'Doing different', though, requires more than our individual and collective commitment. The existing differences and confidences were reinforced by external responses, even from other feminists. At times what we managed to create internally was undermined by these interactions. Exploring these issues explicitly and systematically also threatened the collectivity we managed to maintain most of the time. This echoes with our experiences in women's groups, where issues of power and responsibility remain major areas of conflict, division and uncertainty, and where attempts to address them directly are fraught and frequently resisted.

Conclusions

We are suggesting that reworking an unhelpful system of polarities reproduces confusions between epistemology, method and methodology. We regard methods as ways of doing research, asking questions, collecting and collating information and making sense of it. It is epistemology which defines what counts as valid knowledge and why. If we begin from this position then it is possible to bring a feminist standpoint to a range of methods; we do not have to accept the 'scientistic' model of surveys or reject surveys as necessarily 'non-feminist'.

As Catharine MacKinnon says:

> Objectivity, as the epistemological stance of which objectification is the social process, creates the reality it apprehends . . . feminist method has a distinctive theory of the relation between method and truth, the individual and her social surroundings, the presence and place of the natural and the spiritual in culture and society, social being and causality itself. Having been objectified as sexual beings while stigmatized as ruled by subjective passions, women reject the distinction between knowing subject and known object — the division between subjective and objective postures — as the means to comprehend social life . . . women's interest lies in overthrowing *the distinction itself*. (MacKinnon, 1989, pp. 114, 120–1)

Note

We would like to acknowledge Routledge for permission to reprint a table from Shulamit Reinharz's chapter in *Theories of Women's Studies*, edited by Gloria Bowles and Renate Duelli Klein.

References

CAIN, MAUREEN (1990) 'Realist Philosophy and Standpoint Epistemologies OR Feminist Criminology as a Successor Science', in GELSTHORPE, L. and MORRIS, A. *Feminist Perspectives in Criminology,* Milton Keynes, Open University Press.
HARDING, SANDRA (Ed.) (1986) *The Science Question in Feminism,* Milton Keynes, Open University Press.

Liz Kelly, Linda Regan and Sheila Burton

KLEIN, RENATE DUELLI (1983) 'How to Do what We Want to Do: Thoughts about Feminist Methodology', in BOWLES, GLORIA and KLEIN, RENATE DUELLI (Eds) *Theories of Women's Studies,* London, Routledge and Kegan Paul.

MCGIBBON, ALISON, COOPER, LIBBY and KELLY, LIZ (1989) *'What Support?' An Exploratory Study of Council Policy and Practice and Local Support Services in the Area of Domestic Violence within Hammersmith and Fulham,* Final Report, Council Community and Police Unit, London Borough of Hammersmith and Fulham.

MACKINNON, CATHARINE (1989) *Towards a Feminist Theory of the State,* Cambridge, MA, Harvard University Press.

OAKLEY, ANN (1980) 'Interviewing Women', in ROBERTS, HELEN (Ed.) *Doing Feminist Research,* London, Routledge and Kegan Paul.

RAYMOND, JANICE (1986) *A Passion for Friends: Towards a Philosophy of Female Affection,* London, Women's Press.

REINHARZ, SHULAMIT (1983) 'Experiential Analysis: a Contribution to Feminist Research', in BOWLES, GLORIA and KLEIN, RENATE DUELLI (Eds) *Theories of Women's Studies,* London, Routledge and Kegan Paul.

SCHECTER, SUSAN (1989) 'Why Battered Women Don't Use Women's Services', unpublished paper.

STANLEY, LIZ (Ed.) (1990) *Feminist Praxis: Research Theory and Epistemology in Feminist Sociology,* London, Routledge.

STANLEY, LIZ and WISE, SUE (1983) *Breaking Out: Feminist Consciousness and Feminist Research,* London, Routledge and Kegan Paul.

Chapter 14

Epistemological Issues in Researching Lesbian History: The Case of Romantic Friendship[1]

Liz Stanley

Introduction

An increasingly important strand in feminist history explores women's friendship circles and relationships (examples include Smith-Rosenberg, 1975; Faderman, 1981, 1983; Vicinus, 1985, 1991; Caine, 1986; Thompson, 1987; Oldfield, 1984; Levine, 1990; Alberti, 1990; Stanley, 1985, 1988). Like other strands in feminist history, it involves partly the recovery of this 'lost' aspect of women's history and partly the reconceptualization of such friendships. Important lines of development are: the recognition of a 'women's world' of love and ritual existing within, or perhaps beneath, patriarchal relationships; the argument that until comparatively recently women's 'romantic friendships' were a socially sanctioned parallel to heterosexual attachments and not seen as sexual or deviant; and a more recent attention to how feminist friendship patterns constituted an informal feminist organization that could subvert formal separations, disagreements and divisions. The first two of these developments have been the most influential to date, with particularly the notion of 'romantic friendship' occasioning impassioned responses, both positive and negative.

The idea of 'romantic friendship' has become a site of controversy and debate. One controversy concerns whether the notion of romantic friendship is itself a romantic idea that denies the erotic and/or sexual element in such relationships through operating as a form of conceptual imperialism: the theory says that such friendships were not sexual, and the nature of actual friendships is then deduced from the theory. A related controversy concerns the specification of lesbianism as a late-nineteenth-century phenomenon, rather than either a form of conduct with earlier origins, or indeed origins which lie in behaviours which predate the invention of labels which gloss them. A third controversy overlaps with the concerns of predominantly, if not exclusively, gay male historians with the 'essentialist v. constructionist' debate concerning 'the homosexual' (Boswell, 1991; Halperin, 1991; Padgug, 1991; Altman *et al.*, 1989). Proponents of romantic friendship see 'the lesbian' as the invention of a group of male 'sexologists', who constructed 'the lesbian' as a specific and different kind of person who was, as part of her condition, 'mannish' (Faderman, 1981; Jackson, 1984; Newton, 1984), and then applied this stereotype to erstwhile romantic friends in order to discredit these relationships.

The establishment of a specifically 'lesbian history' (e.g. Lesbian History Group, 1989; Hall Carpenter Archives, 1989; Vicinus, 1989) is composed partly by recovery work and partly by reconceptualization, with the emphasis to date being more on recovery. It also considerably overlaps with developments concerning friendship. All three controversies, not just the third, raise crucial issues concerning claims made about who and what 'the lesbian' is, how to identify 'her' and in what historical periods, who has the (theoretical, political or other) expertise to do this, and how competing knowledge-claims about 'her' should be dealt with. The establishment of a lesbian history is thus placed in the eye of the epistemological storm that characterizes contemporary academic feminism, for it raises questions concerned with essentialism, difference, the category 'women', and the nature of 'the self' (Fuss, 1989; Riley, 1988; Spelman, 1990; Stanley, 1992).

In this chapter I focus on one aspect of these epistemological issues, the question of 'romantic friendship', which I explore in relation to two linked questions. Firstly, under what circumstances and using what kind of historical evidence is it possible to specify, one way or another, whether women's close and loving relationships of the past were romantic friendships or involved erotic/sexual behaviours? And secondly, to what extent does historical evidence support the view that the 'mannish lesbian' was mythic, the invention of male sexologists? I examine these questions both abstractly and in relation to a case study of some actual historical relationships between women. In the following section, 'Feminism and Friendship', I argue for the importance of a concern with women's friendships within feminist history, including by examining the strengths but also the limitations of the 'romantic friendship' approach. Then in 'Dear Edward Carpenter . . .' I show that one example of what present-day lesbian/feminist historians have specified as 'romantic friendship' was seen by the woman herself as her lesbianism, as, in contemporary terms, her 'inversion'; and I use related further evidence to show that the 'mannish lesbian' pre-dates the work of sexologists such as Havelock Ellis and that at least some women saw themselves as 'mannish' in the absence of sexological influences.

Feminism and Friendship

Conventional historians and biographers ignore or fail to see women's close relationships with other women: women are not 'seen' at all or seen as appendages of men or deemed to be alone. It has been feminist researchers who have valued and investigated women's inter-relationships, including patterns of friendship among earlier generations of feminists. However, even when the importance of women's friendship links and patterns *is* conceded, choices in themselves epistemologically consequential still remain.

Lillian Faderman (1981), for example, conceptualizes close friendships between women until the early twentieth century as romantic friendships involving passionate emotional commitment openly expressed. Faderman argues, using many historical secondary sources, that these passionate friendships were neither seen as 'unnatural' nor as sexual, even though their romantic character was widely recognized and accepted. Faderman's approach recognizes two important things: that there are large temporal differences in how friendship is defined and treated (i.e. its meaning is socially constructed), and that in past times women's friendships were seen as a central social relationship; while the focus in present-day research is usually on marriage or other kinds of heterosexual sexual relationships and denigrates friendship, reflecting *current* definitions and understandings, not those of the times and places of historical subjects.

But as well as its undoubted strengths, Faderman's approach romanticizes the past by constructing a lost age of innocence, a time before patriarchal oppressiveness in the work of Victorian/Edwardian sexologists invented 'lesbianism' as a sexualized mannish stereotype and imposed it on passionate relationships between women in order to condemn them. Romantic friendships in Faderman's terms are not sexual relationships; and in an examination of the historical case study of Jane Pirie and Marianne Woods (Faderman, 1983) she argues her grounds for this. However, again there are problems with Faderman's approach. It proceeds from the assumption that 'sexual' means the same things now that it meant in the late eighteenth century, and the early, mid and late nineteenth century. It makes a clear distinction between 'the sexual' as genital acts of various kinds and 'the non-sexual', thereby defining much erotic behaviour as non-sexual. It defines as 'lesbian' only a very narrow set of genital sexual relationships. And it ignores what the protagonists of such romantic relationships thought and wrote, their definitions and understandings, in favour of a researcher-imposed set of understandings and meanings.

A paradigmatic example of Faderman's approach concerns the 'Ladies of Llangollen', Sarah Ponsonby and Eleanor Butler (Mavor, 1971), who ran away from Ireland in 1778 and then lived together in Llangollen a life of 'sweet contentment' in rural retreat from the corruptions of urban social life. Faderman argues that everybody knew they were romantic friends, everybody approved, nobody thought it was a sexual relationship, nobody shunned them because they thought the relationship was 'unnatural'. There are, however, good reasons for suggesting that the facts were otherwise: the diarist Hester Thrale Piozzi[2] refers to the ladies and their friends as 'damned sapphists' and writes that this is why various literary women will not visit them overnight unless accompanied by men; while the recently decoded diary of one of their circle, Anne Lister (Whitbread, 1988), contains details of her explicitly sexual conquests of women and opens up the possibility that other members of the circle were as genitally aware as she.

I am *not* arguing that these women were 'really lesbian' and constituted a lesbian subculture: claims concerning the synonymity of their behaviour and relationships and present-day lesbianism are not intended; but neither am I arguing that 'the lesbian' did not exist then. My view is that drawing *either* conclusion from the historical record is problematic; these women were seen as lesbians by various of their friends and acquaintances, and they may have seen themselves in these terms too, *but* 'lesbian' meant something very different then, and something to which we now have no access.

However, whatever its problems, Faderman's work does at least conceptualize women's historical friendships outside of present-day heterosexist convention that the ties of women's friendships give way to the presumed-to-be-more-important ones of marriage and family. What is needed is a broader view of friendship than Faderman's, one which similarly rejects the assumptions of the convention but does so in favour of a detailed investigative approach rather than a reliance on secondary sources and a style of deductivism which constitutes a form of theoretical imperialism.

While recognizing the influences on them, it is crucial to treat historical persons as agents of their lives and not as puppets whose thoughts and actions were determined: it would be ironic indeed if a feminist approach to friendship, by wanting to recognize women's oppression in the past as well as the present, should treat these friendships as merely the products of patriarchy. In the following section, 'Dear Edward Carpenter . . . ', I counter such a view by discussing material from the Carpenter Archive which addresses Faderman's claim that Havelock Ellis morbidified not only lesbianism in general but the romantic friendships of his wife Edith Lees Ellis in particular, and the related claim (Jackson, 1984; Newton, 1984) that he and other sexologists invented the 'mannish' lesbian stereotype which was then imposed on women's romantic and/or erotic relationships.

Dear Edward Carpenter . . .

From the letters that survive in the Edward Carpenter Archive,[3] Carpenter's three main women correspondents were Kate Salt,[4] Olive Schreiner and Edith Lees Ellis, but with smaller numbers of letters being received from feminist women such as Isabella Ford, Annie Besant, Charlotte Despard, Stella Browne, Constance Lytton, Marie Stopes, Dora Montefiore and others. Edith Lees, married to Havelock Ellis, has been seen as a woman whose non-sexual romantic friendships with women were 'morbidified' by Ellis: effectively, that he created her as a lesbian when in fact she was not. Thus Lillian Faderman argues that her case history in Ellis's *Sexual Inversion*[5] (1897) suggests that Lees experienced romantic friendships with women rather than erotic or sexual feelings for them.

Faderman's general argument is that romantic friendships were 'love relationships in every sense except perhaps the sexual' (Faderman, 1981, p. 16) and were condoned and indeed widely accepted except where one of the partners crossdressed, thus violating men's presumptive property rights over women. What changed this was the activity of late-nineteenth and early-twentieth-century sexologists who defined such love as a medical problem. Faderman argues that sexologists, Krafft-Ebing and Ellis in particular, codified and propagated the punitive ideas of von Westphal (pp. 239–53), which focused on transvestite women. Relatedly, Margaret Jackson's (1984) discussion of sexology accepts Faderman's estimation of the role and centrality of sexologists in creating 'the lesbian', and her analysis focuses on the role of Havelock Ellis in particular. Esther Newton's (1984) discussion of the 'mythic mannish lesbian' similarly insists that women's romantic friendships were a quasi-legitimate parallel to marriage and sees Krafft-Ebing and Ellis as the protagonists in the invention of 'the lesbian'.

Ellis's role, Faderman suggests, was to promote Krafft-Ebing's morbidification of love between women, presenting it as a degeneracy, and she sees Ellis's book as 'one of the most successful treatises on homosexuality written in English' (Faderman, 1981, p. 241). Ellis distinguishes between the 'true invert' and the 'spurious imitation'; and Faderman sees the term 'invert' as a pejorative technical term invented and used by the sexologists; she comments that:

> one wonders how many romantic friends, who had felt themselves to be perfectly normal before, suddenly saw themselves as sick, even though their behaviour had in no way changed, as a result of the sexologists' formulations. (Faderman, 1981, p. 244)

It is at this point that she footnotes comments on Edith Lees; she was, Faderman claims, a victim of Ellis's theories:

> From his own account, Ellis apparently convinced her that she was a congenital invert, while she believed herself to be only a romantic friend to other women. . . . He thus encouraged her to see herself as an invert and to regard her subsequent love relations with women as a manifestation of her inversion. (Faderman, 1981, p. 454)

It is curious that Ellis, portrayed as the author of a sexual political 'fall' as consequential for women as that from Eden, is believed by Faderman. His hints concerning *his* creation of Edith Lees's sexual interest in women are taken as unquestionably true, perhaps because this is one of the few pieces of actual evidence that Faderman has for demonstrating that Ellis's ideas had *any* influence on how women thought of their love and/or desire for other women, whatever influence they may have had on the writing of other sexologists. Faderman does not ask whether Ellis might have had other motives for claiming such influence, nor does she consider whether contrary evidence about Lees's feelings might exist. However, it will come as little surprise to married bisexual or lesbian women to hear of a husband claiming that his wife's desire for women is actually his invention, for bruised male egos frequently respond in this way. It is clear from Ellis's autobiography *My Life* (1940) that considerable tensions existed in his and Edith Lees's relationship and that he took a good deal of trouble in textually locating these as her problem and not his. In examining whether Ellis 'morbidified' Edith Lees's feelings for women, Faderman's complete trust in his statement should therefore be suspended and instead the circumstances of his claim investigated. Also, contrary evidence about Edith Lees's feelings *does* exist, in the form of two particular letters written to her close friend Edward Carpenter.[6]

These two letters are undated, although they appear in an archive sequence which suggests they were written in about 1915, probably because of Edith Lees's reference in the first letter to a lecture on Hinton, for a posthumously published book on Hinton appeared in 1916. However, it is likely that they were written considerably before this: Lees started lecturing on Hinton many years before 1915; and in the first letter it is clear that when it was written Carpenter's sister Alice still did not know, although she suspected, that her brother was homosexual; Edith Lees's first letter notes that:

> she has a fear for your reputation & hers & the religion through you. She said she felt sure I knew you were that & it wd hurt your message & mine etc etc.

Given Carpenter's publications, by 1915 Alice Carpenter could have had no doubt about her brother's homosexuality for a number of years.[7]

In the first of these letters Edith Lees writes about being questioned by Alice Carpenter:

> this of *course* between us — my inversion is the 'talk' in that higher thought. How it has got out heaven knows or whether they only *think* it or know it I don't quite realise but when I went to your sister the other day with

trembling lips & hands she questioned me about what she had heard ['higher thought' is a sarcastic reference to Carpenter's sister Alice's trumpeted piety].

She goes on,

your sister wrote me a long letter after in which she called me 'a fine, loving teacher' etc. — but but — you know.

Lees's main response to Alice Carpenter's questioning was to add to a public lecture some statement concerning such issues in her personal life (this could have been her lecture on 'Eugenics and Abnormality', although she also lectured on 'Oscar Wilde: A Problem in Eugenics'). Certainly during her 1914 lecture tour of America she had already considerably startled many audiences by speaking of her own 'inversion', so this is certainly before November 1914. The letter concludes by Lees writing that 'I'm so thankful for these last ten years of lying low'.

The second of the letters is written in reply to Carpenter's response to her first. Among other matters, she says that 'I've had a vision — as clear & inspiring as ever St Paul had & it's just altered everything for me'; she also discusses how she thought the gossip got out, and her feelings for the woman, now dead, she had been overwhelmingly in love with.[8]

Interpreting these letters is difficult, not least because they do not directly pronounce on the claims made on her behalf by Ellis and by Faderman. However, it is clear that Edith Lees herself definitely thinks that she is an 'invert', was startled to be questioned but responded through public statement about her 'inversion', and is grateful for ten years of 'lying low'. Edith Lees wrote to Carpenter because they shared 'inversion' and Alice's questioning concerned them both. She responded to Alice's 'accusation' not only by writing that '*if* it is true it wd be sheer purity & sweetness to me and so for *me* the best the world cd have for me', but also by publicly speaking about her sexuality. I certainly prefer to accept what Edith Lees says about herself than either what Ellis claims concerning his creation of her as a lesbian or Faderman's acceptance of Ellis's claims.

In addition to the Edith Lees material, there is a group of letters in the Carpenter Archive[9] written to Carpenter after publication of *The Intermediate Sex* in 1908 which throw an additional light upon the question of the 'invention' of the sexualized and mannish lesbian through sexologists' morbidification of love between women. They were sent between July 1913 and March 1925; and, as there are many letters from gay men in the Archive, it is likely that Carpenter received more from women but only these have survived.

On 21 July 1913 AT[10] wrote Carpenter a detailed letter about her 'condition'. Against the backdrop of the women's movement and the possibility of women gaining financial and thus familial independence, AT outlines her first memories, of wanting to wear boys' clothes and doing so in secret; her attempts to end her 'unnatural life' in marriage but her engagement accentuating her feelings for women; her thwarted wish for a career; and her duty fixed at caring for her mother. The women who attract AT are gentle and 'feminine' and have 'that wonderful maternal instinct'; and she expresses her relations with women as 'masculine' and feels 'a deference for them as women'. She loved and lost one woman, and then in her late thirties met 'the woman of my dreams', who reciprocated her great love even though because of joint family commitments they could not live together. However, six years later, and a month before the letter was written, this woman became engaged following her family's sudden loss of income and consequent inability to maintain her at home. AT sadly states her 'agony of suffering' and her 'unspeakable loss' of the woman she considered her wife and the 'mother of my children'.

On 25 October 1915 KO wrote to Carpenter that her reading of *The Intermediate Sex* had made it clear 'that I myself belong to that class', it 'made everything fall into place'. KO outlines her 'horrible loneliness' and need to meet other like-minded women: she is a feminist and in touch with many other feminist women, and 'the average woman does not easily attract me'. KO writes that a letter to a feminist newspaper[11] about her spinsterhood and rejection of marriage brought sixteen replies and with one of these women she has become friends; indeed, although this woman is 'absolutely normal' she gave KO *The Intermediate Sex*. KO is also in correspondence with two women who are physically lovers and longs to meet 'my other half' (a reference to Plato's *Symposium*). KO says she felt no physical desire until she was 28 (two years before), but she had felt a strong desire to kiss and fondle one woman she was in love with, apparently seeing kissing and fondling and desire as different.

On 19 August 1921 EC wrote to Carpenter, having consulted her friend Charles Lazenby who in turn consulted Havelock Ellis who suggested a letter to Carpenter. She outlines her idea 'in my mind for some time of getting together a group of Uranian women to form the nucleus of a club' and asks for the names and addresses of any women he thinks 'would be glad of companionship'. EC notes that living in London she must perpetually come across like-minded women and she needs their companionship: she knows only too well the loneliness of her present situation. She is a 'pagan' and believes in the beauty of sex; and she portrays herself as 'not of the masculine type', being 'fairly evenly mixed male and female'. *The Intermediate Sex*, however, was a revelation to her: 'it was like being given sight'. She thanks Carpenter for what he has done to change society; and she now wants 'to do something however small to help with that work', for the more public recognition, the more consequent suppression there will be.

The last of the four letters was written on 16 March 1925 by BR, who, although 'physically a girl', chooses to call herself by a man's name. BR now teaches 'slum boys' in Derby, but at college two years before (she is now 21) she met a girl she was attracted to but thought wouldn't be interested in her. The girl later showed BR a letter of rejection from the girl who had been her lover for three years. Now BR and her friend have become lovers and will live together soon; and BR says that 'in almost every respect [she] is quite different from me — small, dainty & feminine'. BR and her lover met and remained in contact with six boys who are lovers 'like that' who they have talked to about their own situation.

None of these women mention the ideas of Havelock Ellis or any sexologist other than Carpenter. Carpenter himself discounted the 'inversion' theory of Ulrichs and Hirschfeld; his writing does however outline and discuss it. Ellis appears tangentially in EC's letter, but *not* as a source of ideas about 'Uranianism'. For each of these women it is reading Carpenter's work that acts 'like being given sight', 'a revelation', 'making everything fall into place'; and for KO in particular, although for the others in a different way, this enables her to give a name to, and thus gain a new understanding of, her longstanding feelings.

Three of these women, KO, EC and BR, are relatively open, albeit in different ways, about their 'inversion': BR by having a lover at 21 and being in contact with a group of gay men, EC by wanting to start a club for 'Uranian' women and to change public ideas about 'inversion', KO through feminism and the ability to be fairly open about her feelings and analyses with women who share her political stance. Only the older AT, in her mid-forties and of a more 'genteel' class, appears to locate her feelings within the framework of romantic friendship rather than of sexual as well as 'spiritual' responses to women. Nevertheless AT wrote to Carpenter, author of a book about homosexuality and known to be homosexual himself, and presumably would not have done so had she not construed her responses to women in similar terms. Indeed, the terms of her letter make this incontrovertible. Interestingly, KO is the only one of these women who appears not to have had some kind of conceptual or analytical appreciation of her feelings before reading Carpenter's work: she literally could not 'name' herself and her feelings, and only as she came to do so through debate with other feminists did she learn to experience desire itself.

At least two of these women, AT and BR, position themselves as unlike 'normal', i.e. 'feminine', women and correspondingly identify themselves as 'masculine', while EC sees herself as 'evenly mixed male and female'. Carpenter's conceptualization of 'homogenic love', 'comrade love', 'inversion', 'uranianism', the 'intermediate sex' (all terms used by him, sometimes critically) follows even where (as with 'inversion') it discounts the earlier pioneering work of Karl Heinrich Ulrichs in the 1860s. However, Magnus Hirschfeld and the Scientific Humanitarian Committee from 1897 on strongly promoted Ulrichs's theory of a 'third sex', of a literal inversion of one sex's mind with the other sex's body: the Committee's Yearbook, published from 1899 to 1923, was 'for Intermediate Sexual Types'.

It was in fact the work of these and other gay men as scientists of homosexuality, supported by many other gay men and women, that promoted the idea of 'inversion' and its accompanying 'mannish' lesbian and 'effeminate' gay male categories. Inversion offered an essentialist framework of understanding for many people whose self-experience accorded with it; but even for those who did not, it offered a powerful legitimating rhetoric to compel tolerance if not acceptance. Sexologists such as Krafft-Ebing (in fact a supporter of the early German homosexual rights movement) and Havelock Ellis (who counted a number of openly gay men among his closest friends) followed gay custom and practice, not the other way about. Thus AT, BR and EC position themselves both in relation to experiential feelings and responses and in relation to existing gay-derived conceptualizations of the 'homosexual condition'. Only KO, working within a feminist framework that in practice if not so clearly in theory challenged conventional ideas of 'feminine' and 'masculine', outlines her feelings without reference to 'inversion' and 'intermediacy'. It is therefore ironic indeed that she does so through a debate which Sheila Jeffreys (1985) sees as indicative of heterosexual oppressiveness towards 'spinsters' in general and tacitly towards lesbianism in particular within feminism of the time.[12]

Each of these women experienced themselves as 'different' in their attraction to women. Each of them experienced their difference 'pre-textually', in that Carpenter's work seems to have been the first writing on the subject they had come across, hence its powerful impact on them. For the women who experienced their feelings for women as 'masculine', this derived from a context in which the only difference possible from 'feminine' was 'masculine'. However, it is worth noting that the source of their 'masculine' feelings was longstanding and material: their everyday life and struggles to understand their place within it, *not* the imposition of theoretical ideas by patriarchal male sexologists.

Not surprisingly, these letters do not address in a direct way the terms of the 'romantic friendship v. lesbianism' debate as it has been constructed by present-day feminist theorists. However, they do suggest that the experience and expression of their feelings and desires differs between these four women; that those of them most influenced by Carpenter's writing understand their feelings within the framework of 'inversion'; and no other writing about 'inversion' or 'Uranianism' than Carpenter's is mentioned by any of them. Condemning sexology out of hand, as Faderman and Jackson appear to do, ignores the origins in gay writings of most of the key ideas and terms used within sexology. Such condemnation also sees sexology as deterministic of how lesbian women understood their lives and experiences and at best is simplistic and at worst dismisses what such women themselves said about their situations.

Pursuing Friendship, Recovering Lesbian History?

There is certainly a need to conceptualize women's historical patterns of friendship, as well as to record these. However, as I have shown, there are epistemological and other problems with the main feminist conceptualization of friendship. This not only sees friendship between women before the advent of sexology as a kind of paradise before a fall brought about by evil men, and accords far more power and influence to these men than they actually had, it also imposes on the past what are present-day definitions and understandings of friendship, love and sexuality. In addition, there are factual problems in relation to various of the examples used: there *was* an understanding that the Ladies of Llangollen were sapphists or lesbians among at least some of their friends and acquaintances, and some of their women friends *were* involved in genital sexual relations with each other; Edith Lees most certainly *did* see herself as an 'invert' and later in her life publicly lectured about her situation; and 'mannishness' *was* already existent in particular women's behaviours and identifications in the absence of a demonstrable influence on them of sexologists' pejorative writings about lesbianism.

Much of the feminist debate on romantic friendships of the past is concerned with recovering lesbian history from its present near-invisibility. This is an aim I wholeheartedly support; but it can also lead to a temporal chauvinism which assumes that women's relationships and behaviours have a meaning which has remained constant over the last 200 years or more. This is certainly insufficient. However, understanding these relationships in the terms they were understood by their protagonists is an impossibility: we now can *never* understand the past as it was understood by those who lived it. What is needed is a middle way, one which does not impose a theoretical structure on the lives and experiences of historical people, but which recognizes that love between women could take many shapes and meanings, one of which was an erotic genital sexual involvement which had meaning specific to these persons and their time and social location.

Teasing out these complexities can best be done through a combination of historical and biographical means, looking closely at particular lives and how these are intertwined with others in patterns of friendship within a particular milieu. However, there are two opposing tensions for those of us involved in constructing a lesbian history. There is the felt need to construct, quite literally, a history for ourselves: to be able to see that there were other women, something like us, who went before. But there is also the equal need to recognize that women's relationships in the past, like those of the present, were highly complex and multidimensional, and the label 'lesbian' or 'invert' or 'sapphist' or any other only very imperfectly fits them. For me, spelling out and confronting even if not solving these epistemological problematics is fundamental, for doing so is the bedrock on which a lesbian history — one which is neither crude recovery work, nor the denial of women's sexual relationships with each other, nor treated as a pale shadow of that of gay men — should be based.

Notes

1 The material discussed here appears in Stanley (1992). I am grateful to the British Academy for funding my research on Edith Lees, to Sheffield Public Library and to the Humanities Research Center (HRC) at the University of Texas at Austin. My thanks to Treva Broughton, Hilary Hinds, Celia Lury and David Morgan for comments on a previous incarnation of this piece of writing.

2 Hester Thrale Piozzi's manuscript diarists are in the John Rylands University of Manchester Library.

3 Located in the Archives Department of Sheffield Public Library.

4 Kate Salt with brother Jim Joynes and husband Henry Salt were involved in the Fellowship of the New Life, a 'simple life' socialist group through which they met Carpenter. The marriage of Kate Joynes and Henry Salt has been described as celibate (Marsh, 1986; Brandon, 1990) and Kate (including by George Bernard Shaw, an acquaintance) as a lesbian. In spite of this, and like Sheila Rowbotham (1977), I have found interpreting Kate Salt's letters to Edward Carpenter a good deal more complex than such certain statements by others suggest.

5 Despite Faderman's assumption, there is no clear evidence that this case history is that of Edith Lees; the grounds for the claim are circumstantial only. Strong circumstantial evidence to support my following argument also exists in an exchange of letters between Havelock Ellis and Radclyffe Hall and in fictional material written by Edith Lees herself, both held in the HRC.

6 These exist in the Carpenter Archive and are, in the order in which I discuss them, Carpenter Archive letters numbers 358.15 and 358.16.

7 Carpenter's pamphlet *Homogenic Love* . . . was published in 1894. A collection of essays, *Love's Coming-of-Age*, one of which was entitled 'The intermediate sex', was to have been published as Carpenter's response to the Oscar Wilde trial of 1895; pressures from the publisher forced the removal of this particular essay from the 1896 edition. The excised essay was, however, published in the 1906 second edition, and then with a group of related essays on gay themes it appeared in 1908 as *The Intermediate Sex*. After 1895 Carpenter's relative openness about his sexuality and increasing fame made him and his work a rallying point for other gay women and men.

8 Ellis refers to this woman as 'Lily' and suggests it occurred early in their marriage. There are major questions as to Ellis's reliability; and Edith Lees's papers and diaries appear to have been destroyed after her death. Ellis fails to mention except in pseudonyms any of Edith Lees's women friends, so tracing these relationships using other historical evidence is not possible.

9   Carpenter Archive letters numbers 386.218, 386.262, 386.355 and 386.409 respectively in the order I discuss them.
10   I have used initials only for these four correspondents, as they wrote to Carpenter personal letters clearly not intended for other eyes.
11   This appeared in *The Freewoman*, published from November 1911 to October 1912, and was part of a controversy concerning 'the spinster' and her sexual and other status that appeared in its pages.
12   It was within this debate that KO contributed her letter to *The Freewoman*, a letter which put her in touch with the two feminist women who were lovers that her letter to Carpenter mentions.

References

ALBERTI, JOHANNA (1990) 'Inside Out: Elizabeth Haldane as a Women's Suffrage Survivor in the 1920s and 1930s', *Women's Studies International Forum*, 13, pp. 117–26.
ALTMAN, DENNIS *et al.* (1989) *Which Homosexuality? Essays from the International Scientific Conference on Gay and Lesbian Studies*, London, Gay Men's Press.
BOSWELL, JOHN (1991) 'Revolutions, Universals, and Sexual Categories' in DUBERMAN, MARTIN BAUML, VICINUS, MARTHA and CHAUNCEY, GEORGE, JR. (Eds) *Hidden From History: Reclaiming the Gay and Lesbian Past*, London, Penguin, pp. 17–36.
BRANDON, RUTH (1990) *The New Women and The Old Men: Love, Sex and The Woman Question*, London, Secker and Warburg.
CAINE, BARBARA (1986) *Destined To Be Wives: The Sisters of Beatrice Webb*, Oxford, Clarendon Press.
CARPENTER, EDWARD (1883) *Towards Democracy*, London, Allen and Unwin.
CARPENTER, EDWARD (1894) *Homogenic Love and its Place in a Free Society*, Manchester, Manchester Labour Press Society Ltd.
CARPENTER, EDWARD (1906) *Love's Coming-of-Age*, 2nd ed., London, Allen and Unwin.
CARPENTER, EDWARD (1908) *The Intermediate Sex*, London, Allen and Unwin.
CLAUS, RUTH (1977) 'Confronting Homosexuality: A Letter from Frances Wilder', *Signs*, 2, pp. 928–33.
DUBERMAN, MARTIN BAUML, VICINUS, MARTHA and CHAUNCEY, GEORGE, JR. (Eds) (1991) *Hidden From History: Reclaiming the Gay and Lesbian Past*, London, Penguin.
ELLIS, HAVELOCK (1897) *Sexual Inversion*, London, Wilson and Macmillan (later republished in 1915 as *Studies in Sex Psychology, Vol. II*, Philadelphia, F.A. Davis).
ELLIS, HAVELOCK (1940) *My Life*, London, Heinemann.
FADERMAN, LILLIAN (n.d., but 1981) *Surpassing the Love of Men*, London, Junction Books.
FADERMAN, LILLIAN (1983) *Scotch Verdict: Miss Pirie and Miss Woods v. Dame Cumming Gordon*, New York, Quill.
FUSS, DIANA (1989) *Essentially Speaking: Feminism, Nature and Difference*, London, Routledge.
HALL CARPENTER ARCHIVES (1989) *Inventing Ourselves: Lesbian Life Stories*, London, Routledge.
HALPERIN, DAVID (1991) 'Sex Before Sexuality: Pederasty, Politics, and Power in Classical Athens', in DUBERMAN, MARTIN BAUML, VICINUS, MARTHA and CHAUNCEY, GEORGE, JR. (Eds) *Hidden From History: Reclaiming the Gay and Lesbian Past*, London, Penguin, pp. 37–53.
JACKSON, MARGARET (1984) 'Sex Research and the Construction of Sexuality: A Tool of Male Supremacy?', *Women's Studies International Forum*, 7, pp. 43–52.
JEFFREYS, SHEILA (1985) *The Spinster and Her Enemies: Feminism and Sexuality 1880–1930*, London, Pandora.

LESBIAN HISTORY GROUP (1989) *Not a Passing Phase: Reclaiming Lesbians in History 1840–1985*, London, Women's Press.

LEVINE, PHILIPPA (1990) 'Love, Friendship and Feminism in Later Nineteenth Century England', *Women's Studies International Forum*, 13, pp. 63–78.

MARSH, JAN (1986) *Jane and May Morris: A Biographical Story 1839–1938*, London, Pandora.

MAVOR, ELIZABETH (1971) *The Ladies of Llangollen*, Harmondsworth, Penguin.

NEWTON, ESTHER (1984) 'The Mythic Mannish Lesbian: Radclyffe Hall and the New Woman', *Signs*, 9, pp. 557–75.

OLDFIELD, SYBIL (1984) *Spinsters of This Parish*, London, Virago.

PADGUG, ROBERT DAVID (1991) 'Sexual Matters: Rethinking Sexuality in History', in DUBERMAN, MARTIN BAUML, VICINUS, MARTHA and CHAUNCEY, GEORGE, JR. (Eds) *Hidden From History: Reclaiming the Gay and Lesbian Past*, London, Penguin, pp. 54–64.

RILEY, DENISE (1988) *'Am I That Name?' Feminism and the Category of 'Women' in History*, London, Macmillan.

ROWBOTHAM, SHEILA (1977) 'Edward Carpenter', in ROWBOTHAM, SHEILA and WEEKS, JEFF, *Socialism and the New Life*, London, Pluto, pp. 27–138.

SMITH-ROSENBERG, CARROLL (1975) 'The Female World of Love and Ritual: Relations Between Women in Nineteenth-Century America', *Signs*, 1, pp. 1–29.

SPELMAN, ELIZABETH V. (1988) *Inessential Woman*, London, Women's Press.

STANLEY, LIZ (1985) 'Feminism and Friendship: Two Essays on Olive Schreiner', *Studies in Sexual Politics*, No. 8, University of Manchester, Sociology Department.

STANLEY, LIZ (1988) *The Life and Death of Emily Wilding Davison*, London, Women's Press.

STANLEY, LIZ (1992) *The Auto/Biographical I: The Theory and Practice of Feminist Auto/Biography*, Manchester, Manchester University Press.

THOMPSON, TIERL (Ed.) (1987) *Dear Girl: The Diaries and Letters of Two Working Women*, London, Women's Press.

VICINUS, MARTHA (1985) *Independent Women: Work and Community for Single Women, 1850–1920*, London, Virago.

VICINUS, MARTHA (1989) ' "They Wonder to Which Sex I Belong": The Historical Roots of the Modern Lesbian Identity', in ALTMAN, DENNIS *et al.*, *Which Homosexuality? Essays from the International Scientific Conference on Gay and Lesbian Studies*, London, Gay Men's Press, pp. 171–98.

VICINUS, MARTHA (1991) 'Distance and Desire: English Boarding School Friendships, 1870–1920', in DUBERMAN, MARTIN BAUML, VICINUS, MARTHA and CHAUNCEY, GEORGE, JR. (Eds) *Hidden From History: Reclaiming the Gay and Lesbian Past*, London, Penguin, pp. 212–29.

WHITBREAD, HELENA (Ed.) (1988) *The Diaries of Anne Lister 1791–1840*, London, Virago Press.

Chapter 15

Gender and the Labour Market: Old Theory for New?

Lisa Adkins and Celia Lury

Introduction

This chapter explores the relationship between gender and the labour market, and, in particular, the notion that gender acts as a structuring principle in the labour market. It was, in part, prompted by the current view that some sectors of the labour market are being feminized (see for example Jenson, Hagen, and Reddy, 1988). The intended meaning of the term seems to us to be somewhat ill-defined, but its use is clearly more than simply an acknowledgment of the fact that women are increasingly active in the labour market. Rather, it refers to the set of processes which have led to an increase in the kinds of jobs which have traditionally been done by women — that is, rather than referring to the gender of the personnel employed, it is more usually used to refer to the gender of jobs in the labour market. The emergence of the term feminization is indicative of the increasing recognition accorded to this phenomenon, which in turn is related to the growth in the number of caring and servicing jobs, and their perceived significance for an understanding of contemporary economies. However, we would suggest that the gendering of jobs has had a more long-term significance than the current emphasis on feminization would suggest. In other words, we would like to consider the possibility that feminization is the latest stage of the gendering of the labour market rather than a radically new phenomenon.

Unfortunately, there seem to be few theoretical frameworks within which this phenomenon — the gendering of the labour market — can be investigated. Nevertheless, it was with this question in mind that we turned to the feminist literature on the labour market, taking as our starting point the publication of 'The Unhappy Marriage of Marxism and Feminism: A Debate on Class and Patriarchy' in 1981. This collection of essays promoted the analysis of the labour market as a privileged site for feminist investigations of gender divisions. It simultaneously foregrounded men's control of women's labour in the labour market as the material basis of patriarchy and challenged the unthinking application of marxist categories to the analysis of women's oppression. The lead article in the collection, to which all the others responded, is 'The Unhappy Marriage of Marxism and Feminism' by Heidi Hartmann. She started her article with an elaboration of the metaphor which she employed in the title:

> The 'marriage' of marxism and feminism has been like the marriage of
> husband and wife depicted in English common law: marxism and feminism
> are one, and that one is marxism. (Hartmann, 1981, p. 2)

She went on to argue that marxism and feminism should either work towards a
healthier marriage or get divorced.

Until the publication of this collection many of the theorists who argued for
a combination of patriarchal and capitalist principles in explanations of social
inequality theorized each as having a different institutional base and as being located
in different parts of the social structure. Thus some argued that capitalist relations
were operative in the paid labour market, while patriarchal relations were operative
in the sphere of 'reproduction' and the family (Barrett, 1980; Barrett and McIntosh,
1982; Mitchell, 1975). In this view, gender inequality is theorized as originating
in the sphere of 'reproduction', and is merely carried over into other social
institutions such as the labour market.

One of the most challenging aspects of Hartmann's work for marxist feminism — which previously had provided the dominant explanatory framework for
the analysis of gender divisions in the labour market — was her identification of
autonomous patriarchal relations within the labour market, and her argument that
these relations were the primary cause of women's oppression. This argument —
that the labour market was an autonomous site where gender divisions were
constructed — was supported by Sylvia Walby's work (1986). Walby pointed to
the strength of patriarchal agents, including trade unions, employers, and the state
in determining the pattern of women's employment in Britain between 1800 and
1945. Thus, as part of their analyses, both Hartmann and Walby argued for the
importance of patriarchal agents in the formation of occupational segregation,
which they saw as key in terms of an explanation of women's oppression.

The fundamental assumption which led to this concentration upon occupational segregation can be traced back to Hartmann's assertion that

> The material base upon which patriarchy rests lies most fundamentally in
> men's control over women's labor power. (Hartmann, 1981, p. 15)

More specifically it derives from her suggestion that while capitalism creates the
places for a hierarchy of workers, gender and racial hierarchies determine who fill
which places:

> Men maintain this control by excluding women from access to some
> essential productive resources (in capitalist societies, for example, jobs
> that pay living wages) and by restricting women's sexuality. (Hartmann,
> 1981, p. 15)

Thus, her emphasis on occupational segregation results from the conceptualization
of control in terms of exclusion of access to economic resources.

We wish to challenge both the view that occupational segregation is an outcome
of this form of control, and the assumption that control operates primarily in
terms of exclusion from economic resources. This assumption, we will suggest,
conflates the economic and the material. The persistence of this conflation, we
believe, is indicative of the continuing dominance of marxism within Hartmann's

analysis, which limits her ability to conceptualize other forms of gender inequality in the labour market.

We will develop this argument through a critical exploration of recent feminist work on gender and the labour market which builds upon this conclusion. We have taken *Gendered Jobs and Social Change* by Rosemary Crompton and Kay Sanderson (1990) as an example of such work for critical discussion for two reasons. Firstly, it seems to us to offer a number of new insights into the structuring of the labour market. Secondly, as we shall argue, the difficulties which the authors display in following through these insights seem to us to be symptomatic of the ill effects of the marriage between marxism and feminism as it continues to inform feminist study of the labour market.

The Gendered Dynamics of the Occupational Structure

In order to develop our argument, we will first present a brief account of the distinctive analysis of occupational segregation developed by Crompton and Sanderson. They propose an analytical framework which makes use of three broad assumptions. The first of these is that occupations are not standard units, but rather are organized in remarkably different ways. Secondly, in line with Giddens's structuration theory (Giddens, 1984) they suggest that the occupational structure is both the medium and the outcome of social acts; that is, they make explicit the duality of the occupational structure and the division of labour itself. In doing this, they employ Giddens's understanding of the recursive organization of structure, consciousness and action to look at changes in the structuring of occupations.

Thirdly, they challenge what they see as the monocausality of earlier explanations of divisions in the labour market. In particular, they criticize economically reductionist explanations which have focused upon the patriarchal control of women's labour, such as those of Hartmann and Walby. Such accounts, they argue, downplay the significance of non-economic processes with respect to the production of occupational segregation and gender itself. Instead, they stress the heterogeneity of inputs into occupational structuring, including what they describe as ideological or socio-cultural factors. In these ways, they are able to propose a dynamic model of the structuring of occupational segregation which incorporates a multi-factor conception of social change.

We contend, however, that in spite of claiming to offer new understandings of the gendered dynamics of the occupational structure, Crompton and Sanderson do not really do so. For their resulting analysis of the production of the gendered division of labour in relation to the occupations they study is highly pluralistic: a multitude of disparate processes are located as being involved in the formation and gendered constitution of particular occupations. The most problematic feature of their analysis from our point of view is that the structuring aspects of gender are highly diffused and dispersed amongst these processes. Where gender is seen to be of significance in terms of particular occupations, its importance is understood in terms of processes external to the labour market: in particular, processes which they locate as operating at an ideological level.

What is more, the actual significance of non-economic processes remains hazy: for example, 'economic behaviour' is argued to be generally 'constrained and influenced by "social" factors' (p. 38). Indeed, they suggest that certain 'beliefs' can, in certain unspecified conditions, produce a profound form of fatalism in women which is termed 'moral despotism'.[1] The use of this latter term contributes to what we shall argue is an overly voluntaristic notion of gender.

However, all this is not to say that we do not agree with their critique of Walby and Hartmann, for we do. Rather we take issue with the model of social formation Crompton and Sanderson employ for considering the significance of so-called non-economic processes, which we will suggest not only downplays the significance of such processes, but actually precludes the ability to recognize forms of gendered inequality and control which operate in the labour market, precisely because within this model such processes are not defined as economic. In conclusion, then, we shall argue that this pluralistic conceptualization of factors does little to move beyond previous understandings of the gendered dynamics of the labour market, and, indeed, in many ways, marks a regression in that such pluralism understates the significance of gender in the formation of occupations, occupational segregation, and forms of gendered inequality and exploitation.

Their downplaying of the significance of gender and this failure to theorize the significance of so-called non-economic processes is, we argue, a direct outcome of an unwillingness or inability to step outside a marxist paradigm.[2] There are two interrelated features of this conceptual framework which are particularly important in this respect: first, the use of a model of social formation which assumes an already fixed distinction between what is at times called the material and the normative and at other times called production and the cultural or ideological; and second, related to the first, the use of a purely economic understanding of the material or production.

The first feature — the use of a model of social formation which assumes a particular distinction between production and the cultural, is characteristic of much sociological as well as marxist analysis. Whilst the assumption of this model is widespread, its use is rarely acknowledged, let alone explicated. Yet it has two major drawbacks for feminist theory, the first of which is intrinsic to the model and the second of which is common but not inevitable. First, the model makes it difficult to theorize certain aspects of social life which feminists have always acknowledged to be important for an understanding of gender inequality, such as, for example, sexual violence. Second, it contributes to the tendency to locate certain aspects of that inequality in certain sites — such as, for example, the common implicit assumption that sexuality is primarily located in the domestic sphere (Barrett, 1980; Mitchell, 1975).

Before moving on to discuss the problems associated with the use of this framework in more detail, we want first to look more closely at some examples of the analysis of the structuration of occupations that Crompton and Sanderson present. In particular, we will discuss two occupations whose gendered characteristics, they argue, have been formed through non-economic gendered processes — pharmacy and the school meals service, and a set of occupations which they argue have been structured through non-gendered processes — namely, those within the hotel trade. In doing this, our aim is to, firstly, demonstrate the ways in which they fail to offer an adequate theorization of the significance of non-economic processes for understanding the gender dynamics of the labour market; and, secondly, to indicate the the ways in which they downplay gender in their analysis of these occupations. We will do this through both the use of conceptual argument and the introduction of some concrete material. Thirdly, we will begin to develop our critique of the model of social formation they use. We will suggest that it simply reproduces many of the characteristics of existing feminist analyses of gender divisions within the labour market, including those which they have criticized for economic reductionism.

In relation to the occupation of pharmacy, Crompton and Sanderson argue that ideologies of motherhood, in particular what they refer to as the moral despotism of motherhood, is the most significant factor for understanding the pattern of women's employment within the occupation. They suggest that it is responsible for women's movement in and out of the occupation in accordance with particular stages in their life cycles, and for patterns of women's part-time employment. In a similar vein, they suggest that for the school meals service, exclusive gender segregation and the gendered construction of the occupation can only be understood in terms of the normative stereotyping of the female role, in particular the maternal and caring aspects of this stereotype. In contrast, for the hotel trade, they argue that gender is not significant in terms of the distribution of labour. That is, they argue that whilst at the level of individual firms there may be high degrees of gender segregation, occupations within the trade have not been sex-typed. As a result, employers have increasingly substituted for women workers cheaper and more convenient forms of labour, such as young people. This strategy has, they argue, rendered the hotel trade indifferent to the sex of workers, particularly those within lower-level jobs.

Motherhood and the Gendering of the Labour Market

First, let us consider pharmacy. Here we see the location by Crompton and Sanderson of what they define as a non-economic gendered process as the key to understanding the gendered dynamics of the occupation. In particular, they argue that the ideological construction of motherhood, especially the promotion of beliefs which emphasized the responsibility of individual mothers for the welfare of children, resulted in a moral despotism of motherhood which had significant effects in terms of women's participation rates within pharmacy. For example, they suggest that during the post-war period,

> messages being received by women regarding work and employment were contradictory. On the one hand, slow moves were in progress towards their treatment (in principle) as equal 'citizens' in the market place. On the other, mothers (and most women are actual or potential mothers) were being told that their real work lay at home in caring for children. (Crompton and Sanderson, 1990, p. 52)

The actual effects of 'motherhood' in terms of women's participation rates within the labour market are here seen to take place at an ideological level. More particularly, it is the contradictions between the ideologies of citizenship and motherhood which Crompton and Sanderson see to be the key to understanding women's position within pharmacy. Both these ideologies are seen to originate and operate outside the labour market; in particular they suggest that the ideology of motherhood is produced within the family.

A similar analysis is put forward in relation to the school meals service: Crompton and Sanderson assert that gender segregation is the result of normative stereotyping of the female role. This stereotyping is seen to function through processes external to the labour market, and to operate in terms of its effects at an ideological level. This ideological stereotyping is once again seen to be produced within the family. In terms of the occupation, this stereotyping is argued to produce occupational segregation because women are devoted to caring for children (the consumers of the services they produce). So firm is the grasp of this moral despotism that women within this occupation are seen to have a capacity for 'self-exploitation' (Crompton and Sanderson, 1990, p. 146).

Here we note the voluntarism of Crompton and Sanderson's theorization of gender inequality and exploitation within the labour market: women workers within the school meals service are positioned as responsible for their own exploitation. We would contest such a voluntaristic interpretation of the formation of gender inequalities, and suggest that whilst caring is a characteristic of the occupation, it is not an outcome of women willingly carrying out this work because they have picked up ideas about their roles as mothers in the family. Surely the massive concentration of women workers within occupations that are defined as caring, and the conditions within these occupations, cannot reasonably be reduced to women workers producing these conditions themselves? Rather, we would suggest that caring comes to be a characteristic of occupations, including the school meals service, because of the relations of production in which women exist in relation to men, where the exploitation and appropriation of labour which defines this relationship includes that of caring labour.

To support this argument we would draw on the work of Adrienne Rich (1977) to suggest that the post-war institutionalization of motherhood was operating both in the home *and* in the labour market. If the institution of motherhood is understood as a set of social relations within which caring labour is exploited, it can be conceptualized as a structuring process of gender, which is not confined to the domestic sphere, but is also in operation within the labour market. As such, it can be considered to be potentially not only constitutive of occupations but also, in part, produced in the labour market.

Arlie Hochschild's (1983) work on airline stewardesses, as an example of an occupation which is defined as 'caring' and whose places are overwhelmingly filled by women, is a point in case for the argument that this process was indeed operative in the formation of some occupations in the post-war period. Here she shows that from the 1950s onwards the most outstanding feature of this occupation has been that of the forms of emotional labour which the stewardesses carry out in relation to customers, and in particular to male customers; a form of work which she parallels to the work of motherhood. Importantly she shows that far from this labour being freely carried out by women workers, performing this kind of work was, and remains, a condition of employment for the stewardesses. Thus, her work reveals that during the post-war period the work of women stewardesses within the occupation was increasingly constituted by emotional labouring, a constitution which was produced within the labour market in the sense that carrying out such work came to form a condition of being a stewardess. This shift in the work of being a stewardess can be interpreted as a process of the institutionalization of motherhood occuring *inside* the labour market, through which the exploitation of emotional or caring labour came not only to increasingly both constitute and define the occupation, but to act as a structuring aspect of gender in the sense that it was productive of gendered inequality.

Sexuality and the Gendering of the Labour Market

Finally, we want to consider Crompton and Sanderson's analysis of jobs in the hotel trade. As we have already mentioned, they argue with respect to the hotel trade that whilst gender segregation may be in place at the level of the firm, employer strategies in relation to lower-level occupations mean that these occupations are not sex-typed. Indeed, they suggest that employers are indifferent to the gender of the labour they use in low-level occupations within the trade. They support this argument by pointing to the increasing number of young people employed in the trade. This, they suggest, is the case in spite of extensive gender stereotypes which exist in relation to occupations within the trade such as the glamorous barmaid. However, the claim that employers are indifferent to the gender of the labour they employ is one which we want to dispute.

Within the trade the forms of gender segregation in terms of occupations themselves may indeed differ from firm to firm, but this is not enough of a basis on which to claim that gender does not structure the distribution of labour. This claim assumes that 'young people' are an ungendered category of workers, an assumption which we think is misplaced. Thus, we do not agree that this finding is a sufficient basis to imply, as Crompton and Sanderson do, that women workers are no less exploited than male workers within the trade's occupations.

In contrast to Crompton and Sanderson's analysis, Lisa Adkins's (1991) research into hotel and leisure companies suggests that gender is of central significance for understanding the distribution of labour within the trade's occupations. This research suggests that for women to be workers in this section of the labour market carrying out forms of sexual work is compulsory. So, for example, forms of sexual servicing, such as looking and being sexually attractive, and 'coping' with sexual harassment, are compulsory. The compulsory nature of such work is produced through the reduction of women to sex-objects, a position which forms a condition of employment for women workers. Women workers are, for example, expelled from the labour market for resisting forms of sexual harassment both from male customers and male co-workers, or for refusing to wear sexually degrading uniforms.

Importantly, because women workers in these occupations are defined, and indeed exist, within the workplace as sex-objects, they come to be located in a structurally less powerful position than male workers. For instance, Adkins found that the consistent criteria operating in relation to occupations in which women were clustered in different workplaces related exclusively to attractiveness. In contrast, for occupations in which men were clustered the criteria existed at the level of individual occupations, and were often related to specific occupational skills. The point here is that men can link themselves to specific occupations in a way that women never can. Women's access to specific occupational resources is continually undermined because of their location as sex-objects. As part of this process of objectification, the single and compulsory criterion for employment is attractiveness, and furthermore this is naturalized; that is, attractiveness is assumed to be a quality intrinsic to women themselves rather than a socially achieved criterion. In this set of occupations, women workers cannot, therefore, compete equally with men, as they are not labour market actors in the same way that men are.

At this point we want to return to the issue of Crompton and Sanderson's use of structuration theory where the occupational structure is seen to be both medium and outcome of social acts. Earlier we mentioned that Crompton and Sanderson's use of this framework is problematic in that they assume a neutral or ungendered relation between → *structure* → *consciousness* → *action*; that is, they assume that all social actors share the same relation to → *structure* → *consciousness* → *action*. Adkins's analysis of the hotel and leisure occupations shows that such an assumption denies the ways in which men and women have qualitatively different relations to this process of structuration. In particular, the ability of women workers to be active subjects within the labour market is limited by the position that women workers occupy, in that to be subjects (or workers in this case) women have to be objects, and thus forfeit the capacity to acquire labour market resources. Men, in contrast, can be labour market actors in a different way in that their subject status is not undermined by such an object status (although it is by no means unlimited).

The different relation that men and women have to action means that whilst women are an integral part of the occupational structure, the structure itself can be determined by the actions of male workers in a way that it simply cannot be by female workers. The inability of women workers to determine the occupational structure in the same way as men is exemplified within the leisure companies Adkins looked at, where women's position as objects meant that men could have a monopoly of 'skills' and labour market resources, and therefore help determine the gender constitution of occupations. It is this, we would suggest, which might help explain the women's failure to take industrial action in the case discussed by Crompton and Sanderson, rather than their willingness to make sacrifices 'for the sake of the children'. In sum, we are arguing that men and women have a different relation to the processes of → *structure* → *consciousness* → *action* which we think is an outcome of gendered relations of production.

This leads us to the second major point we want to make. In Adkins's research, it is argued that the social relations of sexuality, and in particular the exploitation of sexual labour within this, are central to an understanding of the gender dynamics of these occupations. Further, Adkins's analysis also suggests that these relations are, in part, produced within the labour market. Importantly, 'sexuality', as is also the case with 'motherhood', would be defined as non-economic, and as ideological within existing marxist and socialist feminist analyses of the labour market.

Clearly we think that both 'sexuality' and 'motherhood' are neither wholly ideological or exogenous to the labour market. Rather, we suggest that the exploitation and control of women's labour within these sets of relations is thoroughly implicated in the ways in which occupations are constituted. We think that Crompton and Sanderson's failure to theorize the significance of 'non-economic' processes and their specificity in the formation of gender divisions is a consequence of their insistence that factors such as motherhood and sexuality are produced outside the labour market and only have a bearing on the labour market at an ideological level. In other words, the problem can be traced back to the model of social formation they use and the assumption that certain aspects of gender inequality are produced, or located, within specific social sites.

This framework and the assumptions within it derive from marxist feminist attempts to theorize women's oppression in terms of the relations of capitalism. Crompton and Sanderson's insistence on, for example, ideologies of motherhood being produced in the family, stems directly from the conventional assumption in marxist feminist analyses that gender divisions are functional for capital in terms of the reproduction of labour power (Beechey, 1978, 1982; Bruegel, 1982). The feminist debate about whether such arguments rely upon a biologism (Leonard, 1984; Friedman, 1982) is simply ignored by Crompton and Sanderson. Similarly, the argument that the exploitation of workers within the hotel trade need only be understood in relation to employers' searches for cheaper sources of labour derives from the assumption that the only real, that is, material, exploitation is that produced by the social relations of the capitalist mode of production, a position which all manner of feminist theorists have challenged (Delphy, 1984; Guillaumin, 1981a, 1981b; Walby, 1986, 1990; Hartmann, 1979, 1981).

Conclusions

In our view, it is remarkable, given the manner in which the marxist paradigm has been deeply problematized by feminist theorizing, that many of its terms are accepted unproblematically. This, moreover, is not simply a characteristic of Crompton and Sanderson's analysis, but is typical of much recent feminist work on the labour market. Even those who recognize that material exploitation is not simply reducible to the capitalist mode of production (Walby, 1990; Hartmann, 1979; Bradley, 1989) still assume that particular areas of women's oppression (sexuality, 'culture') are produced outside the labour market, and that they only have effect in the labour market at an ideological level.

Moreover, such analyses, although recognizing the existence of forms of patriarchal control of women's labour within the labour market, define this control as material only in as much as these forms of control can be related to waged labour, that is, in terms of men's control over women's access to wages, or in access to occupational places. Thus, the dynamics of material relations are implicitly assumed to be determined by an ungendered economic, or capital as it has conventionally been conceptualized. In this way, the conflation of the economic and the material which characterized Hartmann's initial formulation is reproduced.

This, we think, is a fatal error in terms of understanding what constitutes material relations, for, as our examples in relation to sexuality and motherhood have shown, we would argue that the forms of gendered material exploitation which are operative in the labour market are not solely connected to the control of women's access to wages and jobs. Limiting the understanding of the material to the economic in this way leads as we have seen in the case of Crompton and Sanderson to some fairly ad hoc explanations when so-called non-economic processes are considered. The conflation of the material with the economic within Crompton and Sanderson's analysis also leads them to make the problematic assumption that all social actors have the same relation to processes of structuration, precisely because the structures, and therefore forms of consciousness and action, which are defined as being in existence are those which have been identified in relation to the (ungendered) economic. The argument put forward here is that when material relations are not taken to mean marxist-defined economic relations, the locations that men and women occupy in relation to occupational structuration may be seen to be very different.

Our analysis suggests that the continuing dominance of marxism within feminist debates around women's position in the labour market indicates that the 'unhappy marriage' of marxism and feminism is alive and kicking. It further suggests that the continuation of this marriage seriously limits the ability to theorize forms of gender inequality and exploitation operating in the labour market. Most importantly, we have argued that marxism informs three related assumptions to be found in many of the recent attempts to theorize the gender dynamics of the labour market: (1) an unproblematic acceptance of the distinction between production and ideology and the understanding of certain aspects of gender inequality as ideological; (2) the assumption that certain aspects of gender inequality are produced or primarily located within certain sites; and (3) the assumption that material sets of social relations are derivative of the dynamics of an ungendered capitalist mode of production. In the light of the problems that these assumptions generate we recommend nothing other than the divorce of marxism and feminism.

We hope we have begun to develop an explanation of the structuring of the labour market which does not employ these assumptions, but rather draws on aspects of feminist theory formulated elsewhere to develop an analysis of the labour market which recognizes the structuring force of gender. However, we recognize that further analysis of the position of Black women in the labour market is necessary in order to fully understand both the process of gendering and how race acts as a structuring principle. In terms of understanding the dynamics of the labour market we think our analysis points to the conclusion that men and women participate in the labour market within qualitatively different relations of production. These relations mean that not only is what is conventionally seen as the economic labour of women controlled and exploited, but also their sexual and caring labour. Moreover, we think that these relations of production have substantial implications for understanding the ways in which the labour market is organized, and for an understanding of occupational segregation more generally. In addition, we believe that such a framework provides a possible basis from which to investigate the phenomenon of feminization as an example of a shift in the gendering of the labour market, and that, more generally, it enables a way of understanding the labour market as a gendered entity.

Notes

We would like to thank Ann Phoenix, Jackie Stacey, and John Urry for their helpful comments on an earlier version of this paper.

1 This is a term derived from Lockwood's discussion of the concept of fatalism (Lockwood, 1982). He makes a distinction between conditional fatalism, stemming from a person's recognition that he or she is in the grip of circumstances beyond the control of any single individual, and moral despotism, where fatalism results from the individual's socialization into an ideology that provides a comprehensive account which explains the circumstances in question.
2 The interpretation of marxism which we go on to discuss is often implicit, and consequently is not commonly subject to debate. Obviously other understandings of marxism might not have resulted in the problems we identify; nevertheless, what is important for our argument is that this particular interpretation of marxism came to be dominant in feminist analyses of the division of labour.

References

ADKINS, L. (1991) 'Sexual Work and Family Production: A Study of the Gender Division of Labour in the Contemporary British Tourist Industry', unpublished PhD thesis, Department of Sociology, University of Lancaster.

BARRETT, M. (1980) *Women's Oppression Today: Problems in Marxist Feminist Analysis*, London, Verso.

BARRETT, M. and MCINTOSH, M. (1982) *The Anti-Social Family*, London, Verso.

BEECHEY, V. (1978) 'Women and Production: A Critical Analysis of Some Sociological Theories of Women's Work', in KUHN, A. and WOLPE, A. (Eds) *Feminism and Materialism: Women and Modes of Production*, London, Longman.

BEECHEY, V. (1982) 'Some Notes on Female Waged Labour in Capitalist Production', in EVANS, M. (Ed.) *The Woman Question: Readings on the Subordination of Women*, Oxford, Oxford University Press.

BRADLEY, H. (1989) *Men's Work, Women's Work: A Sociological History of the Sexual Division of Labour in Employment*, Cambridge, Polity.

BRUEGEL, I. (1982) 'Women as a Reserve Army of Labour: A Note on the Recent British Experience', in WHITELEGG, E. *et al.* (Eds) *The Changing Experience of Women*, Oxford, Martin Robertson/Open University.

CROMPTON, R. and SANDERSON, K. (1990) *Gendered Jobs and Social Change*, London, Unwin Hyman.

DELPHY, C. (1984) *Close to Home: A Materialist Analysis of Women's Oppression*, London, Hutchinson.

FRIEDMAN, S. (1982) 'The Marxist Paradigm: Radical Feminist Theorists Compared', paper given to British Sociological Association.

GIDDENS, A. (1984) *The Constitution of Society*, Cambridge, Polity.

GUILLAUMIN, C. (1981a) 'The Practice of Power and Belief in Nature, Part I: The Appropriation of Women', *Feminist Issues*, 1, 2.

GUILLAUMIN, C. (1981b) 'The Practice of Power and Belief in Nature, Part II: The Naturalist Discourse', *Feminist Issues*, 1, 3.

HARTMANN, H. (1979) 'Capitalism, Patriarchy and Job Segregation by Sex', in EISENSTEIN, Z.R. (Ed.) *Capitalist Patriarchy and the Case for Socialist Feminism*, New York, Monthly Review Press.

HARTMANN, H. (1981) 'The Unhappy Marriage of Marxism and Feminism: Towards a More Progressive Union', in SARGENT, L. (Ed.) *The Unhappy Marriage of Marxism and Feminism: A Debate on Class and Patriarchy*, London, Pluto.

HOCHSCHILD, A. (1983) *The Managed Heart: The Commercialization of Human Feeling*, Berkeley, University of California Press.

JENSON, J., HAGEN, E. and REDDY, C. (Eds) (1988) *Feminization of the Labour Force: Paradoxes and Promises*, Cambridge, Polity.

LEONARD, D. (1984) 'The Origin of the Family, Private Property and Socialist Feminism?', *Trouble and Strife*, 3.

LOCKWOOD, D. (1982) 'Fatalism: Durkheim's Hidden Theory of Order', in GIDDENS, A. and MACKENZIE, D. (Eds) *Social Class and the Division of Labour*, Cambridge, Cambridge University Press.

MITCHELL, J. (1975) *Psychoanalysis and Feminism*, Harmondsworth, Penguin.

RICH, A. (1977) *Of Woman Born: Motherhood as Experience and Institution*, London, Virago.

SARGENT, L. (Ed.) (1981) *The Unhappy Marriage of Marxism and Feminism: A Debate on Class and Patriarchy*, London, Pluto.

WALBY, S. (1986) *Patriarchy at Work: Patriarchal and Capitalist Relations in Employment*, Cambridge, Polity.

WALBY, S. (1990) *Theorizing Patriarchy*, Oxford, Basil Blackwell.

Chapter 16

Dialogic Theory and Women's Writing

Lynne Pearce

Their strength is the way they know each other, the wordless sensitivity
that has grown between them; a private language constructed to express
their connection with each other and their separation from the authorities:
puns, quotations, riddles, Cockney. They laugh when no-one else does,
because of the exquisite meanings they can give to events which seem
banal to everyone else. Every act, and every movement, they translate
and share, looking at one another secretly, waving private flags. (Roberts,
1978, p. 49)

The 'private language' enjoyed by Julie and Jenny in Michèle Roberts's *A Piece of
the Night* signals the focus of my concerns in this article: namely, the way in which
much contemporary women's writing is involved in the waving of 'private flags'.
I shall be suggesting how some of the key concepts of Mikhail Bakhtin's dialogic
theory can be used as a springboard to understand the gendered exclusivity of
address that exists in literature by and for women; the dialogic intimacy represented
both by female locutors and interlocutors within the text, and between the text
and the ('female') reader (i.e., the reader 'positioned as female').[1] I shall propose
that this dynamic might help us to re-specify what we mean by 'women's writing'
and/or 'feminist writing': texts written not only *by women*, but more especially
written *for them*. Such discussion will lead me, hopefully open-eyed, into a quagmire
of essentialist definitions: treacherous ground in these postmodern times, but
inescapable for those of us who continue to teach courses on 'women authors', or,
indeed, to make the sex of the author a criterion of choice in our private reading.

Bakhtin and the Dialogic

As Michael Holquist points out in his recent introductory book on Bakhtin,
'dialogism' was a term 'never used by Bakhtin himself' (Holquist, 1990, p. 15).
Instead, it must be seen as a convenient epistemological 'catch-all' coined by his
Anglo-American followers in an attempt to conceptualize the notion of *reciprocity*
central to all his writings about language, literature, and what Holquist has called
'the modern history of thinking about thinking' (Holquist, 1990, p. 15). Allowing,
then, for the fact that all we now include under the umbrella of dialogic theory

is, in effect, a broad inference of Bakhtin's own writings, I shall attempt through some selected quotations to convey a sense of the basic principles.

The following extract from the 1929 text *Marxism and the Philosophy of Language* (sometimes attributed to Bakhtin's co-author Voloshinov), provides one of the most suggestive starting points:

> A word is a bridge thrown between myself and another. If one end of the
> bridge belongs to me, then the other depends on my addressee. A word
> is a territory shared by both addresser and addressee, by the speaker and
> his [sic] interlocutor. (Bakhtin/Voloshinov, 1986, pp. 85–6)

We see from this that Bakhtin's notion of dialogue is, at one level, extremely literal: it is predicated upon the everyday occurrence of two people conversing. What interests Bakhtin in such exchange, however, is the power of the addressee in determining the words of the speaker: each word, as he notes elsewhere, is 'directly, blatantly, oriented towards a future answer word' (Bakhtin, 1981, p. 280).

For some literary theorists, the fact that Bakhtinian dialogue has its roots in a model of spoken language has been seen as a problem; they have doubted that a model so firmly grounded in the concrete analysis of 'speech-acts' can bear much relevance to the conditions of dialogue in literary texts.[2] It is true, indeed, that Bakhtin's own accounts of dialogic activity frequently fail to register a difference between the written and the spoken word, but much of his analysis *is* concerned specifically with the written word.

His account of 'doubly-voiced discourse' in *Problems of Dostoevsky's Poetics*, for example, proposes that 'dialogic relationships are possible not only among whole utterances' but 'toward an individual word, if that word is perceived not as the impersonal word of speech but as a sign of someone else's semantic position' (Bakhtin, 1984, pp. 184–5). From this perspective, he shows how the individual words of literary works will frequently betray the controlling presence of another text. This will sometimes take the form of a stylization or parody of the other text or, in certain circumstances, give rise to the *active* category of exchange which Bakhtin called 'hidden polemic'.[3] In *Problems of Dostoevsky's Poetics*, Bakhtin cites Dostoevsky's own *Notes from the Underground* as an example of a text in which the narrator's words are frequently in 'hidden polemic' with censorious 'answer words' not present in the text itself. It is, indeed, the recasting of words and discourses as dynamic sites of reciprocal exchange, rather than fixed semantic positions, that makes Bakhtin's model so exciting for the literary critic: a sentiment summed up in Bakhtin's own observation:

> Within the arena of . . . every utterance an intense conflict between one's
> own and another's word is being fought out. . . . The utterance so
> conceived is a considerably more complex and dynamic organism than it
> appears when consumed simply as a thing that articulates the intention of
> the person uttering it. (Clark and Holquist, 1984, p. 220)

One final point needs to be made here concerning the ambiguous nature of the 'addressee' in Bakhtin's writings: namely, the way in which the interlocutor inside the text is frequently conflated with the reader outside it. While there may be problems with this in terms of theoretical agency (Hirschkop and Shepherd, 1989, pp. 92–3) (i.e. the reader is an active participant in the creation of 'meaning'; the textual addressee, a mere 'actualizer'), one finds that in practice there is frequently an elision between the two positions.[4] I want to move on now to illustrate this point, and the dialogic interaction between speaker and addressee in general, through some specific textual examples.

'I' as a Function of 'We': The Relationship Between Speaker and Addressee in Contemporary Women's Fiction[5]

One of two recent books (see also Bauer, 1989) to specifically address themselves to the relationship between feminism and dialogic theory is Ann Herrmann's *The Dialogic and Difference: 'An/Other Woman' in Virginia Woolf and Christa Wolf* (1989). In a fascinating comparison of the two writers, Herrmann shows that where Woolf's texts always have one ear pointed towards an adversarial male (a graphic instance of Bakhtin's 'hidden polemic'), Wolf casts hers as a sympathetic female 'ally'. She writes:

> The rhetorical difference [i.e. the difference between Woolf and Wolf] lies in the difference of the addressee; Woolf constructs her addressee as *antagonist*, whose otherness is attributed to difference in gender and class. Wolf constructs her interlocutor as ally, as someone who mirrors her own point of view . . . for [Christa Wolf] any construction of the subject implies the inclusion of another subjectivity as a way of guarding against objectification. (Herrmann, 1989, p. 43)

Although, according to Bakhtin/Voloshinov writing in 'Discourse in Life and Discourse in Poetry', this is only one of the relationships that may be held by the two parties, it is, he concedes, the most familiar one: 'Speaking figuratively, the listener is normally found *next to* the author as his [sic] ally' (Shukman, 1983, p. 24). Similarly, although all writing by women certainly does not position the reader as an ally (we have already seen the case of Virginia Woolf, for example), I would suggest that that which we would wish to call 'feminist' invariably does. In contemporary women's fiction, moreover, that comradeship — that sense of 'community' — has frequently been brought to metafictional consciousness. Marge Piercy's novel, *Small Changes*, for example, opens with the dedication, 'For me. For you. For us. Even for them', a statement which deftly registers the bond between the self and the female 'Other', and positions it against the (implicitly) masculine third person plural. As a dedication it thus acknowledges that while men are free to read the text — they cannot, indeed, be prevented from reading it — they are positioned outside the boundaries of the inclusive address (Me/You/Us) which represents a specifically female continuum.

While a dedication is perhaps the most overtly political way in which a writer can identify her readership, many other fictional works postulate a special relationship between speaker and addressee. The narrator of Margaret Atwood's *The Handmaid's Tale*, for example, tells her story to a nameless ally who can be seen both as a fictional character in the text and also as the reader. This ambiguity is brought to metafictional self-consciousness when, in one of several asides, Offred observes:

A story is like a letter. *Dear You*, I'll say. Just You, without a name. Attaching a name attaches you to the world of fact, which is riskier, more hazardous: who knows what the chances are out there, of survival, yours? I will say *you, you*, like an old love song. *You* can mean more than one.

    You can mean thousands. (Atwood, 1986, p. 50)

What is fascinating about this particular address is that it forces the reader to enter the text almost against her own better judgment. Offred's intimacy carries with it the risk of danger ('who knows what the chances are out there?'). Brought into the action of the text, into the dangerous future Offred inhabits, we are cautioned about our own slim chances of survival. By joining with Offred and reciprocating her need, we, too, risk punishment and death: a risk, indeed, which may also be read as an ironic metaphor for what it always means to accept our positioning as a feminist (as opposed to a 'female'?) reader. Atwood's novel is thus an excellent example of a text which conflates the addressee inside the text with the addressee, or reader, on the outside; and this is a device, I would suggest, that is used repeatedly in contemporary women's writing; especially writing which desires political engagement.

    Christa Wolf, in her famous post-war novel *The Quest for Christa T.*, makes devastating use of 'us' and 'we' in telling her heroine's story. Once again, we have a situation in which pronouns which might *technically* refer to the narrator and her friends in the novel — the people who shared the life of Christa T. — also look outwards to us, the reader. By means of the inclusive term we are brought into the experience of Christa T.'s loss; and, most importantly, forced to share in the responsibility of her death:

She really might have died, almost. But she mustn't leave us. This is the time at which to think more of her, to think her further, to let her live and grow older as other people do. . . . At the last moment, one has the thought of working on her. . . .
    Useless to pretend it's for her sake. Once and for all, she doesn't need us. So we should be certain of one thing: that it's for our sake. Because it seems that we need her. (Wolf, 1982, p. 5)

    The intimacy and involvement that authors like Atwood and Christa Wolf make a strategy of address is seen elsewhere in contemporary women's writing in the relationship between the fictional characters. I want to move on now to look at some examples of texts which are descriptive of dialogic relationships: relationships between female characters in which intimacy has given rise to what Michèle Roberts in the extract from *A Piece of the Night* referred to as 'a private language constructed to express their connection with each other and their separation from the authorities' (Roberts, 1978, p. 49).

'A territory shared': The Private Languages of Women

The mode of writing which brings this exclusivity of address most prominently to light is the letter; and letters between women have obtained a special significance in contemporary feminist criticism precisely on account of their marginality to male literary genres. The letters of friends and lovers are invariably exclusive in their intimacy, their codes and shorthands sometimes proving an impenetrable barrier to any outsider trying to make sense of them. It is therefore no coincidence, I think, that research on letters written between women has become a major preoccupation of feminist critics who have discovered, in their cryptic surfaces, an intimacy that is highly political in its exclusivity. This has been especially true of women researching lesbian writing: a good half of Lillian Faderman's *Surpassing the Love of Men*, for example, involves the re-reading and reconstruction of letters between women whose inferences had previously gone unseen.

It is significant, too, that many contemporary women writers have chosen the epistolary form to represent intimate relationships between women. The success of Alice Walker's *The Color Purple* is acknowledged to depend largely on her inventive re-working of the oldest of novelistic forms. Celie's letters — addressed first to God, then to her sister Nettie — give a new immediacy to the oppressions of black women. I would suggest, moreover, that the hostility with which this text was received by reviewers critical of its representation of black men can be explained by the gynocentricism of its address. As one of my students recently pointed out in an essay on the book, the *story* actually moves towards a reconciliation with the men: more threatening is their total exclusion from the circle of address.

Another text which does something extraordinary in terms of address is Jane Rule's novel *This Is Not For You* (1982). It is a rare example of a fictional work — outside the epistolary — written entirely in the second person. The first chapter opens like this:

> This is not a letter. I wrote you for the last time over a year ago to offer the little understanding I had, to say good-bye. I could have written again, but somehow your forsaking the world for the sake of the world left me nothing to say. Your vow of silence must also stop my tongue, or so it seemed. What a way to win an argument! (Rule, 1987, p. 61)

The dynamic established between the narrator (Kate) and her addressee (Esther) in this arresting 'first and last' paragraph returns us to the mechanics of Bakhtinian dialogue. Kate establishes the conditions of address by taking us to the point at which address is no longer possible: the point at which her words have lost their 'future answer words' in the voice of the woman to whom the text is addressed. Esther's vow of silence (she has literally become a nun!) stops Kate's tongue. Without an interlocutor to realize themselves against, words are not possible, and Kate can only go on to tell the story she does by addressing Esther in the past, according to the terms of their 'old argument'.

Yet despite the fact that this dialogue between Kate and Esther is created retrospectively, its dynamic demonstrates as well as anything I've yet found the peculiar exclusivity of address that may occur between women. The image of two minds locked together in cryptic sympathy is symbolized by Kate's ability to decipher Esther's postcards:

> When I got back to Washington, the first of your cathedral cards had arrived. The message read, 'Mother likes Italy', which meant obviously that you didn't. Or you were recovering your sense of security enough to find your mother's company increasingly difficult. (Rule, 1987, p. 209)

Such 'writing in code' — which I've referred to several times in passing already — may be taken as a distinguishing feature of dialogic activity in feminist texts: a form of address that suggests a private conspiracy between one woman and another; a dialogue whose interests remain hidden, unseen by the outside world. This brings me to the final aspect of Bakhtinian theory I want to raise in this chapter: the importance of intonation and extra-literary context in the gendering of the addressee.

Intonation and Extra-Literary Context

According to Bakhtin, the intonation of an utterance is the element which registers most accurately the relationship between the speaker and the addressee in any verbal exchange. Clark and Holquist describe it like this:

> The purest expression of the values assumed in any utterance is found at the level of intonation, for the reason that intonation always lies at the border of the verbal and the non-verbal, the I and the other. Intonation clearly registers the other's presence, creating a kind of picture in sound of the addressee to whom the speaker imagines she is speaking. . . . Intonation serves as the material means for stitching together the sound, in the speech of the speaker, and the unsaid, in the context of the situation. (Clark and Holquist, 1984, p. 12)

It will be seen from this description that what Bakhtin means by intonation translates roughly into what we refer to in everyday speech as 'tone of voice'; the premise that the voice in which something is spoken — whether it is comforting, angry, pleading, or ironic — often matters more than the words themselves. It is the reason, as Clark and Holquist explain, that when we overhear someone's telephone conversation we can quickly establish their relationship to the person at the other end even if we don't know who they are or what they are talking about. In the essay 'Discourse in Life and Discourse in Art' Bakhtin/Voloshinov makes the same point by means of a short story. It goes like this:

> Two people are sitting in a room. They are both silent. Then one of them says 'Well!'. The other does not respond. [End of story] (Shukman, 1983, p. 99)

In the subsequent analysis, Bakhtin proves that the listener-reader can only make sense of the word 'Well!' if he or she knows more about the extra-verbal context in which the statement is made, and the particular intonation with which it is spoken. On the latter he speculates:

> Let us suppose that the intonation with which this word was pronounced is known to us: indignation and reproach moderated by a certain amount of humour. This intonation somehow fills in the semantic void of the adverb *well*, but still does not reveal the meaning of the whole. . . . (Shukman, 1983, p. 99)

whereupon he invokes the additional necessity of being familiar with the 'extra-verbal context' of the situation, in this case the fact that

> At the time the colloquy took place, both interlocutors *looked up* at the window and *saw* that it had begun to snow; *both knew* that it was already May and that it was high time for spring to come; finally, *both* were *sick and tired* of the protracted winter — *they were both looking forward* to spring and 'both were *bitterly disappointed* by the late snow fall'. (Shukman, 1983, p. 99 [author's emphasis])

What I am proposing here is that it is precisely these two elements, 'intonation' and 'extra-verbal context', that make possible the existence of Roberts's 'private languages'. Jordan, the male narrator of Jeanette Winterson's *Sexing the Cherry*, at one point registers this exclusion when he says:

> I noticed that women have a private language. A language not dependent on the constructions of men but structured by signs and expressions, and that uses ordinary words as code words meaning something other. (Winterson, 1989, p. 29)

While the feminist theories of, for example, Elaine Showalter and Julia Kristeva have attempted to explain this 'difference' in terms of cultural/psychological *marginality*, Bakhtin's model allows us to positively re-appropriate that space in terms of the *communality* which exists within the oppressed or minority group.[6] An important inference here is, of course, that the 'conspiratorial' dialogue we find in women's writing is predicated upon women's own exclusion from the dominant (masculine) 'interpretive community'; what the Roberts quotation referred to as 'their separation from the authorities' (Roberts, 1978, p. 49). The reason why Jordan cannot understand the language of women is because they have developed a model of communication that functions according to different codes: a new linguistic 'territory' in which words, disguised and ironized by the subtleties of intonation and extra-verbal context do, indeed, mean 'something other'. Meaning, according to this system, depends upon a highly developed sense of relationship between speaker and addressee; it exists, indeed, in the space between them.

Conclusion

Whether or not the model of dialogic address and interaction found in the texts I have been looking at is necessarily a strategy of opposition I have not finally decided. The pervasiveness with which the model occurs is, however, sufficient for me to propose it as a defining characteristic of the contemporary women's writing that we would wish to call 'feminist'. Feminist writing is not merely writing by women, it is also writing *for women*. It is writing which enacts or describes a dialogue between women: a dialogue in which the meaning of any utterance depends upon, and is defined by, reciprocity of address.

I am aware, of course, that once such generalizations have been made they exist to be knocked down. I am aware of this, but still feel that for theory to advance, 'the grand and totalizing narratives' have sometimes to be made. In anticipation of this particular dialogic encounter, I will therefore attempt to anticipate some of the most obvious protests.

In the first instance there are those who will probably say, why bother with definitions of women's writing anyway? As Toril Moi observed in *Sexual/Textual Politics*, 'to define Woman is necessarily to essentialize her' (Moi, 1985, p. 139). My reply to this is the justification that I offered at the beginning of this article: that as long as we persist in arranging our reading and teaching around such categories as 'women's writing' or 'feminist writing' we need to know what it is. In this belief I am, at least, supported by other feminist theorists who continue to plague themselves with the same questions. Teresa de Lauretis recently reviewed her own political commitment as a feminist film critic via an interrogation of the terms 'women's cinema' and 'feminist cinema', concluding:

> In sum, what I would call alternative films in women's cinema are those which engage the current problems, the real issues, the things actually at stake in feminist communities on a local scale, and which, although informed by a global perspective, do not assume or aim at a universal, multinational audience, but address a particular one in its specific history of struggles and emergency. (de Lauretis, 1990, p. 17)

While it could be argued that de Lauretis's position causes her to be unnecessarily dismissive of feminist readings of 'non-feminist' texts, her statement does, once again, help us focus on the specificity of address that makes a text of itself 'feminist'. Although, elsewhere, my own work has been based on the assumption that if a reader is able to intervene in the production of a text's meaning it may be rendered feminist, I now believe, like de Lauretis, that we need to distinguish between those texts which have to be 'appropriated' and those which speak to us directly. Like her, I also see the reason for this as one of political urgency: after spending ten years of my own life reading male-produced texts 'against the grain' I now want to engage with those which posit me as an 'ally'.

The de Lauretis quotation, with its focus on particular audiences, brings me to the second of the objections that may be raised against my hypothesis as it stands: that is, its universalized conception of the female addressee. As someone attending an earlier version of this paper pointed out, it is surely reductive to assume that one female addressee is the same as another. In my attempt to theorize what seemed to me a pervasive feature of contemporary women's writing, I overlooked the many other factors — race, class, sexual orientation — which position female addressees both inside and outside texts. In many ways it would, for example, be more productive to look at the differences between the addressees of *The Color Purple* and *The Handmaid's Tale*. Both construct female addressees, but there is a fascinating tension in Walker's text between the black addressee in the text and the appropriation of that subject position by a white readership. In such instances, the gender of the addressee is clearly a starting point rather than an end in itself: as de Lauretis has proposed, we must envisage 'a female social subject engendered, constructed and defined by *multiple* social relations' (de Lauretis, 1990, p. 14).

There is the ultimate advantage, however, that a theory of feminism based upon 'relationship' can, with some artistry, side-step the more blatant essentialisms.

Although the subtext of this paper has been to add yet another voice to the old question 'do women write differently?', it has avoided the supposition that this 'difference' has anything to do with the biological sex of the author or, indeed, the reader: simply that the texts concerned construct *gendered positions* for their speakers and addressees. Although I personally feel that much of the anxiety about essentialism in theory is misplaced, the notion of 'positionality' has been seized upon by critics like Julia Kristeva in order to show the importance of gender in 'women's lived experience' without naturalizing it (see Moi, 1985, p. 166). As Linda Alcoff has neatly summarized: 'Woman is a position from which a feminist politics can emerge rather than a set of attributes that are objectively identifiable' (Alcoff, 1988, p. 433). With this criterion in mind, it is possible for me to propose a redefinition of 'women's writing' or, more specifically, 'feminist writing' which makes gender at once central and provisional. A theory of feminist dialogics is not concerned with the relationship between 'women' *per se* but with gendered subject positions ('speaker'/'addressee') which are not fixed, but historically specific and politically strategic. Furthermore, the 'feminism' of the texts I have considered rests finally in neither of the positions *per se* but, more radically, in the dialogue between them.

Notes

1 Teresa de Lauretis (1990) identifies these two terms — 'by' and 'for' — as the criteria by which we may identify *women's cinema*.
2 See Ken Hirschkop's criticism of Voloshinov/Bakhtin in his essay on 'Bakhtin and Cultural Theory' (Hirschkop and Shepherd, 1989, p. 14).
3 David Lodge offers a clear summary of these different types of 'doubly-voiced discourse' in his essay 'Lawrence, Dostoevsky, Bakhtin' (1985), now reproduced in his collected essays *After Bakhtin* (1990).
4 In Wolfgang Iser's reader-response theory, the role of the reader is not to engage in active dialogue with the text, but simply to 'actualize' its structures (see Iser, 1974, p. xii).
5 This subheading derives from Clark and Holquist's formulation: 'For Bakhtin, individual intention is a relative matter, in as much as the "I" is a function of "we"' (1984, p. 224).
6 Showalter's two key essays which define 'women' in terms of cultural marginality are 'Towards a Feminist Poetics' and 'Feminist Criticism in the Wilderness' (see Showalter, 1987). Julia Kristeva's theories of marginality are explicated by Toril Moi in *Sexual/Textual Politics* (Moi, 1985, pp. 150–73).

References

ALCOFF, LINDA (1988) 'Cultural Feminism vs Poststructuralism: The Identity Crisis', *Signs*, Spring, pp. 405–36.
ATWOOD, MARGARET (1986) *The Handmaid's Tale*, London, Jonathan Cape.
BAKHTIN, MIKHAIL (1981) *The Dialogic Imagination* (1941), ed. HOLQUIST, MICHAEL, trans. EMERSON, CARYL and HOLQUIST, MICHAEL, Austin, TX, University of Texas Press.
BAKHTIN, MIKHAIL (1984) *Problems of Dostoevsky's Poetics* (1929), trans. EMERSON, CARYL, Manchester, Manchester University Press.
BAKHTIN, MIKHAIL (1986) *Speech Genres and Other Late Essays* (1952–3), ed. EMERSON,

CARYL and HOLQUIST, MICHAEL, trans. MCGEE, VERN, Austin, TX, University of Texas Press.

BAKHTIN, MIKHAIL/MEDVEDEV, P.N. (1985) *The Formal Method in Literary Scholarship* (1928), trans. WEHRLE, ALBERT J., Cambridge, MA, Harvard University Press.

BAKHTIN, MIKHAIL/VOLOSHINOV, V.N. (1976) *Freudianism: A Marxist Critique* (1927), trans. TITUNIK, I.R., New York, Academic Press.

BAKHTIN, MIKHAIL/VOLOSHINOV, V.N. (1986) *Marxism and the Philosophy of Language* (1929), trans. MATEJKA, LADISLAW and TITUNIK, I.R., Cambridge, MA, Harvard University Press.

BAUER, DALE (1989) *Feminist Dialogics: A Theory of Failed Community*, New York, State University of New York Press.

CLARK, KATARINA and HOLQUIST, MICHAEL (1984) *Mikhail Bakhtin*, Cambridge, MA, Harvard University Press.

DE LAURETIS, TERESA (1990) 'Guerilla in the Midst: Women's Cinema in the 80s', *Screen*, 31 (1), Spring, pp. 6–25.

FADERMAN, LILLIAN (1985) *Surpassing the Love of Men* (orig. 1981), London, Women's Press.

FISH, STANLEY (1980) *Is there a Text in this Class? The Authority of Interpretive Communities*, Cambridge, MA, Harvard University Press.

FLYNN, ELIZABETH A. and SCHWEICKART, PATROCINIO (Eds) (1986) *Gender and Reading: Essays on Readers, Texts, and Contexts*, Baltimore and London, Johns Hopkins University Press. Includes Patrocinio Schweickart's essay 'Reading Ourselves: Towards a Theory of Feminist Reading'.

HERRMANN, ANN (1989) *The Dialogic and Difference: 'An/Other Woman' in Virginia Woolf and Christa Wolf*, New York, Columbia University Press.

HIRSCHKOP, KEN and SHEPHERD, DAVID (1989) *Bakhtin and Cultural Theory*, Manchester and New York, Manchester University Press.

HOLQUIST, MICHAEL (1990) *Dialogism: Bakhtin and his World*, London and New York, Routledge.

ISER, WOLFGANG (1974) *The Implied Reader*, Baltimore and London, Johns Hopkins University Press.

LODGE, DAVID (1990) *After Bakhtin: Essays on Fiction and Criticism*, London and New York, Routledge.

MOI, TORIL (1985) *Sexual/Textual Politics*, London, Methuen.

PIERCY, MARGE (1974) *Small Changes*, New York, Fawcett Crest.

ROBERTS, MICHÈLE (1978) *A Piece of the Night*, London, Women's Press.

RULE, JANE (1987) *This Is Not For You* (1982), London, Pandora Press.

SHOWALTER, ELAINE (1987) *New Feminist Criticism*, London, Virago. Includes the essays 'Towards a Feminist Poetics' and 'Feminist Criticism in the Wilderness'.

SHUKMAN, ANN (Ed.) (1983) *The Bakhtin School Papers*, Oxford, RPT Publications. Includes the essay 'Discourse in Life and Discourse in Art' attributed to V. N. Voloshinov.

WALKER, ALICE (1983) *The Color Purple*, London, Women's Press.

WINTERSON, JEANETTE (1989) *Sexing the Cherry*, London, Bloomsbury.

WOLF, CHRISTA (1982) *The Quest for Christa T.* (1968), London, Virago.

Notes on Contributors

Lisa Adkins is a lecturer in Women's Studies and Sociology at Lancaster University. She has recently completed a PhD which examines the significance of sexuality and family work relations for production in the British tourist industry.

Nasa Begum is currently researching the needs and wishes of Asian people with disabilities. Before this she worked as a policy adviser in a local government women's unit. She continues to be actively involved in the disability rights, women's and race fields in a personal and professional capacity.

Sheila Burton's note appears with Liz Kelly's.

Beatrix Campbell is a freelance journalist, author of *Wigan Pier Revisited, Iron Ladies: Why do Women Vote Tory?*, and *Unofficial Secrets*, a book about child sexual abuse in Cleveland. She has also made several television documentaries and is currently writing two books, one on recent child abuse controversies and another on Britain in the 1990s.

Helen (charles) likes the shape of her name to be respected. The fact that the 'family' names of many Black people originate from the slaveocracy means that naming has not been a matter of free choice for centuries. She is an active member of the Brighton and Hove Black Women's Group and is involved in lesbian politics.

Chris Corrin lives and works in Glasgow, teaching Politics. Her main work has been with women in Hungary. Her two books are: *Magyar Women: Hungarian Women's Lives, 1940s–1990s*, Macmillan, 1992 and an edited collection, *Superwomen and the Double Burden: Women's Experiences of Change in Central and Eastern Europe and the Former Soviet Union*, Scarlet Press, 1992. She continues to work in these fields.

Gill Dunne is a mature student at Cambridge University. She is currently completing a PhD on the life-styles of lesbian women, hoping to broaden the debate about sexuality to take account of some of the economic consequences of compulsory heterosexuality. She is also seeking a well-paid and stress-free job, as an antidote to postgraduate work.

194

Hilary Hinds teaches Literature at Fircroft College of Adult Education in Birmingham. She is co-editor of *Her Own Life: Autobiographical Writings by Seventeenth-Century Englishwomen* (Routledge, 1989), and is currently working on another anthology of seventeenth-century women's writing with Elaine Hobby.

Naila Kabeer is a Research Fellow at the Institute of Development Studies, Sussex. She specializes in training, teaching and research on gender issues in development, focusing mainly on household economics, rural production and poverty, and reproductive rights. She is a member of the Feminist Review Collective and on the board of Panos Institute. She is currently working on a book on feminist critiques of development policy and practice which will be published by Verso in 1992/1993.

Liz Kelly, **Linda Regan** and **Sheila Burton** have worked together at the Child Abuse Studies Unit, Polytechnic of North London, for two and a half years. Apart from conducting research CASU offers advice and consultancy, organizes networking, training and conferences on the abuse of children and adult women from a feminist perspective. They intend to continue developing a collective approach to feminist research/practice.

Celia Lury lectures in Women's Studies and Cultural Studies in the Sociology Department, Lancaster University. She is currently researching the culture industries, and is interested in the relationship between feminist theory and cultural theory.

Maureen McNeil is Senior Lecturer in the Cultural Studies Department at the University of Birmingham. Her publications include *Under the Banner of Science: Erasmus Darwin and His Age* (Manchester University Press, 1987); an edited collection *Gender and Expertise*; and, edited with Ian Varcoe and Steven Yearley, *New Reproductive Technologies*.

Siobhan Mullally is a lecturer in Law at the University of Hull. She is currently undertaking research on feminist perspectives on law, with particular reference to the Women's Convention and its relevance for Ireland.

Lynne Pearce teaches English and Women's Studies at Lancaster University. She is co-author of *Feminist Readings/Feminists Reading* (Harvester Wheatsheaf, 1989) and author of *Woman/Image/Text: Readings in Pre-Raphaelite Art and Literature* (Harvester Wheatsheaf, 1991). She is currently working on a book on dialogic theory for the Edward Arnold *Working with Theory* series.

Deborah Philips teaches Literature and Women's Studies at West London Institute. She was a co-founder and editor of *Women's Review*.

Ann Phoenix works at the Thomas Coram Research Unit, Institute of Education, University of London. She is currently working on a project on social identities in adolescence. Her previous books are *Young Mothers?*, Polity, 1991 and (jointly edited with Anne Woollett and Eva Lloyd) *Motherhood: Meanings, Practices and Ideologies*, Sage, 1991.

Linda Regan's note appears with Liz Kelly's.

Shaheen Sardar-Ali is Associate Professor of Law at the University of Peshawar in Pakistan. She has written widely on the status of women in Islam, and is currently undertaking research in International Human Rights law and its relevance for women in the Muslim world.

Felly Nkweto Simmonds is Senior Lecturer in Sociology at Newcastle Polytechnic. She is from Zambia and has taught in Zambia, Tanzania and Sierra Leone. She has worked as a development education worker for Oxfam's education department, and as a freelance Women and Development consultant. Her previous publications are: *Images of Women in Development Education*, in *Links 27* (WUS/Third World First, 1986); *She's Gotta Have It: The Representation of Black Female Sexuality on Film*, in Lovell, T. (Ed.) *British Feminist Thought* (Basil Blackwell, 1990). Her main interest is in the making of an inclusive feminist theory and practice. An impossible task. She is bringing up a daughter and two sons. A less impossible task.

Jackie Stacey teaches Women's Studies and Film Studies in the Department of Sociology at Lancaster University. She is co-editor of *Off Centre: Feminism and Cultural Studies* (Harper Collins/Routledge, 1991), and has published articles on feminist and cultural theory in journals such as *Feminist Review, Media, Culture and Society* and *Screen*. During the compilation of this collection, she discovered she had cancer, against which she has so far, with the help of friends and family, been fighting a winning battle.

Liz Stanley is working-class and Romany by birth, a lesbian by luck and a northerner in England by choice. She has taught in the Sociology Department at Manchester University since 1977. Most recently her research interests have focused on historical topics and feminist autobiography, although her abiding sociological and feminist concern is with the processes by which 'knowledge' is produced. Publications include *The Diaries of Hannah Cullwick* (Rutgers University Press, 1984); *The Life and Death of Emily Wilding Davison* (Women's Press, 1988); *Feminist Praxis: Research, Theory and Epistemology in Feminist Sociology* (Routledge, 1990) and *The Auto/Biographical I: The Theory and Practice of Feminist Auto/Biography* (Manchester University Press, 1992).

Ella Westland holds Literature degrees from Bristol, Oxford and Harvard Universities. She began the project described in this book when she was teaching at West London Institute. She is now a Cornwall-based lecturer in the Department of Continuing and Adult Education of Exeter University, running Access and evening classes for mature students (mainly women). Ella lives near Mevagissey with her baby daughter Anna.

Christine Wieneke works in the Social Ecology Centre at the University of Western Sydney, Nepean in New South Wales, Australia, and, until recently, was the Equal Opportunity Officer and Co-Director of its Women's Research Centre. She has undertaken extensive research on equal employment opportunity and affirmative action in Australia, as well as research relating to academic and general staff women in universities, women in trade unions and an oral history of women in Western Sydney. She has published a range of articles concerned with these areas of women's inequality at work.

Tamsin Wilton is a Lecturer in Health Studies and Women's Studies at Bristol Polytechnic, and occasionally teaches Lesbian Studies at the Department of Continuing Education at Bristol University. She is the co-author of *AIDS — Working with Young People* (AVERT, 1990) and author of *Antibody Politic — AIDS and Society* (New Clarion Press, in press). She is currently researching a multidisciplinary lesbian studies 'primer', and lives with her pretended family and enough black cats to worry the Spanish Inquisition.

Index

Index

exclusion politics 29, 30, 31, 33, 65
expectations 88–91, 92–6, 127, 129
experience
  essentialism and 192
  feminist methodology and 149–50,
    154
  see also personal as political

Faderman, Lillian 81, 161, 162–5, 169,
    188
family 75
  disabled women and 65, 68
  and human rights 114
  research on, in Hungary 129
Fanon, Frantz 52
fatalism 176
Fellowship of the New Life 164(n4)
femininity/feminine culture 23–4, 76
feminism
  and academia 150
  'addresses' 16, 20
  backlash against 20, 81
  capitalism and 4, 14–15
  changes in 15, 16, 20
  Conservative Party and 13–14, 15
  and definitions of lesbianism 168
  and disability 51, 61
  divisions/perspectives 6–9, 55
  in East-Central Europe 130–2
  and heterosexuality 75
  impact on education/disciplines 4,
    5–6
  liberal 6, 7, 104–5, 106
  marxism and *see under* marxism
  materialist 7
  moralism 23
  and motherhood 24
  and other political traditions 15–16
  and political institutions 14
  principles 16–17
  'professional' 20, 22
  radical 6–8, 52, 80–1, 83–4
  and representation of sexuality 83–4
  and research methods 20, 156, 158,
    163
  revolutionary 6–7, 55, 80–1, 83–4
  socialist 6, 55, 108
    see also marxism
  and teaching *see under* teaching
  and Women's Studies 1, 20, 26
  see also Women's Liberation
    Movement
feminist epistemology 149, 159
feminist fiction *see under* fiction

feminist methodology 149–50, 151–9
feminist theory 23, 26, 174, 181
  Black feminists and 52–9
  and difference 52, 54–9, 74
  and disabled women's experience
    70–1
  and history of lesbianism/women's
    friendships 163–4
  on legislation 134–5
  marxism and *see* marxism
  and men on Women's Studies courses
    43
  and research 20, 156, 158, 163
Feminist Theory Conference (Glasgow,
    1991) 26(n9)
feminization of labour market 128, 173,
    182
femocrats 143
fertility 102, 130
fiction 184, 186–92
  addressee 186–9, 191, 192
  feminist 25, 32, 184, 186–9, 190,
    191
  romances 23–4
film 83, 157, 184(n1), 191
film studies 4, 23, 78
Fine, M. 62–3, 67, 69
food production 102, 103, 104
Ford, Isabella 164
Foucault, Michel 75, 83
Franzway, Suzanne 135
Freewoman, The 167(n11), 168(n12)
Frenchay Health Authority 80
Friedman, S. 181
friendship 161–70
Frutchey, Chuck 78
Fusco, Coco 31
Fuss, Diana 21, 23, 162

Galler, R. 70
Game, Ann 135
Gatens, Moira 74, 77
Gates, H.L. 31
Gavey, Nicola 75, 76, 77, 80, 83
gay men 75, 79
  historical theories 161
  HIV/AIDS health promotion material
    aimed at 78–9, 80
  see also homosexuality
gender 108
  as construct 74, 192
  and development 108–11
  inequality, internalization 110
  labour market and 173–82